Reading Drills

for Speed and Comprehension

Second Edition

Edward B. Fry, Ph.D.
Director, Reading Center
Rutgers University

Jamestown Publishers
Providence, Rhode Island

READING DRILLS
FOR SPEED AND COMPREHENSION

Catalog No. 751

Copyright ©1975 by Edward B. Fry

Cover Design by Stephen R. Anthony

Text Design and Illustrations
by Mary M. Macdonald

Printed in the United States on Recycled Paper

79 80 81 82 9 8 7 6 5 4 3

ISBN 0-89061-039-8

Foreword

I am most pleased by the wide reception this drill book has had in many colleges and some secondary schools. Apparently, improving reading skills is a subject that is becoming more accepted at the upper levels of education.

Curiously enough, reading is widely taught in the elementary schools and in adult and business management schools. The secondary schools and colleges chose to ignore reading skills improvement until recently. It seemed to be proper to improve students' speaking skills or writing skills, but reading skills were presumed to be completed by the end of the elementary years. Reading specialists have long known that this was not true, but it apparently took expensive, adult reading speed courses to remind secondary and college educators that much could be done for older students.

Much credit is due to Professor Frederick L. Westover of the University of Alabama for helping us take out many of the errors that somehow crept into the first edition. His influence on the new graphs that appear in this edition is also gratefully acknowledged. By diligently preparing for his own reading improvement classes, he has helped many others. May that serve as a model for all of us.

EF

Contents

How To Use This Book

1. Have the students time themselves while reading a passage. On an individual basis this can best be done using a stop watch but on a group basis the teacher can write down the elapsed time every 10 seconds on the chalkboard using any watch with a second hand as a timer. The students should *write down the time* it took them to read the passage as soon as they have completed reading it.

2. Have the students answer the comprehension drills without looking back at the passage. The student would normally do all the drills but if time is short just the multiple choice questions may be done.

3. Score the drill passages and enter both comprehension and rate scores on the graphs at the end of the book.

4. Interpretation of progress is important. The introduction gives many suggestions. Comprehension is generally of five types:
   a. The first five multiple choice questions tend to be of *a factual nature.*

   b. The second five multiple choice tend to be of a *subjective nature.*
   c. The first cloze passage has *subject matter* word deletions and tends to show if the student has understood the content of this particular segment.
   d. The second cloze passage has *structure word* deletions and tends to show the student's familiarity and skills with the syntax of English. These passages tend to be easy for native speakers of English who are good readers but particularly valuable for remedial, bilingual or English-as-a-second-language students.
   e. The ten vocabulary in context items give the student an opportunity to develop his ability to use the context (the surrounding words) as an aid to word recognition. The meaning of a word may change, depending on how it is used. Understanding the context helps the student understand the word.

5. Encouragement is important. Students need both the discipline of regular assignments and class drill time and the encouragement of both self progress and teacher praise. Depending on the particular student's needs, he should be encouraged to read a little faster or to improve comprehension. Generally, students who tend to score below 70% on the multiple choice drill should stress comprehension and students who regularly score 90% or 100% should be urged to speed up. Look at each student's scores and/or graph each day. Most do-it-yourself or home-improvement-only type reading courses fail because of lack of teacher encouragement, stimulation and discipline.

6. Assignments. There are 30 passages in the book, each followed by multiple choice, cloze comprehension and vocabulary drills. The teacher may use these in any way he or she wishes. Some teachers would use a passage three times a week in class for ten weeks. Others would have only one in-class drill a week and two homework drills per week. Some would complete the book in five weeks and some would stretch it out over a semester. Personally, I like ten weeks but I'm only one teacher.

The drills may be used in an untimed fashion if the teacher is interested in just comprehension improvement.

The drills also may be used in a variety of situations to stimulate discussion of comprehension or even for oral reading. Good class discussions can be obtained by having students "prove" that their answer is right by finding the part of the passage that backs up their point. It is good that the students sometimes disagree with the author; it teaches them that books aren't infallible.

The drill pages are perforated so that they can be torn out and turned in if the teacher wishes. Also the answer key pages can be easily removed if that is desired.

Introduction

This book is designed as a drill book to help students at the university or advanced secondary level improve their reading speed and comprehension. It may be used alone or in conjunction with its companion workbook, *Skimming & Scanning* (© 1978, Edward Fry). Combining these two texts creates an effective program for building reading rate and comprehension.

This drill book emphasizes timed reading passages followed by two types of comprehension questions, two types of cloze passages and a vocabulary in context drill. Timed reading is the best known method of improving reading speed. The comprehension drills are a way of continually pointing out to the student that there is no point of reading at any speed if there is no understanding of what is read.

Readability of the Passages

The 30 reading passages have all been graded for readability and arranged in the following order: the first passage, Passage A, for each set is of medium difficulty (reading levels 8 and 9); the second passage, Passage B, is the most difficult (reading level 10); and the third passage of the set is the easiest (reading level 7). Thus, the student has the advantage of reading passages of varying difficulty. However, for measuring growth in reading rate you need passages of equal difficulty. Note that the progress graphs on pages 186 and 187 have columns for each passage in the book. We recommend that the student graph only the first passage in a set, however, or an average of the three passages. The reason that we do not ask the student to put every passage on the graph is that it tends to show a lot of variability, and it is easier to see progress when either the averages or the first passages are used. Another reason is that in some courses only one passage is used in class (usually Passage A) and the other two are used as homework. The reading rate of passages done as homework show a lot of variability due to many factors, from inaccurate timing to disruptive environmental conditions. Reading rate tends to jump around quite a bit anyway from fluctuations in motivation, fatigue, previous knowledge of the subject, and many other factors. Hence, we are suggesting you control at least a few of these causes for fluctuation by consistently using either Passage A or a unit average.

There is no fixed time for completing a unit, but I tend to think of it as a week's work, along with whatever other things that the instructor may decide upon. Ten week periods have often been found to be a satisfactory time period to work on reading rate improvement—short enough to hold interest and long enough to gain some practice experience and start to establish new habits.

We will discuss fluctuations in rate, but you should be aware that there will be fluctuations in comprehension, also from the same causes. There is a further cause for fluctuations in comprehension, and that is that the questions and cloze passages are really drills, not reliable test instruments. Hence, look upon them as indications of comprehension achievement. Unit averaging (of 3 scores), of course, gives more stable scores, but even working passage-by-passage, the student and instructor will see trends in comprehension ability. Just don't expect the scores to be terribly accurate; after all, their chief purpose is to teach the student the importance of getting comprehension while reading at an improving rate.

One more point, the last passage in the book is also of medium difficulty in case instructors wish to compare beginning and ending rate on passages of the same difficulty level.

Reading Speed Improvement

The improvement of reading speed, at any level, is for the normal or superior student. Students having difficulty in reading should concentrate on comprehension before working to improve speed. This drill book may be used primarily for comprehension improvement, if that is what the teacher wishes to emphasize. (See column two.)

As a rule, the passages in a reading speed improvement book should be relatively easy for the student. He should not have difficulty with the vocabulary or the subject matter. Hence, most of the passages in this book should be fairly easy for advanced secondary or university students. Do not worry about their being too easy; let the students see how fast and efficiently they can read them. One mark of a good reader is that he can speed up and read easy material rapidly, with good comprehension.

Conversely, one mark of a poor reader is that he reads everything at the same speed, usually slow.

Reading speed training can benefit almost everyone. In the United States some of the most enthusiastic students in reading improvement courses are university graduates who realize how important even a slight improvement in their reading skill can be. I am happy to report that reading rate training is becoming a regular part of many university and secondary school curricula.

Comprehension

There is nothing more important than comprehension in reading. The main purpose in reading is to understand the author's thoughts.

The multiple choice questions that follow each of the selections in this drill book are roughly divided into two types of questions. Usually, the first five questions are matters of fact and the second five questions require a little more thinking than rote recall of facts, such as the ability to find what is meant even though it is not specifically stated or the ability to put several different ideas together to form a new idea. These latter questions might be called subjective because they require some thinking on the part of the reader.

You should look over the mistakes you make on these exercises and if you tend to miss questions more in the first half of the drills rather than the second half, perhaps you are missing too many facts. If, on the other hand, you tend to miss questions in the second half of drills, maybe you are getting facts all right but you are not thinking hard enough about what you are reading so that you can extend or "think about" what you have read.

Very few students can read these passages once and get all of the multiple choice questions correct. Usually a score of about 70 or 80 percent correct is normal. If you get 90 or 100 percent correct, you are probably reading too slowly for the purposes of the exercises in this course and you should speed up. But, if your comprehension score is below 70 percent, this is not good and you should strive to improve it.

One method of improving your comprehension is to go back and study all of the multiple choice questions you missed. The first thing to do is to read the question again very carefully. It is surprising how many students get the wrong answer simply because they have not carefully read the question. After doing this, the student should then look back in the story to see if he can find the part where the question is answered. If the question is from the first half of the drill, that is, an objective or factual question, this should be fairly easy. If on the other hand, the question is from the latter half and requires more thought or inference, the student may have to reread portions of the story which deal with the nature of the question and then think about those portions to see how the correct answer is arrived at. The important work here is for the student to see what a correct answer looks like when it is embedded in the text. Teacher guidance or class discussion is often important in teaching comprehension.

Sometimes the student will disagree with the author's answer to a question. This is natural, particularly in the second half or subjective questions. It is quite possible for errors to creep into a book of this type or even legitimate differences of opinion as to the correct answer. The student should remember that these questions are for purposes of a drill only and that if the questions succeed in focusing the student's attention on the importance of comprehension, then they have succeeded in doing their work.

It is important that the comprehension drills be scored immediately after they are taken while the whole subject is fresh in the student's mind. If he is going to study his wrong answers further, it should be done right after the drill rather than at some later time.

It is not unusual for students who have made a rapid increase in speed in the first few weeks of a reading improvement course to have their comprehension gradually or rapidly go down. What should happen in this case is that the student should attempt to level off his speed, *but not lower it,* and concentrate more on comprehension. Usually what will happen if the student levels off his speed and concentrates on comprehension is that the comprehension will gradually rise in a week or two to a normal level of 70 or 80 percent. The *wrong* thing to do is to lower speed. Lowering speed will almost immediately

bring up comprehension but the student may be in the awkward position of being right back where he started after several weeks of work. Study carefully the illustration which follows if you have the problem of rising speed and falling comprehension.

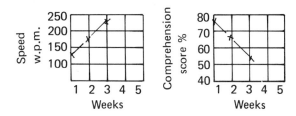

The Problem: Student makes rapid speed increase but loses comprehension.

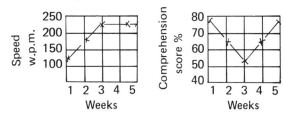

The Correct Solution: Level off speed increase and concentrate on improving comprehension.

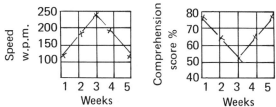

The Wrong Solution: It is wrong to lower speed (lose the gain) in order to raise comprehension.

Note: In the wrong solution the student has exactly the same speed and comprehension at the fifth week as he did at the first week; hence no improvement has taken place.

You should be keeping your own speed and comprehension graphs in the back of this drill book. Achieving a proper balance between speed and comprehension is one of the most important things that you will learn in this course. A bad reader is typically one who reads everything at the same speed, usually a slow speed. Another type of bad reader is one who reads so rapidly that he never has any good comprehension. Hence, the important thing for a good reader to achieve is balance between speed and comprehension. And, through training such as you are getting in this drill book, you should be able to increase your speed while maintaining a normal level of comprehension.

It is not easy to improve your reading skills. Therefore, in taking the drills that follow, you must put forth your full effort to increase your speed and achieve good comprehension.

Cloze Technique

A feature of this drill book is the cloze technique passages following the more traditional multiple choice questions. These passages are a relatively new way of teaching comprehension. Traditional comprehension instruction uses questions to be answered following reading of a passage. The cloze technique, by leaving out words, provides a method of questioning during the reading of a passage. These cloze techniques are of two types:

1. One type of cloze technique has subject matter words omitted in the passages. Subject matter words are the nouns, verbs, adjectives and adverbs which make one passage uniquely different from another. For example, a story of dinosaurs and a story on automobiles would tend to use the same structure words but different subject matter words. The cloze passage with subject matter words omitted is a useful means of measuring the comprehension of all students and *teaching* comprehension to all students.

2. This type of cloze technique has structure words omitted in passages. Linguists define structure words as those little words such as "the" and "of," which are necessary mechanically for holding the language together, but which contribute little to the unique meaning of a passage. Structure cloze passages are probably most useful for instructing students for whom English is difficult or is a second language.

Psychologically, multiple choice questions are a recognition task, while the cloze technique involves knowledge of English structure and recall. All of these are important parts of reading comprehension, and, as a bonus, they are the type of skills which will help the students do well on many kinds of examinations.

The cloze passages are taken from passages in the article. The student can locate the sentences and correct his own responses or use the key to get the correct answer. One difficulty is that the student may use a synonym or a word which is equally applicable. Research with the cloze technique has shown that, for testing or training, allowing the student to use synonyms is no better than requiring him to supply the author's exact words. For example, in a test situation the same students will come out on top and the same students will come out on the bottom of the class whether exact words are required or synonyms are allowed though, of course, the exact word score will always be a little lower. For our purposes, improvement in comprehension will be reflected from week to week if either exact words or synonym scores are used. Experience has shown that students are a little happier if synonyms are allowed, but the allowance of synonyms presents much more difficulty in correction.

In any event, either or both cloze technique passages are an optional part of the reading improvement course or the use of this drill book.

Vocabulary in Context

Accompanying each selection is a vocabulary in context exercise. These exercises consist of ten words from the selection reprinted in context. Following each word, four meanings are given. The student's task is to select the best meaning for the word as used in this selection.

The precise meaning of a word depends largely on how it is used. As you know, dictionaries often list several meanings for a single word. Only by understanding the context in which a word appears is the reader able to associate the word with an appropriate meaning.

In the vocabulary exercises each word is printed in the sentence or expression from the selection to help the student recall how the word was originally used. Also given is the location of the word in the selection so that, if necessary, the reader can return to that section and reread the entire context to understand the word better.

Remember to keep context in mind when completing the vocabulary exercises. All four choices given for a word may be "dictionary correct," but only one is the best meaning for the word as used in this selection.

At the end of each exercise a single vocabulary word is examined further. These thirty brief sections give the student an opportunity to see how words are structured from prefixes, suffixes and roots.

Self Correction

All of the drills in this book are designed to be corrected by the student immediately after he has taken them. An answer key is provided on page 179. Perhaps the most obvious benefit of this is that it saves the teacher work. However, the more valid reason is that it is a better learning situation for the student. Psychologists have consistently found that the more immediate the knowledge of results (right or wrong), the better the learning.

Common Faults and Eye Movements

Good readers have less body movement. This means they do not point at words, turn their head or talk to themselves while reading. Here are a few don'ts for better reading:

1. Don't point at words or hold a pencil or ruler under the line while you are reading. This might help little children or illiterate adults. However, if you can read the stories in this book, you certainly don't need any mechanical help for your eyes.

2. Don't move your head from side to side while reading. Some students, especially when trying to read fast, move their head from side to side. Neck muscles cannot be moved as rapidly as eye muscles.

3. Don't say the words to yourself. Some poor readers often think that it is necessary to mumble the words to themselves while reading. In bad cases even their lips move. This should be avoided.

A more subtle type of talking to yourself while reading is called subvocalization. This means that you are saying words to yourself but not actually moving your lips or tongue. In short, you are thinking each word as you read. Good readers subvocalize very little, while poor readers place a heavy emphasis on subvocalization.

Curing excessive subvocalization is not easy. The best cure is to place your emphasis on trying to go faster and to think about what the author is saying. You should be asking the author questions or commenting on the material. You should be thinking, "that is a good point," "that will be an answer to a question," "this doesn't compare with what I already know" or "I don't believe that." The important point here is that you are not subvocalizing each of the author's words as though you were a phonograph record. Rather, you are thinking about what the author is saying.

One difficulty with subvocalization is that, if you think about it while you are reading, you are most surely going to do it. Hence, if you simply say "I will not subvocalize, I will not subvocalize," you will find yourself doing it and your speed will not be helped. The cure for too much subvocalization is to go faster and think about the author's ideas.

The Importance of Faster Reading

You probably talk at the average rate of 150 words a minute, but, if you are a reader of average ability in the United States, you read at the rate of 250 words a minute. Thus, your reading speed, before starting the reading improvement course, is already nearly twice as fast as your speaking or listening speed. Hence, reading is one of the fastest ways of putting verbal knowledge into your mind. The flexibility and inexpensiveness of printing also make printed verbal information by far the cheapest means of transmitting this kind of information.

The following figure showing the number of books read over a period of ten years, illustrates rather dramatically, what an increase in reading speed can do for you. Look at the differences in the piles of books read by a slow reader and those read by a good reader.

The speed of 350 words a minute that we have selected for a good reader is far lower than the speeds achieved by really fast readers. However, if you are reading at a rate of 250 words a minute and can increase your speed to 350 words a minute, in the course of ten years it can make a tremendous difference in the amount of knowledge which you acquire. This illustration assumes that you will read one hour a day, six days a week, and that the books you read are of an average length of 70,000 words. Please do not assume that you must read a book for at least an hour every day. Many people do not read this much, but many would if they could learn to read better.

Faster reading, once it is mastered, makes reading more interesting, not more work.

	1 week	1 month	2 years	10 years
Slow reader 150 words per min.	¾ book	3 books	36 books	360 books
Fair reader 250 words per min.	1¼ books	5½ books	66 books	660 books
Good reader 350 words per min.	1¾ books	7½ books	90 books	900 books

Common Questions Asked by Students

Here are the answers to a few questions that students frequently ask at the beginning of a reading improvement course:

1. *How much gain in speed can I expect to make during a reading improvement course?* Students can frequently double their reading speed in a test situation on material of average difficulty. This means that some students will do a little better than doubling their speed and others will improve less. However, even if you achieve and maintain a 30 or 40 percent increase in reading speed, think what this can mean when spread out through the rest of your life.

2. *Does reading faster lower comprehension?* Generally not. On the average, most classes end with the same comprehension that they begin with. Individual students who have below normal comprehension at the beginning of a class usually manage to bring it up to normal. Other students who are reading very slowly because of extremely high comprehension frequently find it more advantageous to lower their comprehension slightly and greatly increase their speed. Flexibility is really the goal of rate training. This is the ability to go fast when you want or need to.

3. *Can people learn to read 2,000 words a minute or faster?* Usually not. Good readers, reading material with which they are not familiar and getting normal comprehension, seldom exceed speeds of five or six hundred words a minute. This same good reader can often skim material at a thousand to twelve hundred words per minute. However, skimming is a special skill in which part of the material is not read and an intentional acceptance of lowered comprehension is implied. Tests have been conducted with people who claim to read 2,000 words a minute and better by giving them material in which every other line is left out. These extremely fast readers never noticed the difference. Hence, by the standards of what most people call reading, it cannot be done at 2,000 words a minute. It is possible for somebody who knows the subject matter to flip the pages of

a book rather rapidly and give an idea of what is contained in the book. This, however, can hardly be called reading and determining a words per minute score for this type of activity is unfair.

4. *Does training in one type of reading matter help on other types of reading matter?* Yes, it really does not make much difference what type of material you read to improve your reading. Reading ability seems to be a more general skill which can be transferred to a wide variety of material. This, however, does not mean you will or should read all material at the same rate. You will naturally read difficult material more slowly. Training to read faster on easy types of material will improve your reading speed on more difficult types of material.

5. *Can you be too old to learn to improve reading?* No, high school seniors, college freshmen and business executives all can improve their reading speed and by about the same percentage. A study done in Scotland compared students over 40 years old with those under 40 years old and found no difference.

6. *Will reading speed gain stay with me after the course has ended?* Yes, most of it will. When studies have been done of students who have completed reading speed improvement courses, they usually find that most of the increase has stayed with the students. However, many invesitgators have found a slight decrease. Hence, it is fairly safe to say that the retention of the gain made will be between 60 and 100 percent, six months to a year after taking the course. If it lasts this long, it will probably last for life.

7. *Is skimming different from reading?* Yes. Skimming is a very fast reading rate with different purposes. In regular reading a person usually tries to get good comprehension and leave out nothing. In skimming a person purposely skips or leaves out small portions of the material in order to attain a very high rate. A skimmer also knows that he is only trying to get the main idea of a passage and a few of the facts, not all. A skilled reader can skim at twice his fastest normal reading rate, but he gets a little lower comprehension. With a little practice most people can learn to skim—you can try it on some of the drills in this book—you may surprise yourself.

8. *Do all people make the same rate progress?* No, there are a lot of different types of reading ability. Some people are especially gifted in reading just as others have music ability. However, almost everyone can learn to read with a fairly high degree of efficiency and nearly everyone can improve his reading ability with training. But it is not unusual for some students to be able to read twice as fast as others. Also, during reading rate or comprehension training some students will have different improvement patterns; some make progress immediately and others seem to make no progress for a while then improve as the drills continue.

9. *How can I fail to improve?* There are a lot of ways to fail. Perhaps the easiest and most often used is to fail *to try* to improve. It takes effort to change reading habits. The next best way is to stop halfway through.

It is necessary to have good vision to read effectively. If you have any symptoms of eye strain or blurry vision (near or far) visit your optometrist or opthalmologist for a checkup.

To benefit from these drills they should be fairly easy reading. If not, get an easier drillbook.

A good environment also helps. This is why most reading improvement is done in classes—the teacher structures a good learning environment free of distractions that are found at home.

Set 1

Set 1·A
Magic

Starting Time: Minutes_____ Seconds_____

Magic, or conjuring, is a form of entertainment that is based on pretending to do things which are impossible. The magician is a specially trained actor. He tries to make the audience believe that he has the power to do things which are against the laws of nature.

Magic shows are entertaining as long as the audience does not discover how the tricks are done. The magician always tries to keep his tricks a secret.

The magician usually depends on his skill with his hands, on his knowledge of psychology, and, sometimes, on mechanical devices. Since magic tricks are meant to fool people, the use of psychology is important. The magician must keep people from noticing all the movements of his hands and from thinking about the secret parts of his equipment. He must also lead the audience to draw false conclusions. The magician's success depends on the fact that many things seen by the eye do not register on the mind.

Two basic magic tricks are making objects seem to appear and making objects seem to disappear. A combination of these two tricks makes for some interesting effects. For example, the magician puts a small ball under one of several cups. The ball then seems to jump from one cup to another or to change color. What actually happens is that the magician, employing quick hand movements or a mechanical device, hides one ball. While doing this he talks to the audience and waves a brightly colored cloth with one hand. The audience is too busy watching the cloth and listening to the magician's words to notice that his other hand is hiding the ball.

Another favorite trick is to cut or burn something, and then make it appear whole again. What actually happens is that the magician makes the cut or burned object disappear by quickly hiding it while the audience watches something else. Then he "magically" makes it appear whole again by displaying another object that has not been cut or burned.

There are a number of so-called "mind-reading" tricks in which the magician purports to tell a person what he is thinking about. For some of these tricks the magician has a person write down his thoughts. Then the magician secretly obtains the paper. Another "mind-reading" technique is to have a trained helper blindfold the magician. Then the helper has the audience hand him various objects. The helper can tell the magician what the objects are, without mentioning their names, by using keywords or code words as he talks to the magician. This trick may take the magician and his helper many months to learn.

A magician's powers are really quite limited, but he makes people believe that he can do most anything by changing or combining several tricks.

Tricks in which the magician apparently cuts people in half or makes them disappear are called illusions. The word illusion derives from the fact that mirrors are often used to perform these tricks. A famous illusion trick is to saw a woman in half. The woman is put into a long box with her head sticking out of one end and her feet sticking out of the other end. The magician takes an ordinary wood saw and cuts the box into two halves. The audience is shocked, thinking that perhaps he has killed the woman. A few moments later, however, the magician puts his "magic" cape over the box and the woman comes out. The woman that the audience saw being cut in two was only an image in a mirror—an illusion.

Conjuring is as popular today as it was in ancient times. Records show that over 2,000 years ago magic performances were being given in ancient Egypt, India, Rome, China and Greece. These early magicians only performed for small groups of people on a street corner or for a king and his friends. The magicians in those days used only small objects that they could carry with them or borrow, such as cups, pebbles, knives, and string.

Early conjurers frequently wore a large apron with many pockets in which they could carry their props. The bag-like apron served as identification and as a place to hide things while performing. Conjurers also carried a small folding table on which to perform their tricks.

About 1400, more elaborate tricks were invented which used larger equipment, such as boxes and barrels with false bottoms. Under these false bottoms the magician could hide a bird, rabbit, plant, or whatever he wanted to make appear suddenly. From one barrel he could make several different liquids pour forth while he told the audience that he was changing the entire contents of the barrel by magic. People of that time knew very little about mechanical devices, so it was easier for the magician to deceive them.

Some conjurers made enough money to buy a donkey, a horse, or even a horse and wagon so that they could carry bigger equipment. Conjurers also began to rent halls or empty stores so that they could give their shows indoors. Some conjurers used a large room in a local inn to give their performances. Others had a large van that could be opened in the rear to make a stage.

The most successful magicians would move only three or four times a year. They decorated their stages with lots of equipment, but used only a small part of it in each show. In this way they could entice the same people back over and over again. Some of their equipment was of no use at all. It was only used to decorate the stage and impress the audience.

Modern magic did not really start until the 1800s. Its father is considered to be Jean Houdin, a Frenchman, who developed rules for conjuring. Houdin was also a highly skilled mechanic and watchmaker. Today modern magicians can perform feats of magic that would have been impossible years ago because they now have better mechanical equipment and greater knowledge of audience psychology.

Finishing Time: Minutes_____ Seconds_____

Magic

COMPREHENSION: Answer the questions without looking back at the passage. When finished, correct your answers by checking with the answer key on page 179. Find your words per minute by looking in the chart on page 185. Enter both scores on graphs provided at the end of this book.

1. The magician pretends to do things which
   ☐ a. people like.
   ☐ b. are impossible.
   ☐ c. are secret.
   ☐ d. make people laugh.

2. An important part of a magic trick is that
   ☐ a. it does not take too long.
   ☐ b. it has a combination of interesting effects.
   ☐ c. the audience doesn't discover how it is done.
   ☐ d. a bright colored cloth is used.

3. If a magician cuts something, such as a cloth, he usually makes it appear whole again by
   ☐ a. displaying a duplicate.
   ☐ b. using special glue.
   ☐ c. not really cutting it.
   ☐ d. showing you only the part not cut.

4. In the 1400s some of the favorite new tricks used
   ☐ a. cups and balls.
   ☐ b. cloth and knives.
   ☐ c. mind reading.
   ☐ d. false bottoms.

5. A mark of a magician's success was that
   ☐ a. he used big equipment.
   ☐ b. he didn't move often.
   ☐ c. he performed in an inn.
   ☐ d. his tricks involved illusions.

6. Psychology is an important part of magic tricks because
   ☐ a. magicians are psychologists.
   ☐ b. there is no such thing as magic.
   ☐ c. it tells you how much people see.
   ☐ d. there is a special branch of psychology devoted to magic.

7. The audience draws false conclusions because
   ☐ a. the magician is smart.
   ☐ b. they are led to believe them by the conjurer.
   ☐ c. they like to be deceived.
   ☐ d. there could be no other explanation.

8. After reading this article, you would conclude that mind reading
   ☐ a. couldn't really work.
   ☐ b. requires much concentration.
   ☐ c. requires a special talent.
   ☐ d. could work only for some people.

9. What is one valid conclusion you can draw from this article?
   ☐ a. Magicians are now extinct.
   ☐ b. People today don't like to be fooled.
   ☐ c. Magic is only for children.
   ☐ d. It is more difficult to be a magician today than it was 400 years ago.

10. Another good title for this article would be
   ☐ a. "Magic Is a Lost Art."
   ☐ b. "How to Fool Your Friends."
   ☐ c. "The First Actors."
   ☐ d. "An Introduction to Conjuring."

Name _____ Date _____ Class _____

Reading Time: _____ _____ _____ _____ _____
              Minutes Seconds Words per minute Total number right Percent

Magic

CLOZE TEST: The following passage, taken from the selection you have just read, has words omitted from it. Fill in the blank without looking back at the passage. When finished, correct your answers by checking with the answer key on page 179.

A. Subject Matter Words Missing

Some conjurors made enough _____ 1 to buy a donkey, a horse, or even a horse and _____ 2 so that they could carry _____ 3 equipment. Conjurors also began to _____ 4 halls or empty stores so that they could give their shows _____ 5. Some conjurors used a large _____ 6 in a local inn to give their performances. Others had a large van that _____ 7 be opened in the rear to make a _____ 8. The most _____ 9 magicians would move only three or four _____ 10 a year.

B. Structure Words Missing

Magic, _____ 1 conjuring, is a form of entertainment that is based _____ 2 pretending to do things which are impossible. The magician is _____ 3 specially trained actor. He tries to make _____ 4 audience believe that he has the power _____ 5 do things which are against the laws _____ 6 nature. Magic shows are entertaining as long _____ 7 the audience does _____ 8 discover how the tricks are done. The magician always tries _____ 9 keep his tricks _____ 10 secret.

_____ Name   _____ Date   _____ Class

_____ A. Number Right   _____ Percent   _____ B. Number Right   _____ Percent

Magic

VOCABULARY: The following words have been taken from the selection you have just read. Put an X in the box before the best meaning or synonym for the word as used in the selection.

1. **conclusions**, page 18, col. 1, par. 3
"He must also lead the audience to draw false conclusions."
☐ a. false hopes
☐ b. strange notions
☐ c. wrong judgments
☐ d. quick reactions

2. **register**, page 18, col. 1, par. 3
"... many things seen by the eye do not register on the mind."
☐ a. easily avoid
☐ b. really interest
☐ c. hardly interest
☐ d. seem to impress

3. **purports**, page 18, col. 2, par. 3
"... the magician purports to tell a person what he is thinking about."
☐ a. to force
☐ b. to pretend
☐ c. to attempt to hide
☐ d. to claim

4. **technique**, page 18, col. 2, par. 3
"Another 'mind-reading' technique ..."
☐ a. continued deception
☐ b. method of performance
☐ c. unusual position
☐ d. quick move

5. **limited**, page 19, col. 1, par. 2
"A magician's powers are really quite limited, but he makes people believe that he can do most anything ..."
☐ a. easily stopped
☐ b. difficult to develop
☐ c. confined to certain things
☐ d. unable to be learned

6. **apparently**, page 19, col. 1, par. 3
"Tricks in which the magician apparently cuts people in half ... are called illusions."
☐ a. to attempt to
☐ b. to distract
☐ c. to seem to
☐ d. to fail at

7. **derives**, page 19, col. 1, par. 3
"The word illusion derives from the fact that mirrors are often used ..."
☐ a. comes from a source
☐ b. comes from an untruth
☐ c. is difficult to understand
☐ d. cannot be explained

8. **props**, page 19, col. 1, par. 5
"... a large apron with many pockets in which they could carry their props."
☐ a. something to lean on
☐ b. objects or devices
☐ c. strong supports
☐ d. mechanical devices

9. **deceive**, page 19, col. 1, par. 6
"People of that time knew very little ... so it was easier ... to deceive them."
☐ a. to deliberately lie to
☐ b. to mislead
☐ c. to betray
☐ d. to influence badly

10. **entice**, page 19, col. 2, par. 2
"In this way they could entice the same people back ..."
☐ a. to mislead
☐ b. to cheat
☐ c. to invite
☐ d. to lure

The word **entice** has an interesting origin. It is derived from a Latin word *titio* which means *firebrand*. The word we have today is a modification of the old French *enticier, to incite*. The suffix **ment** added to **entice** gives us the state of being **enticed**.

Name _____ Date _____ Class _____

Total Number Right _____ Percent _____

22

Starting Time: Minutes_____ Seconds_____

For thousands of years, people thought of glass as something beautiful to look *at*. Only recently have they come to think of it as something to look *through*. Stores display their goods in large glass windows. Glass bottles and jars that hold food and drink allow us to see the contents. Glass is used to make spectacles, microscopes, telescopes, and many other extremely useful and necessary objects. Spectacles, or glasses, are used by people who cannot see perfectly or by people who want to protect their eyes from bright light. Microscopes make tiny things larger so that we can examine them. Telescopes make objects that are far away appear much closer to us.

Glass was discovered a very long time ago. The Roman historian Pliny describes one discovery this way: the crew of a Phoenician boat landed at the mouth of a river in Syria. The crew could not find any stones to support their kettle, so they used lumps of nitre, a sodium compound, from the ship. When the heat of the fire melted the nitre, it mixed with the sand under it and the mixture became liquid glass. After this discovery the glass factories at Tyre and Sidon became quite famous, and the Phoenicians learned how to blow glass.

The Egyptians also knew how to make glass thousands of years ago. The glass they made was green because the sand contained iron. They found they could change the color by adding other minerals to the sand.

The Greeks were not famous for their glass-making. They seemed more interested in making pottery. However, the Romans made large amounts of glass and began using it for windows. They made dishes and cups out of glass, and they decorated their palaces with glass mosaics (pictures made by putting together small bits of colored glass).

The Romans took the art of glass-making to the lands they colonized in Europe and the near East. During the Middle Ages, Constantinople (Istanbul) was an important glass center. When the Venetians took control of Constantinople, they sent many of the expert glassmakers back to Venice, and Venice became very famous for its glass. The Venetians made their glass on the island of Murano, near Venice, for two reasons: to prevent the hot fires from spreading to the city and to keep the process a secret. The glassmakers were not allowed to divulge their knowledge of glassmaking to other cities or countries. Those who did were punished or killed.

The Venetians developed a kind of glass that was so clear it could be made into lenses. Using this special glass it was possible to make spectacles and other optical instruments. In the seventeenth century, Venetian artists were taken to Paris to make mirrors for the Palace of Versailles, built by King Louis XIV.

In former centuries glass was shaped by blowing through a long pipe into a ball of very hot, soft, molten glass. The air could make the glass thick or thin and give it different shapes. The final shaping was done with special tools. Sometimes the glass was reheated several times before it was finally worked into the desired shape. Today, compressed air machines and molds are used to blow and shape glass.

In the present century, safety glass was invented for use in modern cars and planes. Safety glass is made by placing a layer of plastic between two layers of plate glass. When the outside layer of glass is broken, the pieces do not scatter and injure people. Some glass of this type is strong enough to resist bullets.

Until World War II, most of the glass used for optical instruments was exported from Europe. However, during the war Americans could not get European glass, and they were forced to make their own. As a result, new kinds of glass were developed that had been previously unknown. These new effects were achieved by mixing other chemical elements with the sand. Some of these new glasses are very strong and can resist many kinds of shocks. Legend has it that a very hard glass, similar to that recently developed, was invented by a Roman who showed his discovery to the Emperor. When the Emperor saw the glass he feared that it would become more valuable than gold and silver, making his treasury worthless. Consequently, he had the glassmaker killed, and the secret was not discovered again for hundreds of years.

Foamglass is made by mixing finely crushed glass with carbon dust. Gas from the heated carbon makes the glass foam up as it melts. When this glass cools, it is black and very light. It floats and it can be sawed or drilled. As is true of all glass, foamglass resists heat, does not burn, does not rot, is not eaten by rats and is not rotted by water.

This kind of glass can be used for floats for fishing nets or for insulating houses to keep them warm in winter and cool in summer. It also can be used for the lining of refrigerators and for the insulators on poles that carry telephone and electric wires. Its resistance to acids makes it very useful in the making of pipes carrying chemicals that would eat away metals. It is also useful in carrying milk, which might be contaminated by metal pipes. Small drops of glass can be used instead of jewels in many electric instruments, such as those in airplanes.

While many utilitarian uses for glass have been developed, its original aesthetic value has not been forgotten. Bowls and vases of cut glass ornament many homes. The designs are cut into thick glass by wheels that turn extremely fast. Designs are etched into polished glass with acid.

Although in recent years plastics have replaced glass under conditions where glass might be easily broken, there are new uses being developed for glass that were never imagined in the past. Perhaps the greatest advantage of glass is that its constituent parts are inexpensive and can be found all over the world.

Finishing Time: Minutes_____ Seconds_____

Glass

COMPREHENSION: Answer the questions without looking back at the passage. When finished, correct your answers by checking with the answer key on page 179. Find your words per minute by looking in the chart on page 185. Enter both scores on graphs provided at the end of this book.

1. How did the Greeks use glass?
   □ a. For windows
   □ b. For telescopes
   □ c. For ornaments.
   □ d. They did not use glass.

2. Glass was used for windows by the
   □ a. Romans.
   □ b. Greeks.
   □ c. Egyptians.
   □ d. Phoenicians.

3. Venice kept its monopoly on glass by
   □ a. keeping invaders out.
   □ b. punishing glassmakers who left Venice.
   □ c. destroying Constantinople.
   □ d. paying glassmakers very well.

4. Safety glass is used for cars and planes because
   □ a. it cannot break.
   □ b. it cannot crack.
   □ c. it resists bullets.
   □ d. if it is broken, the pieces do not scatter.

5. Glass is useful in chemical laboratories because
   □ a. it does not break easily.
   □ b. it is transparent.
   □ c. it resists acids.
   □ d. it does not get dirty.

6. Glass that could be used for lenses was first developed by
   □ a. the Phoenicians.
   □ b. the French.
   □ c. the Venetians.
   □ d. the Romans.

7. The Phoenicians discovered glass when
   □ a. a bag of sand fell into the ashes.
   □ b. their nitre combined with the carbon in the sand.
   □ c. their nitre combined with the sand.
   □ d. their heated carbon spilled into the sand.

8. Egyptian glass was green because
   □ a. the sand contained iron.
   □ b. their nitre contained iron.
   □ c. their sand was multi-pigmented.
   □ d. green was the royal color of the Nile.

9. The materials used for glassmaking are
   □ a. expensive and rare.
   □ b. inexpensive and easily obtained.
   □ c. fragile and difficult to transport.
   □ d. simple and easy to combine.

10. Many new types of glass were invented in America because of
   □ a. the new inventions such as cars and airplanes.
   □ b. World War II.
   □ c. the discovery of new chemical elements.
   □ d. the need for safety glass and microscopes.

Name   Date   Class

Reading Time: _____ _____ _____ _____ _____
               Minutes   Seconds   Words per minute   Total number right   Percent

Glass

CLOZE TEST: The following passage, taken from the selection you have just read, has words omitted from it. Fill in the blank without looking back at the passage. When finished, correct your answers by checking with the answer key on page 179.

A. Subject Matter Words Missing

The Romans took the _____ 1 of glass-making to the lands they _____ 2 in Europe and the near East. During the Middle Ages, Constantinople (Istanbul) was an _____ 3 center. When the Venetians took _____ 4 of Constantinople, they sent many of the _____ 5 glassmakers back to Venice, and Venice became very _____ 6 for its glass. The Venetians made their glass on the _____ 7 of Murano, near Venice, for two reasons: to _____ 8 the hot fires from spreading to the city and to keep the process a _____ 9. The glassmakers were not allowed to _____ 10 their knowledge of glassmaking to other cities or countries.

B. Structure Words Missing

The Venetians developed a kind of glass that was _____ 1 clear it could be made _____ 2 lenses. Using this special glass it was possible _____ 3 make spectacles and other optical instruments. _____ 4 the seventeenth century, Venetian artists were taken _____ 5 Paris to make mirrors for the Palace _____ 6 Versailles, built by King Louis XIV. _____ 7 French had developed other kinds of glass—notably the stained glass used _____ 8 churches. In former centuries glass was shaped by blowing _____ 9 a long pipe into a ball _____ 10 very hot, soft, molten glass.

Name		Date	Class
A. Number Right	Percent	B. Number Right	Percent

26

Glass

VOCABULARY: The following words have been taken from the selection you have just read. Put an *X* in the box before the best meaning or synonym for the word as used in the selection.

1. **compound**, page 23, col. 1, par. 2
"... they used lumps of nitre, a sodium compound, from the ship."
□ a. a piece of wood
□ b. a crystal formation
□ c. a combination of elements
□ d. a place of containment

2. **colonized**, page 23, col. 2, par. 3
"... lands they colonized in Europe ..."
□ a. to overcome by force
□ b. to establish a settlement
□ c. to buy lands
□ d. to join similar groups together

3. **process**, page 23, col. 2, par. 3
"The Venetians made their glass on the island ... to keep the process a secret."
□ a. an artificial method
□ b. a system of doing something
□ c. a series of changes
□ d. a written order

4. **divulge**, page 23, col. 2, par. 3
"The glassmakers were not allowed to divulge their knowledge of glass-making ..."
□ a. to reveal something secret
□ b. to reveal only stolen information
□ c. to separate from
□ d. to announce without permission

5. **optical**, page 24, col. 1, par. 1
"... to make spectacles and other optical instruments."
□ a. expensive instruments
□ b. exclusive products
□ c. carefully made
□ d. pertaining to sight

6. **compressed**, page 24, col. 1, par. 2
"Today compressed air machines and molds ..."
□ a. made cool
□ b. able to explode
□ c. forced into less space
□ d. made useable

7. **contaminated**, page 24, col. 2, par. 1
"It is also useful in carrying milk, which might be contaminated ..."
□ a. to make sour
□ b. to make impure by contact
□ c. to cause to be warm
□ d. to give a bad taste to

8. **utilitarian**, page 24, col. 2, par. 2
"While many utilitarian uses for glass have been developed ..."
□ a. for practical use
□ b. for creativity reasons
□ c. for public service
□ d. for industry

9. **etched**, page 24, col. 2, par. 2
"Designs are etched into polished glass with acid."
□ a. to damage
□ b. to experiment
□ c. to copy
□ d. to engrave

10. **constituent**, page 24, col. 2, par. 3
"... constituent parts are inexpensive ..."
□ a. to be most important
□ b. to be less valuable
□ c. to help make up a thing
□ d. to be least important

Divulge is a word which means to disclose or reveal. It comes from the Latin word *divulgare, to make common. Vulgaris* means *pertaining to the common people.* **Divulge** is made up of *di (de)* and *vulgare* and **to divulge** usually means to reveal something private, secret or previously unknown.

_____   _____   _____
Name   Date   Class

_____   _____
Total Number Right   Percent

Set 1·C
How Well Do
You See?

Starting Time: Minutes_____ Seconds_____

When we can see well, we do not think about our eyes very often. It is only when we cannot see perfectly that we realize how important our eyes are.

People who are nearsighted can only see things that are very close to their eyes. Everything else seems blurry. Many people who do a lot of close work, such as writing, reading and sewing, become nearsighted. Then they have to wear glasses in order to see distant objects clearly.

People who are farsighted suffer from just the opposite problem. They can see things that are far away, but they have difficulty reading a book unless they hold it at arm's length. If they want to do much reading, they must get glasses too.

Other people do not see clearly because their eyes are not exactly the right shape. They have what is called astigmatism. This, too, can be corrected by glasses. Some people's eyes become cloudy because of cataracts. Long ago these people often became blind. Now, however, it is possible to operate on the cataracts and remove them.

When night falls, colors become fainter to the eye and finally disappear. After your eyes have grown accustomed to the dark, you can see better if you use the sides of your eyes rather than the centers. Sometimes, after dark, you see a small object to one side of you, which seems to disappear if you turn your head in its direction. This is because, when you turn your head, you are looking at the object too directly. Men on guard duty sometimes think they see something moving to one side of them. When they turn to look straight at it, they cannot see it any more, and they believe they were mistaken. However, this misapprehension occurs because the center of the eye, which is very sensitive in daylight, is not as sensitive as the sides of the eye after dark.

The eye is very similar to a camera: to take a picture there must be enough light, but not too much. On a camera, the opening of the lens can usually be adjusted. If there is not much light outside, you open the lens diaphragm wide. If the sun is shining brightly, you close the lens diaphragm. This is what your eye pupil does automatically. When the light is bright, your pupil grows small; when there is not much light, the pupil grows larger.

In a camera, the lens must be focused on the object to be photographed. This is done by changing the distance between the lens and the film inside the camera. Your eye has muscles which make such changes automatically. If you are looking at something far away, things which are close by will not appear very clear. However, if you are looking at some object close to you, distant objects will appear indistinct.

You can see how the lens works if you ask someone to stand at a window and look into the distance and then to look at a speck on the window glass. You will be able to see his eye change shape slightly as he looks from one area to the other. The eyes, in fact, relax more if they are looking into the distance. Therefore, it is a good idea to look up now and then if you are concentrating on some work close to your eyes.

What you see depends, to a great extent, on what you are in the habit of looking for. You might see many things in front of your eyes, but they will not mean anything to you if you cannot recognize them. A paper covered with complicated mathematical problems, for example, will not mean very much to someone unacquainted with higher mathematics.

Having two good eyes is important for judging distances. Each eye sees things from a slightly different angle. To prove this to yourself, look at an object out of one eye; then look at the same object out of your other eye. You will find the object's relation to the background and other things around it has changed. The difference between these two different eye views helps us to judge how far away an object is. People who have only one eye cannot judge distance as well as people with two eyes.

Your eye retains the image of what it has seen for a short time after it has finished seeing it. This is obvious when you go to see a moving picture. The film is really a succession of small pictures. Each picture stays in front of the lens for a fraction of a second before the next picture takes its place. Yet, when the pictures move fast enough, we get the impression that the people on the screen are really moving in a normal way, and not in a jumpy fashion.

Sometimes moving pictures can be taken at a faster speed than normal, and then shown at a normal speed. This gives the impression of "slow motion"—people or animals running very slowly and gracefully. On the other hand, a picture may be taken at a

slower speed than normal, then shown at a normal speed. This process gives the impression of people moving much faster than possible and is consequently quite amusing.

To demonstrate to yourself how important the mind's interpretation of what you see is, try the following experiment. Take three pieces of paper of the same size. On the first piece draw a picture of a man five inches high. On the second sheet draw the picture of a hand five inches high. On the third sheet draw a picture of a fish five inches high. Now, if you place the picture of the fish next to the picture of the hand, the fish will seem very small—not at all worth catching. However, if you place the picture of the fish next to the picture of the man, the fish will look big enough to feed a small village.

Finishing Time: Minutes_____ Seconds_____

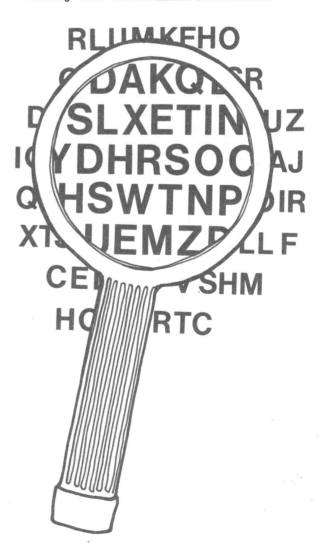

How Well Do You See?

COMPREHENSION: Answer the questions without looking back at the passage. When finished, correct your answers by checking with the answer key on page 179. Find your words per minute by looking in the chart on page 185. Enter both scores on graphs provided at the end of this book.

1. When things far away seem indistinct, one is probably
   ☐ a. nearsighted.
   ☐ b. farsighted.
   ☐ c. astigmatic.
   ☐ d. suffering from cataracts.

2. To see a small object at night, it is best
   ☐ a. to look straight at it.
   ☐ b. to blink your eyes often.
   ☐ c. to look in a slightly different direction.
   ☐ d. to squint your eyes.

3. To take a picture in dim light, you
   ☐ a. close the lens diaphragm.
   ☐ b. open the lens diaphragm.
   ☐ c. use a faster speed than normal.
   ☐ d. adjust the focus of the camera.

4. Having two eyes, instead of one, is particularly useful for
   ☐ a. seeing at night.
   ☐ b. seeing objects far away.
   ☐ c. looking over a wide area.
   ☐ d. judging distances.

5. People who suffer from astigmatism
   ☐ a. have eyes that are not exactly the right shape.
   ☐ b. have a curable virus in their eyes.
   ☐ c. have a difficulty that can be corrected by an operation.
   ☐ d. have an eye difficulty that cannot be corrected by glasses.

6. A detective may notice different things from another person because
   ☐ a. detectives are specially chosen for their excellent eyesight.
   ☐ b. he is equipped with special glasses.
   ☐ c. he is accustomed to looking for certain details.
   ☐ d. he is able to focus his eyes quickly.

7. To make a tree in a picture seem big, we could
   ☐ a. put it in a big frame.
   ☐ b. put a small person in the picture.
   ☐ c. put it in a small frame.
   ☐ d. put a large person in the foreground.

8. An eye is different from a camera in that
   ☐ a. it does not need to focus on an object to see it clearly.
   ☐ b. it focuses automatically.
   ☐ c. it adjusts to different lights.
   ☐ d. it opens and shuts.

9. When doing work requiring close attention, it is good
   ☐ a. to look up from time to time.
   ☐ b. to keep looking at the work to avoid changing focus.
   ☐ c. to work in a very bright light.
   ☐ d. to work in a very soft light.

10. To make slow motion pictures, the film is
   ☐ a. taken at a faster speed than normal.
   ☐ b. taken at a slower speed than normal.
   ☐ c. shown at a faster speed than normal.
   ☐ d. shown at a slower speed than normal.

Name _____ Date _____ Class _____

Reading Time: _____ _____ _____ _____ _____
              Minutes   Seconds   Words per minute   Total number right   Percent

30

How Well Do You See?

CLOZE TEST: The following passage, taken from the selection you have just read, has words omitted from it. Fill in the blank without looking back at the passage. When finished, correct your answers by checking with the answer key on page 179.

A. Subject Matter Words Missing

People who are nearsighted can only _____1_____ things that are very close to their eyes. Everything else seems _____2_____. Many people who do a lot of close work, such as writing, reading, and sewing, _____3_____ nearsighted. Then they have to wear glasses in order to see _____4_____ objects clearly. People who are farsighted suffer from just the _____5_____ problem. They can see things that are far away, but they have difficulty _____6_____ a book unless they _____7_____ it at arm's length. If they want to do much reading, they must get _____8_____ too. Other people do not see _____9_____ because their eyes are not exactly the right _____10_____.

B. Structure Words Missing

Having two good eyes is important _____1_____ judging distances. Each eye sees things _____2_____ a slightly different angle. To prove this _____3_____ yourself, look at an object out _____4_____ one eye; _____5_____ look at the same object out of your other eye. You will find the object's relation to the background _____6_____ other things _____7_____ it has changed. The difference _____8_____ these two different eye views helps us to judge how far _____9_____ an object _____10_____.

Name		Date	Class	

A. Number Right	Percent	B. Number Right	Percent

How Well Do You See?

VOCABULARY: The following words have been taken from the selection you have just read. Put an *X* in the box before the best meaning or synonym for the word as used in the selection.

1. **nearsighted**, page 28, col. 1, par. 2
"Many people who do a lot of close work, ... become nearsighted."
☐ a. to be partially sighted
☐ b. to see things near at hand
☐ c. to nearly see
☐ d. to ignore distance

2. **suffer**, page 28, col. 1, par. 3
"People who are farsighted suffer from just the opposite problem."
☐ a. to experience
☐ b. to react
☐ c. to feel pain
☐ d. to imagine

3. **sensitive**, page 28, col. 2, par. 1
"... the center of the eye ... is not as sensitive as the sides of the eye after dark."
☐ a. to be easily hurt
☐ b. to feel
☐ c. to be conscious
☐ d. to be sharp

4. **automatically**, page 28, col. 2, par. 2
"This is what your eye pupil does automatically."
☐ a. in an involuntary way
☐ b. with deliberation
☐ c. much like an automobile
☐ d. with compliance.

5. **complicated**, page 29, col. 1, par. 3
"A paper covered with complicated mathematical problems ..."
☐ a. easily solved
☐ b. more selective
☐ c. difficult to understand
☐ d. made up of two parts

6. **relation**, page 29, col. 1, par. 4
"You will find the object's relation to the background ... has changed."
☐ a. a necessary explanation
☐ b. an important similarity
☐ c. an existing connection
☐ d. an intimate attachment

7. **retains**, page 29, col. 1, par. 5
"Your eye retains the image of what it has seen for a short time after ..."
☐ a. to firmly grasp
☐ b. to continue to keep
☐ c. to surrender unwillingly
☐ d. to hold captive

8. **succession**, page 29, col. 1, par. 5
"The film is really a succession of small pictures."
☐ a. an accomplishment
☐ b. the most important
☐ c. one following another
☐ d. a good imitation

9. **consequently**, page 29, col. 2, par. 1
"gives the impression of people ... and is consequently quite amusing."
☐ a. in the long run
☐ b. on the other hand
☐ c. in some instances
☐ d. as a result

10. **demonstrate**, page 29, col. 2, par. 2
"To demonstrate to yourself how important the mind's interpretation ..."
☐ a. to describe
☐ b. to make evident
☐ c. to hold up
☐ d. to refer

Consequently is composed of a prefix **con** which is from the Latin, and means **with** or **together**. The root of the word is *sequi*. This is also from the Latin and means *to follow*. The general meaning of the word is usually interpreted as following as a result or effect. It rained, **consequently**, we stayed at home.

Name _____ Date _____ Class _____

Total Number Right _____ Percent _____

Set 2·A
What Makes
the Weather?

Starting Time: Minutes_____ Seconds_____

During the early period of the earth's history, the weather on earth apparently fluctuated between bright sun and showers. In recent times, however, the mountains and valleys on land and under water have had a great influence on the earth's weather. They effect the movements of the thin film of water we call the sea and the thin layer of air around the earth. These movements produce changes in the temperature and humidity prevailing at the surface.

Although the sun is approximately 93 million miles away, its rays warm the earth. The areas that receive the sun's rays vertically are, naturally, warmer than those areas that receive only slanting rays. Vertical rays do not need to make as long a journey through the atmosphere before reaching the surface of the earth. Therefore, less of their heat is lost in the air and more of their heat is saved to warm the earth. Furthermore, slanting rays are spread over a wider area than vertical rays, so that less heat is available at a given point.

The sun's rays do not heat the vast stretches of space between the sun and the earth. If they did, we should expect to be warmer on top of a high mountain or riding in an airplane than we are on the ground. Actually, however, we feel cooler at the top of a mountain; and, if we fly a plane high enough, we encounter freezing temperatures, even over the equator.

This is true because the sun's rays are like the waves used in radio broadcasting. Music sent out by a radio transmitter does not fill the air with sounds for all to hear. Instead, the music travels in the form of electromagnetic waves, which must pass through a receiver and an amplifier to be heard. Similarly, the sun's rays cross our atmosphere and are absorbed by the surface of the earth. These rays warm the surface, which sends back some of this heat into the air.

When the air near the earth's surface has been warmed, it rises and is replaced by cooler air which comes down to take its place. This cool air, in turn, is warmed and rises to be replaced by more cool air. As air rises it becomes cooler because it expands and is less concentrated. The air above it weighs less because there is less of it. If the air is suddenly let out of a tire, the air expands rapidly and becomes much cooler. On the other hand, when air is put under greater pressure, it becomes warmer. This is what happens to the cold air that comes down to take the place of rising warm air.

The earth is much cooler than the sun, and the wave length of the earth's radiations is much longer than that of sun rays. These longer heat waves cannot pass through the atmosphere as easily as the short waves coming from the sun. Similarly, radio stations that transmit programs to distant countries broadcast in short waves, which can travel all around the world. Stations that broadcast local programs send out longer waves, which can be received more easily, but only in a limited area.

Heat waves, rising from the earth, meet resistance in the atmosphere from the water vapor there. Many of the waves are stopped by the water vapor and cannot get back out into space. The atmosphere, when it is warmed up, also sends some heat back to the earth's surface.

When the sun's rays strike water surfaces, some of the water becomes absorbed by the air as water vapor. The warmer the air is, the more vapor it can hold. When the air has absorbed its maximum amount of vapor, it is said to be saturated. If the air is then cooled, some of the vapor will condense and clouds will form. These clouds will contain drops of water at temperatures above freezing, or ice crystals at temperatures below freezing.

Clouds can greatly affect the temperature of the earth's surface. When there are many clouds in the sky, all of the sun's rays cannot reach the earth. The cloudy day, then, will be cooler than the cloudless day. Clouds also prevent the earth from cooling off rapidly at night. For this reason, countries such as the British Isles, which are often covered by clouds, have a relatively constant temperature. The weather in these cloudy areas is neither very hot in summer nor very cold in winter. On the other hand, places such as deserts, which have few or no clouds, have very sharp variations in temperature—between night and day as well as between summer and winter.

Wind is caused by air moving between cold and warm regions. The warm air around the equator rises, while the cold air near the poles sinks to the ground. Therefore, in the upper atmosphere there is less air pressure near the poles than near the equator. To compensate for this condition the upper air moves toward the poles in an attempt to equalize the pressure. This makes the sur-face pressure greater at the poles, and sends air toward the equator.

The earth is always spinning from west to east, taking the atmosphere with it. Let us take, for example, a mass of air that is moving at the same speed as the earth at the equator. When some of this air begins moving toward the north pole it will travel in smaller circles as it moves northward. Thus it will pick up speed. This will appear as a west wind. On the other hand, let us take a mass of air that is originally moving as fast as the earth near the pole. As it starts traveling toward the equator it will have to travel in larger circles. Hence it will seem to lose speed. If it moves around more slowly than the earth it will appear as an east wind. Finally, the many variations caused by air masses which become cooler and descend, while other masses become warmer and rise, produce constant changes in the weather.

Finishing Time: Minutes_____ Seconds_____

What Makes the Weather?

COMPREHENSION: Answer the questions without looking back at the passage. When finished, correct your answers by checking with the answer key on page 179. Find your words per minute by looking in the chart on page 185. Enter both scores on graphs provided at the end of this book.

1. It is warmer at the equator because
   □ a. that part of the earth is closer to the sun.
   □ b. the sun's rays are like radio waves.
   □ c. the sun's rays are vertical there.
   □ d. there are no mountains at the equator.

2. It is cooler on top of a mountain because
   □ a. it is closer to the sun.
   □ b. there is less atmosphere to hold the earth's heat waves.
   □ c. there is more humidity there.
   □ d. it is like riding in an aeroplane.

3. When there are clouds, days tend to be
   □ a. warmer than when it is clear.
   □ b. cooler than when it is clear.
   □ c. the same as when it is clear.
   □ d. very uncomfortable.

4. Air can hold more water vapor when it is
   □ a. warm.
   □ b. cool.
   □ c. freezing.
   □ d. rising.

5. The sun's rays are absorbed by
   □ a. clouds.
   □ b. the electromagnetic waves of the atmosphere.
   □ c. the surface of the earth.
   □ d. water vapor.

6. If a country has a relatively constant temperature, it would probably be
   □ a. in a desert.
   □ b. covered by clouds.
   □ c. struck by the vertical rays of the sun.
   □ d. where there are many radio waves in the air.

7. Clouds do not often form over deserts because
   □ a. there is no water to form vapor.
   □ b. the winds blow them away.
   □ c. the sun's rays are too hot.
   □ d. the nights are too cold.

8. The earth's atmosphere is useful because
   □ a. it is transparent.
   □ b. it is thicker near the equator.
   □ c. it goes away at night.
   □ d. it enables the sun's rays to heat the earth.

9. A man who wants to predict the weather must watch
   □ a. the wind.
   □ b. the humidity.
   □ c. the clouds.
   □ d. all of these.

10. This article gives the impression that the weather
   □ a. is easy to predict.
   □ b. is generally the same from one year to the next.
   □ c. is traveling around in circles.
   □ d. is constantly changing.

Name _____   Date _____   Class _____

Reading Time: _____ _____   _____   _____   _____
               Minutes   Seconds   Words per minute   Total number right   Percent

What Makes the Weather?

CLOZE TEST: The following passage, taken from the selection you have just read, has words omitted from it. Fill in the blank without looking back at the passage. When finished, correct your answers by checking with the answer key on page 179.

A. Subject Matter Words Missing

The earth is much _____ 1 than the sun, and the wave length of the _____ 2 radiations is much longer than that of sun _____ 3. These longer heat waves _____ 4 pass through the atmosphere as _____ 5 as the short waves coming from the sun. Similarly, radio stations that transmit _____ 6 to distant countries broadcast in short waves, which can _____ 7 all around the world. Stations that _____ 8 local programs send out _____ 9 waves, which can be received more easily, but only in a limited _____ 10.

B. Structure Words Missing

When the air near _____ 1 earth's surface has been warmed, it rises and is replaced _____ 2 cooler air which comes down _____ 3 take its place. This cool air, _____ 4 turn, is warmed and rises to be replaced _____ 5 more cool air. _____ 6 air rises it becomes cooler because it expands _____ 7 is less concentrated. The air above it weighs less _____ 8 there is less of it. _____ 9 the air is suddenly let out _____ 10 a tire, the air expands rapidly and becomes much cooler.

Name _____ Date _____ Class _____

A. Number Right _____ Percent _____ B. Number Right _____ Percent _____

37

What Makes the Weather?

VOCABULARY: The following words have been taken from the selection you have just read. Put an *X* in the box before the best meaning or synonym for the word as used in the selection.

1. **fluctuated**, page 34, col. 1, par. 1
"... the weather on earth apparently fluctuated ..."
□ a. to change continually
□ b. to be spasmodic
□ c. to generate
□ d. to slowly yield

2. **prevailing**, page 34, col. 1, par. 1
"... in the temperature and humidity prevailing at the surface."
□ a. most effectual
□ b. very obvious
□ c. high above
□ d. most predominant

3. **vast**, page 34, col. 1, par. 3
"The sun's rays do not heat the vast stretches of space ..."
□ a. nearby or close
□ b. wide and immense
□ c. absolutely inaccessible
□ d. well insulated

4. **encounter**, page 34, col. 1, par. 3
"... if we fly a plane high enough, we encounter freezing temperatures, ..."
□ a. to be in conflict with
□ b. to be endangered by
□ c. to come upon
□ d. to be overwhelmed by

5. **concentrated**, page 34, col. 2, par. 3
"As air rises it becomes cooler because it expands and is less concentrated."
□ a. to be centered
□ b. to have more in a cubic unit
□ c. to seem complicated
□ d. to increase quality

6. **pressure**, page 34, col. 2, par. 3
"... when air is put under greater pressure, it becomes warmer."
□ a. an outside influence
□ b. a strong change
□ c. a troubled state
□ d. the force of one thing upon another

7. **maximum**, page 35, col. 1, par. 3
"... has absorbed its maximum amount of vapor, it is said to be saturated."
□ a. the greatest distance
□ b. the greatest width
□ c. the greatest length
□ d. the greatest quantity

8. **saturated**, page 35, col. 1, par. 3
"... has absorbed its maximum amount of vapor, it is said to be saturated."
□ a. to be damaged
□ b. to be fulfilled
□ c. to be soaked thoroughly
□ d. to be nearly soaked

9. **relatively**, page 35, col. 1, par. 4
"... have a relatively constant temperature."
□ a. in comparison or connection with
□ b. in the absence of
□ c. in a very close way
□ d. in an exact way

10. **compensate**, page 35, col. 1, par. 5
"To compensate for this condition the upper air moves toward the poles ..."
□ a. to complete
□ b. to ignore
□ c. to make up for
□ d. to prepare

Concentrated is composed of a root word *centrum* which means *center*. The prefix **con** means **with or together** and the suffix **ate** means **having**. The letters **ed** indicate **past time**. This word is used frequently in ordinary conversation.

Name _____ Date _____ Class _____

Total Number Right _____ Percent _____

38

Starting Time: Minutes_____ Seconds_____

Scientists believe that people "dressed up" long before they made a habit of wearing clothes. Primitive man dressed himself in feathers and ornaments, or painted his body and wrapped himself in animal skins. It was probably some time before man discovered that the decorations kept him warm and protected him from various injuries. Even today, millions of people who wear little clothing use ornaments and decorations.

When primitive people began to wear clothing regularly, they had to make it from the materials at hand. In cold regions, they often used the skins of fur-bearing animals as protection against the cold. In warmer regions of the world, the people dressed themselves in clothing made from leaves, tree bark, and woven grasses. Some people scraped the hair from animal skins to make soft leather for their clothes.

Linen was the first woven material from which clothes were made. From very early times, men have known how to make flax into fine linen. In fact, over four thousand years ago, Egyptians grew flax along the banks of the Nile River. They learned how to make threads from the fiber of the flax plant, and the linen that the ancient Egyptians wore was a softer, finer linen than the linen of today. However, only the very rich Egyptians could afford this fine linen. The poor people of ancient Egypt wore very coarse linen or animal skins, and most of them owned only one garment apiece.

Egyptian and Jewish priests, who lived in warm lands, wore fine linen clothing at religious festivals. The Egyptians wound their mummies in bands of linen before placing them in the tomb. Fine linen was also worn by the wealthy Greeks of ancient times. And, during the Middle Ages, most of the people in Europe wore linen.

Wool was probably the second woven material to be used for clothes, because there are many kinds of sheep that can live in many different climates, and because sheep are easy to raise, they have been raised in many parts of the world for their meat and their soft, warm wool. We do not know when people first thought of cutting off the sheep's wool and spinning it into yarn. However, we do know that, very early in history, rich and poor people alike were wearing wool clothes.

Wool clothes can be worn all the year round because wool is a natural insulator. By protecting the body from outside changes in temperature, wool keeps the body warm in winter and cool in summer.

39

Sheep's wool was not the only wool used by early man. The desert people made clothing from camel's hair; the people of Asia Minor used the fleece of the angora goat; the people of northern India and Tibet wove the fleece of the cashmere goat into soft, warm clothing; and the South American Indians made clothes from the wool of the llama, their beast of burden.

Despite the widespread early use of wool and linen, cotton is the most important source of man's clothing. Today, about three out of every four people in the world wear clothing made of cotton. Cotton has had a long history. Fifteen hundred years before the birth of Christ, the people of India were making cotton into cloth. The Greek historian, Herodotus, who wrote in the fifth century before Christ, described a tree in Asia which bore cotton. He said that "it exceeded in goodness and beauty the wool of any sheep." He also described the way the people of India wove and dyed cotton. For two thousand years the Indian's methods of weaving and dying have remained unchanged.

Cotton was not exported to Europe until the eighth century A.D. It was brought to Spain then by the Moors of North Africa. The Europeans liked this textile and began to make cotton cloth. By the fifteenth century, the cotton industry had spread from Spain to central Europe and the Low Countries.

When Columbus arrived in the West Indies, he found the Indians wearing cotton clothes. Pizarro, the Spanish conqueror of Peru, found that the Incas were growing cotton for use in the making of clothes. Magellan found the Brazilians swinging in cotton hammocks. And Cortes was so impressed by the beauty of the cotton tapestries and rugs that the Aztecs made, that he sent some of them as presents to King Charles II of Spain.

The Chinese were the first people to make silk clothing, and, for more than 2000 years, they were the only people in the world who knew how to make silk. The Chinese guarded the secret of their silk manufacture carefully. Their merchants grew rich in the silk trade with other Asian countries and Europe. Silk, in fact, was so expensive that it was known as the "cloth of kings."

During the reign of Emperor Justinian of Constantinople, two Persian monks who lived in China brought silkworms to Europe. In the years that followed, western Europeans learned how to grow silkworms and use the silk from the cocoons. Silk is still one of the most useful textiles in clothing manufacture because of its extremely strong fibers. A thread of silk is two-thirds as strong as an iron wire of the same size and so smooth that dirt cannot cling to it easily.

Two hundred years ago, most of the people of the world had little or no clothing. Clothing was taken care of very carefully and handed down from parents to children. Many people never owned a new garment in their lives, and, except for the rich, no one had more than one outfit of clothes at a time.

Primitive man made shoes long before he made permanent records on clay tablets or parchment scrolls. For many centuries, the shoemaker was interested only in covering the foot. Although he used fancy leathers and decorated shoes in many ways, he paid little attention to the fit of a shoe. In fact, it was only after 1850 that someone lit upon the idea of making differently-shaped shoes for the left and right foot.

Finishing Time: Minutes_____ Seconds_____

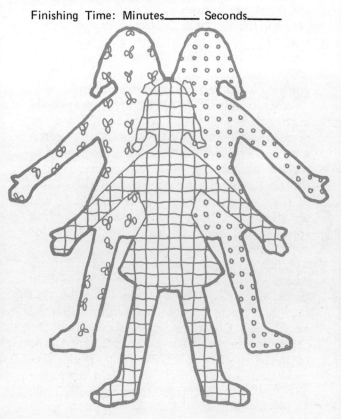

Looking Nice

COMPREHENSION: Answer the questions without looking back at the passage. When finished, correct your answers by checking with the answer key on page 179. Find your words per minute by looking in the chart on page 185. Enter both scores on graphs provided at the end of this book.

1. Linen is made from
   ☐ a. flax.
   ☐ b. grasses.
   ☐ c. cotton.
   ☐ d. skins.

2. The linen of the ancient Egyptians was
   ☐ a. almost as fine as that we see today.
   ☐ b. as fine as that we see today.
   ☐ c. finer than that we see today.
   ☐ d. a different kind of coth from what we see today.

3. The first woven material to be made into clothing was
   ☐ a. cotton.
   ☐ b. wool.
   ☐ c. linen.
   ☐ d. silk.

4. Silkworms were introduced into Europe by
   ☐ a. two Justinian Monks.
   ☐ b. two courtiers of Constantinople.
   ☐ c. two Persian Monks.
   ☐ d. two Egyptian Priests.

5. Pizzaro found the Incas
   ☐ a. using the wool of the llama for clothes.
   ☐ b. swinging on cotton hammocks.
   ☐ c. making beautiful tapestries from cotton.
   ☐ d. growing cotton for clothes.

6. The desert people obtained wool from
   ☐ a. sheep.
   ☐ b. llamas.
   ☐ c. camels.
   ☐ d. goats.

7. Wool can be worn year-round because
   ☐ a. sheep are found in both cold countries and hot countries.
   ☐ b. it has a strong, heat-resistant fiber.
   ☐ c. it is a natural insulator.
   ☐ d. sheep can be shorn year-round.

8. Which is the strongest material?
   ☐ a. Cotton
   ☐ b. Silk
   ☐ c. Wool
   ☐ d. Linen

9. People began making shoes for each foot
   ☐ a. in Roman Times.
   ☐ b. in the Middle Ages.
   ☐ c. in the eighteenth century.
   ☐ d. in the nineteenth century.

10. Cashmere was first used for clothes by
    ☐ a. South American Indians.
    ☐ b. the people of Asia Minor.
    ☐ c. the people of northern India and Tibet.
    ☐ d. the early Greeks.

_____   _____   _____
Name   Date   Class

Reading Time: _____ _____ _____ _____ _____
               Minutes Seconds   Words per minute Total number right Percent

41

Looking Nice

CLOZE TEST: The following passage, taken from the selection you have just read, has words omitted from it. Fill in the blank without looking back at the passage. When finished, correct your answers by checking with the answer key on page 179.

A. Subject Matter Words Missing

The Chinese were the _____ (1) people to make silk clothing, and, for more than 2000 _____ (2), they were the only people in the world who _____ (3) how to make silk. The Chinese _____ (4) the secret of their silk manufacture _____ (5). Their merchants grew rich in the silk _____ (6) with other Asian countries and Europe. Silk, in fact, was so _____ (7) that it was known as the "cloth of kings." During the _____ (8) of Emperor Justinian of Constantinople, two Persian _____ (9) who lived in China brought _____ (10) to Europe.

B. Structure Words Missing

Silk is _____ (1) one of the most useful textiles in clothing manufacture _____ (2) of its extremely strong fibers. A thread _____ (3) silk is two-thirds as strong _____ (4) an iron wire of the same size and _____ (5) smooth that dirt cannot cling _____ (6) it easily. Two hundred years _____ (7), most of the people of the world had little or _____ (8) clothing. Clothing was taken care _____ (9) very carefully and handed down _____ (10) parents to children.

Name _____   Date _____   Class _____

A. Number Right _____   Percent _____   B. Number Right _____   Percent _____

Looking Nice

VOCABULARY: The following words have been taken from the selection you have just read. Put an X in the box before the best meaning or synonym for the word as used in the selection.

1. **primitive**, page 39, col. 1, par. 2
"When primitive people began to wear clothing regularly, ..."
   - ☐ a. old fashioned
   - ☐ b. first or earliest of a kind
   - ☐ c. uncultured and dull
   - ☐ d. unrestrained and savage

2. **apiece**, page 39, col. 2, par. 1
"... and most of them owned only one garment apiece."
   - ☐ a. in several pieces
   - ☐ b. which was special
   - ☐ c. for each person
   - ☐ d. for outside use

3. **festivals**, page 39, col. 2, par. 2
"Egyptian and Jewish priests ... wore fine linen clothing at religious festivals."
   - ☐ a. a church service
   - ☐ b. the celebration of a feast
   - ☐ c. a song celebration
   - ☐ d. a gathering of clergy

4. **insulator**, page 39, col. 2, par. 4
"... wool is a natural insulator."
   - ☐ a. a protector from the elements
   - ☐ b. a scarce material
   - ☐ c. a protector from shock
   - ☐ d. a flexible fiber

5. **exceeded**, page 40, col. 1, par. 2
"... it exceeded in goodness and beauty the wool of any sheep."
   - ☐ a. to be an addition to
   - ☐ b. to come before
   - ☐ c. to be an exchange for
   - ☐ d. to surpass in excellence

6. **exported**, page 40, col. 1, par. 3
"Cotton was not exported to Europe ..."
   - ☐ a. to be found in
   - ☐ b. to be found in excess
   - ☐ c. to be sent to other places
   - ☐ d. to be excluded from

7. **textile**, page 40, col. 1, par. 3
"The Europeans liked this textile and began to make cotton cloth."
   - ☐ a. style of clothing
   - ☐ b. pattern or design
   - ☐ c. a special fabric
   - ☐ d. a woven material

8. **cling**, page 40, col. 2, par. 1
"... and so smooth that dirt cannot cling to it easily."
   - ☐ a. adhere closely
   - ☐ b. remain on top
   - ☐ c. stain permanently
   - ☐ d. fall on

9. **permanent**, page 40, col. 2, par. 3
"... he made permanent records on clay tablets or parchment scrolls."
   - ☐ a. being readable
   - ☐ b. decorative and complete
   - ☐ c. remaining unchanged
   - ☐ d. totally indestructible

10. **lit**, page 40, col. 2, par. 3
"In fact, it was only after 1850 that someome lit upon the idea ..."
   - ☐ a. to descend upon
   - ☐ b. to come upon by chance
   - ☐ c. to be illuminated by
   - ☐ d. to discover

The Latin word *primus* means *first*. Similarly, *primarius* means *of the first rank*. The word **primitive** obviously has its basic meaning in these words. That which is **primitive** is the first of its kind. It is original or primary.

Name _____   Date _____   Class _____

Total Number Right _____   Percent _____

Set 2·C
Engineers
of the Woods

In the forests of North America, where the winters are often long and cold, small ponds can be found along the streams. Sometimes these ponds are natural; sometimes they are man-made; and sometimes they are the constructions of beavers. You can tell a beaver pond by its dam. To make the dams, the beavers lay sticks and branches on top of each other to form an effective barrier against the water of the stream. Near the dam the beavers build a mud-covered, rounded pile of other sticks and branches. Usually this mound is similar to a small island surrounded by the water of the pond. This is the house where a beaver family spends the winter, protected from its enemies and from the cold. The beavers are able to keep dry in the center of the house, which is above water level.

The beavers work hard to make their house. They cut down trees, gather branches and twigs, and put them together with mud. Most of the summer is spent in this kind of work, but in winter the beavers' work proves worthwhile. Their house protects them even from bears.

During the American Revolution, when the armies made roads through the woods, they often tore down the beaver dams to drain swamps and make dry roads. However, the beavers returned again and again to their former dam-sites and rebuilt their dams. Thus, in a very short time, the roads were under water again.

The beaver is related to other rodents, or gnawing animals, such as rats, mice and squirrels. The beaver, however, is much bigger than its rodent cousins. An adult beaver may weigh more than 50 pounds, and his body may be about three feet long. His tail will add ten or twelve more inches to his length. His hind feet are webbed, which helps him swim rapidly. His front paws are similar to a pair of strong hands. With them he can carry logs and stones. His eyes, nose and ears are small, but he has two huge front teeth. These teeth are always growing, and he must keep them sharpened by constant use. The teeth of an adult beaver are yellow from the bark of trees that he gnaws.

The beaver's tail is particularly useful. It is broad and oval, in the shape of a paddle-blade. He uses it as an oar or rudder when he is in the water, and to balance himself when he is sitting on the ground. He often uses his tail to strike the ground as a warning to other beavers that danger is near. He can remain under water for ten minutes, using his tail as a sort of propeller.

Men attach great value to the beaver because of his fur. The beaver has practically disappeared from Europe because fur hunters and trappers killed so many beavers for their pelts. The beaver might easily have become extinct in America, too, but laws were passed to protect the beavers before they were all killed.

The beaver likes family life, and lives with the same mate all of his life. Several young—usually two to five—are born every year. The little beavers stay with their parents two years before mating and setting out on their own. The whole family lives in the same mound, or lodge. Generally there are several lodges in the same area, and the beaver families help each other in their community life. They share the work of building dams, constructing mounds, and raising the young (who require more space to live each year).

When there are too many beavers in one place, some of them will start a new colony in another place. They usually choose a spot near some fairly deep lake or river, where there are birch, poplar or willow trees. The bark of the birch, poplar, or willow is eaten as food. Then the wood is used in building.

Sometimes the lodges are built on the bank of the water, but usually they are built on an island in the water. If there is no island already there, the beavers make one by piling sticks and mud on the bed of the river until the top is a few inches above the level of the water. This top is carpeted with small pieces of wood, leaves, or moss. A dome-shaped roof of sticks and lots of mud is then built over this "floor." Food for the winter is taken to the lodge before the weather gets too cold. Some of it—the larger pieces—is stored on the bottom of the lake or river, near the entrance to a tunnel leading up to the lodge. There are sometimes several such entrances, under the surface of the water. Wood that is kept under water may be stuck in the mud, or weighted down with stones.

Beavers prefer to work at night. One beaver, in a single night, can fell a tree that is eight inches in diameter. After felling the tree, the beaver gnaws the trunk into pieces that can be carried. He uses these as the base for the dam. The dam is built in a straight line, or in a curve, with the outside of the curve facing upstream. A small dam may be enlarged after several years, in order to flood a larger surface and provide living space for more beavers. Under favorable conditions, a dam may last for a hundred years or more. Naturally, other animals use these dams as bridges, forcing the beavers to keep the dams in good repair. The dams must be strong enough to resist the pressure of ice in the spring; and sometimes holes are made by the beavers, after heavy rains, to allow excess water to run off.

Another type of work beavers do is canal-digging. When they have used the good trees near their home, they must bring more wood from farther away. To accomplish this, they may dig a canal to float the trees to the place where they are needed.

Beaver dams help people because they prevent floods and make irrigation easier. It is fortunate that these animals have not been allowed to disappear completely.

Finishing Time: Minutes_____ Seconds_____

Engineers of the Woods

COMPREHENSION: Answer the questions without looking back at the passage. When finished, correct your answers by checking with the answer key on page 179. Find your words per minute by looking in the chart on page 185. Enter both scores on graphs provided at the end of this book.

1. Beaver dams are found mainly in
    ☐ a. tropical regions.
    ☐ b. temperate regions.
    ☐ c. North America.
    ☐ d. Europe.

2. Beavers are related to
    ☐ a. dogs.
    ☐ b. cats.
    ☐ c. rats.
    ☐ d. deer.

3. Beavers use their tails in
    ☐ a. swimming.
    ☐ b. climbing.
    ☐ c. carrying wood.
    ☐ d. cutting trees.

4. The entrances to beaver houses are
    ☐ a. under trees.
    ☐ b. by the dam.
    ☐ c. under the water.
    ☐ d. level with the water surface.

5. The most important reason for the beaver's popularity is his
    ☐ a. ability to cut down trees.
    ☐ b. prevention of floods.
    ☐ c. amusing appearance.
    ☐ d. fur.

6. Beavers build their dams
    ☐ a. to live in them.
    ☐ b. to protect themselves from people.
    ☐ c. to help irrigate the nearby lands.
    ☐ d. to provide themselves with a pool.

7. An interesting feature of beaver life is their
    ☐ a. independence.
    ☐ b. sense of community.
    ☐ c. long, hard work.
    ☐ d. sharing of females.

8. Nowadays, beavers are protected by law because
    ☐ a. people want to have beaver fur.
    ☐ b. hunting is discouraged.
    ☐ c. beavers' work helps conserve natural resources.
    ☐ d. too many people shot beavers just for fun.

9. During the American Revolution, armies often tore down the beaver dams
    ☐ a. to make fur coats.
    ☐ b. as food.
    ☐ c. as temporary shelters.
    ☐ d. to drain swamps.

10. Judging from the text, men are gradually learning that animals
    ☐ a. are often necessary in ways they did not realize.
    ☐ b. often need to be shot in certain numbers.
    ☐ c. should never be protected by laws.
    ☐ d. are a good source of profits.

Name _____   Date _____   Class _____

Reading Time: _____ _____   _____   _____   _____
                Minutes   Seconds   Words per minute   Total number right   Percent

46

Engineers of the Woods

CLOZE TEST: The following passage, taken from the selection you have just read, has words omitted from it. Fill in the blank without looking back at the passage. When finished, correct your answers by checking with the answer key on page 179.

A. Subject Matter Words Missing

Food for the _____ is taken to the lodge before the

1

_____ gets too cold. Some of it—the _____

2   3

pieces—is stored on the bottom of the lake or river, near the _____

4

to a tunnel leading up to the lodge. There are sometimes _____

5

such entrances, under the surface of the _____. Wood that is kept

6

under water may be _____ in the mud, or weighted down with

7

stones. Beavers _____ to work at night. One beaver, in a

8

_____ night, can fell a tree that is eight inches

9

in _____'.

10

B. Structure Words Missing

Sometimes the lodges are built _____ the bank of the water,

1

_____ usually they are built on an island _____

2   3

the water. If there is _____ island already there, the beavers make

4

one _____ piling up sticks and mud on _____

5   6

bed of the river _____ the top is a few inches _____

7   8

the level of the water. This top is carpeted _____ small pieces of wood,

9

leaves, _____ moss.

10

Name _____   Date _____   Class _____

A. Number Right _____   Percent _____   B. Number Right _____   Percent _____

47

Engineers of the Woods

VOCABULARY: The following words have been taken from the selection you have just read. Put an *X* in the box before the best meaning or synonym for the word as used in the selection.

1. **constructions**, page 44, col. 1, par. 1
   "... and sometimes they are the constructions of beavers."
   ☐ a. well made structures
   ☐ b. poor attempts
   ☐ c. new achievements
   ☐ d. pesty obstacles

2. **effective**, page 44, col. 1, par. 1
   "To make dams, the beavers lay sticks ... to form an effective barrier ..."
   ☐ a. really outrageous
   ☐ b. very capable
   ☐ c. almost inconspicuous
   ☐ d. too elaborate

3. **barrier**, page 44, col. 1, par. 1
   "To make dams, the beavers lay sticks ... to form an effective barrier ..."
   ☐ a. a hide out
   ☐ b. a look-out tower
   ☐ c. something to prevent passage
   ☐ d. a weak bridge

4. **sites**, page 44, col. 2, par. 1
   "However, the beavers returned again and again to their former dam-sites ..."
   ☐ a. places or localities
   ☐ b. unsightly locations
   ☐ c. feeding ground
   ☐ d. destroyed structures

5. **gnawing**, page 44, col. 2, par. 2
   "The beaver is related to other rodents, or gnawing animals, ..."
   ☐ a. to wear away by constant biting
   ☐ b. to move swiftly
   ☐ c. to be small
   ☐ d. to be a meat eater

6. **extinct**, page 45, col. 1, par. 1
   "The beaver might easily have become extinct ... but laws were passed ..."
   ☐ a. very rare
   ☐ b. almost supressed
   ☐ c. seriously hunted
   ☐ d. no longer living

7. **generally**, page 45, col. 1, par. 2
   "Generally there are several lodges in the same area ..."
   ☐ a. it is the common thing
   ☐ b. once in a while
   ☐ c. at some time
   ☐ d. with some regularity

8. **felling**, page 45, col. 1, par. 5
   "After felling the tree, the beaver gnaws the trunk into pieces ..."
   ☐ a. to finish off
   ☐ b. to cut or knock down
   ☐ c. to climb up
   ☐ d. to lose balance

9. **surface**, page 45, col. 1, par. 5
   "... may be enlarged after several years in order to flood a larger surface ..."
   ☐ a. rising up
   ☐ b. the very top
   ☐ c. the area of a thing
   ☐ d. the finish

10. **accomplish**, page 45, col. 2, par. 2
    "To accomplish this, they may dig a canal to float the trees ..."
    ☐ a. to make an agreement
    ☐ b. to aid someone
    ☐ c. to increase by growth
    ☐ d. to succeed in doing

The everyday word **surface** contains the prefix **sur**. This is French in origin and means **above**. The Big Sur, in California, is high above the Pacific Ocean. The second part of the word, **face**, is from the Latin *facies* which means *form, shape or face.* The **surface**, then, is the outer face or outside of a thing.

Name _____   Date _____   Class _____

_____   _____
Total Number Right   Percent

48

Set 3

Set 3·A
Animal
Education

Starting Time: Minutes_____ Seconds_____

Animals perform many useful and entertaining jobs. Dogs are particularly valuable in guiding the blind, protecting property, finding lost people, and hunting criminals. Horses are used in guarding herds, carrying men in lands where there are no roads, and helping farmers work their land. Pigeons have long been used to carry messages. Wild animals from the jungles, forests and seas are very popular performers in circuses and moving pictures. People realize that, although animals may not have the same intelligence as human beings, they are smart enough to learn certain things.

The first thing a dog is taught is to obey. It should not take too long for him to learn commands. Simple orders, such as "sit, lie down, stay there, come here," can even be taught by a child.

Training a dog to be a watchdog often produces unexpected results. Some dogs quickly learn the difference between unwanted people and friends. This is because their masters welcome friends and invite them into their houses. However, some dogs will always attack the postman who comes to deliver letters. One explanation for this behavior is that, although the postman comes to the house often, he never enters the house.

Therefore, the dog thinks the postman is someone who is not wanted, but keeps coming back anyway.

Masters of dogs who attack postmen can easily show the dog that the postman is a friend and that the dog does not need to treat him as an unwanted person. A dog is quite ready to do what his master wishes. And a dog is always happy when he is praised for understanding correctly.

Dogs can be taught to obey commands when the sound of a word is connected with a certain act. Two important factors in teaching a dog to obey commands are: using the same word each time for the same act, and teaching only one act at a time. Dogs can learn not only to sit, lie down, come, and stay in place when their masters go away, but also to jump, carry, and fetch.

After a dog learns to carry an object, he can learn to bring something back from a distance. A stick can be thrown far away, and the dog enjoys running after it, and searching for it until he finds it. After a lot of practice, the dog can retrieve a stick (or other object) even when he has not seen it thrown. To teach a dog this skill, the master makes a simple trail by walking some distance in a straight line. Then he leaves the stick at the end of the trail. The dog learns to follow the straight line at first. Then, later, he learns to follow more irregular lines. Eventually, he can learn to follow an odor instead of looking for an object. With this skill he can be very useful in tracking down lost people or criminals.

Dogs are extremely useful as companions for blind people. When a dog has been properly trained, he will always lead his blind master in the right direction and keep him out of danger. For example, seeing-eye dogs learn never to cross a busy road when cars are coming, even if their masters command them to do so.

Horses are also able to learn many things. Horses that are used for guard or police duty must learn never to be frightened of noises, traffic, and other disturbances. Racing horses are able to run much faster than other horses, but they are also quite high strung. Therefore, it is necessary for those people who train them to be very patient and understanding.

Pigeons have a natural instinct to return home, even if they are very far away and the trip is hard or dangerous. Men utilize this homing instinct to send messages on small pieces of paper which are fastened to the pigeons' backs or legs. In war time, pigeons have been known to fly as fast as 75 miles an hour and to cover distances of 500 to 600 miles. These homing pigeons begin their training when they are about four weeks old. After a few weeks they can begin flying and carrying messages. If all goes well, their flying career lasts about four years.

Animals can learn to do many things that, while not necessarily useful, are very amusing to watch. In circuses, animals are taught to do the tricks that are most compatible to their physical and temperamental make-up. Lions and tigers can be taught to leap and spring gracefully when told to do so, or to stay in place on command. Elephants learn to walk in line, to stand on their hind legs, to lie on their sides, and to stand on their heads. They can also learn to dance.

Another trainer had an elephant and a tiger. After many weeks of living in the same cage, the two animals became accustomed to each other. Then the tiger was taught to jump on the elephant's back. Both animals became so interested in the act (as well as the praise and food they received after the act), that they forgot they were natural enemies. Later a lion was added to the act. This also took a lot of patient training. However, when the three animals grew accustomed to each other they made a most successful circus act.

The moving pictures and television can use trained animals too. Some animals, such as skunks and foxes, are easy to film. All you have to do is make a trail in front of the camera by dragging something that smells good to the animals over the ground. Big animals, such as lions and tigers, can be photographed as they bound happily back to their families and dinner. If a movie actor is nearby, the well-trained animal will pay no attention to him. However, the audience may imagine that the actor escaped a terrible death by the skin of his teeth.

Finishing Time: Minutes_____ Seconds_____

Animal Education

COMPREHENSION: Answer the questions without looking back at the passage. When finished, correct your answers by checking with the answer key on page 180. Find your words per minute by looking in the chart on page 185. Enter both scores on graphs provided at the end of this book.

1. A dog feels happiest if, after he has worked well,
   - ☐ a. he gets a good piece of meat.
   - ☐ b. he gets praise from his master.
   - ☐ c. he is allowed to be by himself.
   - ☐ d. he is taken for a walk.

2. Some dogs may be suspicious of postmen because
   - ☐ a. postmen carry large, suspicious-looking bags.
   - ☐ b. postmen wear uniforms.
   - ☐ c. postmen never enter a house.
   - ☐ d. postmen come to a house often.

3. Dogs who accompany blind people must learn
   - ☐ a. to obey all orders.
   - ☐ b. to obey only safe orders.
   - ☐ c. never to cross busy roads.
   - ☐ d. to cross roads when commanded to do so.

4. Race horses are hard to train because they are
   - ☐ a. faster than other horses.
   - ☐ b. smaller than other horses.
   - ☐ c. more suspicious than other horses.
   - ☐ d. more nervous than other horses.

5. Pigeons can carry messages for about
   - ☐ a. two weeks.
   - ☐ b. four weeks.
   - ☐ c. two years.
   - ☐ d. four years.

6. Pigeons have been known to fly as fast as
   - ☐ a. 75 mph.
   - ☐ b. 50 mph.
   - ☐ c. 110 mph.
   - ☐ d. 62 mph.

7. Dogs can be taught to obey commands when the sound of a word
   - ☐ a. is repeated often enough.
   - ☐ b. is connected with a certain act.
   - ☐ c. becomes familiar because of the master's tone of voice.
   - ☐ d. is uttered patiently and with understanding.

8. Lions can be photographed easily when
   - ☐ a. they are following a trail of something that smells good to them.
   - ☐ b. they are returning to their families.
   - ☐ c. they have been trained to work with other animals.
   - ☐ d. they do not know a movie-actor is nearby.

9. Which of the following statements is wrong?
   - ☐ a. Elephants can be graceful.
   - ☐ b. Tigers are too dangerous to be trained.
   - ☐ c. Animals which are natural enemies can be trained to live together.
   - ☐ d. Animals can become interested in their tricks.

10. The first thing a dog needs to learn in order to be trained is
    - ☐ a. obedience.
    - ☐ b. attacking.
    - ☐ c. staying still.
    - ☐ d. heeling.

Name _____ Date _____ Class _____

Reading Time: _____ _____   _____ _____ _____
                Minutes   Seconds   Words per minute   Total number right   Percent

Animal Education

CLOZE TEST: The following passage, taken from the selection you have just read, has words omitted from it. Fill in the blank without looking back at the passage. When finished, correct your answers by checking with the answer key on page 180.

A. Subject Matter Words Missing

The first thing a dog is _____1_____ is to obey. It should not _____2_____ too long for him to learn commands. _____3_____ orders, such as "sit, lie down, stay there, _____4_____ here," can even be taught by a child. Dogs can also learn to bark at _____5_____ and even to attack them. Many people have dogs to _____6_____ undesirable people off of their property. _____7_____ a dog to be a watchdog often produces unexpected results. Some dogs _____8_____ learn the difference between unwanted people and _____9_____. This is because their masters welcome friends and _____10_____ them into their houses.

B. Structure Words Missing

After a dog learns to carry _____1_____ object, he can learn to bring something back _____2_____ a distance. A stick can be thrown far _____3_____, and the dog enjoys running after it, and searching _____4_____ it until he finds it. After a lot _____5_____ practice, the dog can retrieve a stick (_____6_____ other object) even when he has _____7_____ seen it thrown. To teach a dog this skill, the master makes a simple trail _____8_____ walking some distance in a straight line. _____9_____ he leaves the stick at the end _____10_____ the trail.

Name _____   Date _____ Class _____

A. Number Right _____ Percent _____ B. Number Right _____ Percent _____

Animal Education

VOCABULARY: The following words have been taken from the selection you have just read. Put an *X* in the box before the best meaning or synonym for the word as used in the selection.

1. **particularly**, page 50, col. 1, par. 1
   "Dogs are particularly valuable in guiding the blind, ..."
   ☐ a. socially and physically
   ☐ b. especially or uniquely
   ☐ c. only occasionally
   ☐ d. only partially

2. **factors**, page 50, col. 2, par. 3
   "Two important factors in teaching a dog to obey commands are: ..."
   ☐ a. grave concerns
   ☐ b. hereditary characters
   ☐ c. numerical considerations
   ☐ d. basic elements

3. **retrieve**, page 50, col. 2, par. 4
   "... the dog can retrieve a stick even when he has not seen it thrown."
   ☐ a. to be able to recover or regain
   ☐ b. to be able to make good
   ☐ c. to be able to carry
   ☐ d. to be able to perceive.

4. **irregular**, page 51, col. 1, par. 1
   "Then, later, he learns to follow more irregular lines."
   ☐ a. more exciting
   ☐ b. not uniform
   ☐ c. less smooth
   ☐ d. more difficult

5. **strung**, page 51, col. 1, par. 3
   "Racing horses ... are also quite high strung."
   ☐ a. highly nervous
   ☐ b. extremely undependable
   ☐ c. high built
   ☐ d. lowly bred

6. **instinct**, page 51, col. 1, par. 4
   "Pigeons have a natural instinct to return home, ..."
   ☐ a. a physical aid
   ☐ b. a defect in flight
   ☐ c. an inborn tendency
   ☐ d. an unusual gift

7. **compatible**, page 51, col. 1, par. 5
   "... the tricks that are most compatible to their physical ... make-up."
   ☐ a. like or associated with
   ☐ b. accustomed to
   ☐ c. agreeable to
   ☐ d. composed of

8. **temperamental**, page 51, col. 1, par. 5
   "... the tricks that are most compatible to their ... temperamental make-up."
   ☐ a. aggressive nature
   ☐ b. prevailing tendency
   ☐ c. natural disposition
   ☐ d. a particular quality

9. **accustomed**, page 51, col. 1, par. 6
   "... the two animals became accustomed to each other."
   ☐ a. to become tolerant of
   ☐ b. to become habituated to
   ☐ c. to become pleased with
   ☐ d. to become patient with

10. **bound**, page 51, col. 2, par. 2
    "... lions and tigers, can be photographed as they bound happily back ..."
    ☐ a. to run with restriction
    ☐ b. to run in a group
    ☐ c. to leap onward
    ☐ d. to have limits

Compatible is a word often used in discussions about marriage. One definition is worded: capable of existing together without discord or disharmony. In the Latin origin, *compati*, the meaning is expressed as, *to suffer with*. The suffix **ible** indicates **being able to**. A person who is **compatible** is, then, one who can share another's sufferings.

Name _____ Date _____ Class _____

Total Number Right _____ Percent _____

54

Starting Time: Minutes_____ Seconds_____

In the nineteenth century, the invention of the telegraph made it possible to send noises, signals, and even music over wires from one place to another. However, the human voice had never traveled this way. Many inventors tried to find a way to send a voice over wires, and in 1876 some of their efforts were crowned with success. Two American inventors, Alexander Graham Bell and Elisha Gray, succeeded at almost the same time. The United States Supreme Court finally had to decide which of the two was the first inventor of the telephone. The Court decided in Bell's favor.

Born in Edinburgh, Scotland, Bell grew up in a family that was very interested in teaching people to speak. His grandfather had been an actor who left the theatre to teach elocution; his father was a teacher who helped deaf-mutes learn how to speak.

After studying in Edinburgh and London, Bell moved to Canada with his family. Bell was frail and, since two of his brothers had died of tuberculosis, his family felt that the climate of Canada would be less damp and more healthy for Alexander.

In 1871, the year after the Bells' arrival in Canada, young Alexander found a job in the United States. He was hired as a teacher in a new school for the deaf in Boston, Massachusetts. He taught there and at other United States schools. Eventually, he opened a school of his own. One of his pupils later became his wife.

Bell thought that if he could make speech visible by actually showing the vibrations of the voice, he could teach his deaf pupils to make the same vibrations themselves. Bell tried to find a way to reproduce the vibrations by electrical means. He was led to believe that if a wire could carry vibrations, there was no reason why it could not carry the words spoken by a person. After all, he reasoned, spoken words are only a series of different vibrations.

Bell spent his evenings experimenting with tuning forks (forkshaped pieces of metal which always produce the same musical note and which are used to tune pianos), metal springs, and magneto batteries. His assistant, named Watson, worked with him for almost four years. They spent all their spare time, as well as their spare money, on their experiments. When their money ran out, they persuaded some businessmen to help them financially.

Finally, one day in 1874, Bell was at his receiver in one room, trying to catch the signals sent by Watson from another room. Suddenly he heard a faint twang. Rushing into Watson's room, Bell shouted, "What did you do then?" He found that the sound had been made accidentally when two pieces of metal had stuck together and closed the circuit. Watson had pushed the pieces apart, and the metallic vibration had been carried to Bell over the wire. After this discovery, all they had to do was find the best kinds of materials for carrying the human voice over wires. The basic principle had been discovered.

After much experimentation, the first telephone was exhibited at the Centennial Exposition of 1876 in Philadelphia. At first few people paid any attention to the young man whose table held a curious box with an unexciting appearance. There were many other things to see at the exposition, and Bell was not the "barker" type who painted big signs and shouted about the wonders of his display. However, when the judges came to inspect the new machine, they were amazed. Some of the visitors at the exposition included the English scientist, William Thomson (Lord Kelvin), and the Emperor of Brazil, who had previously met Bell. Thomson said the telephone was "the greatest marvel hitherto achieved by the electric telegraph." The Emperor of Brazil exclaimed, "It talks!!" Soon crowds were gathering around the exhibit and, from that time on, Bell was famous.

Bell never lost his interest in helping the deaf. After all, it was because of his work with them that he had begun his search for a way to reproduce the human voice electrically. If he had not tried to make speech visible to the deaf, he might never have discovered the telephone. Bell established a fund for the study of deafness. His studies showed that deafness was increasing in America, because deaf people were kept in institutions where they met and married one another. This policy, he warned, was producing a deaf variety of the human race. He strongly advocated a policy where deaf people could be taught to use language instead of being limited to the use of sign language. Bell said that the deaf should also live among normal people, so that they would not consider themselves inferior to others and fail to develop their powers of speech.

Not long after Bell's invention, telephone companies were established in the United States, Great Britain, France and many other countries. It is said that in Bell's later life, when telephones had become quite common, the telephone disturbed him because it was always ringing and interrupting his experiments.

Bell invented other things besides the telephone, but none of them were as important to mankind as the telephone. One of the most interesting of his inventions was the photophone, which carried the sound of the voice for a short distance over a vibrating beam of light. Another invention of interest was the graphophone, an ancestor of the phonograph, which used wax records similar to those we know today.

However, probably none of these later inventions gave Bell the same feeling of triumph as he had on the day when he spilled some acid from his batteries. It was after he had worked for months to find ways to send something more than metallic twangs over the wires. Thinking Watson, his helper, was in the next room, Bell called, "Mr. Watson, come here. I want you." Watson was not in the next room. He was down in his laboratory, next to the receiver. To Watson's surprise, he heard the words perfectly. He ran to tell Bell the news: the wires had carried Bell's voice perfectly.

Finishing Time: Minutes_____ Seconds_____

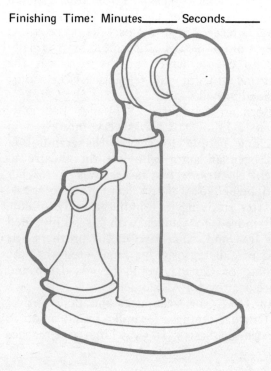

56

The Telephone and Its Inventor

COMPREHENSION: Answer the questions without looking back at the passage. When finished, correct your answwrs by checking with the answer key on page 180. Find your words per minute by looking in the chart on page 185. Enter both scores on graphs provided at the end of this book.

1. Bell was led to invent the telephone by
   - ☐ a. his work with the deaf.
   - ☐ b. his interest in the telegraph.
   - ☐ c. his family background.
   - ☐ d. his desire for money and recognition.

2. Bell's life work was that of
   - ☐ a. a scientist.
   - ☐ b. a teacher.
   - ☐ c. an inventor.
   - ☐ d. an actor.

3. He felt that deaf people were better educated in schools where
   - ☐ a. they were by themselves.
   - ☐ b. they could meet people to marry.
   - ☐ c. they could meet normal people.
   - ☐ d. they could learn the sign language.

4. Bell's work was made difficult by lack of
   - ☐ a. money.
   - ☐ b. family support.
   - ☐ c. time.
   - ☐ d. qualified assistants.

5. After Bell invented the telephone,
   - ☐ a. he invented nothing else of importance.
   - ☐ b he continued to work on other inventions.
   - ☐ c. he conducted displays at many expositions.
   - ☐ d. he died a poor man.

6. Bell probably became interested in the human voice
   - ☐ a. when he was a child.
   - ☐ b. when he had finished his studies.
   - ☐ c. when he married a deaf woman.
   - ☐ d. when he worked with the deaf.

7. The idea of making wires that carry voices had
   - ☐ a. originated with Bell.
   - ☐ b. fascinated many people.
   - ☐ c. never been thought of before.
   - ☐ d. been shown to be possible.

8. Bell's first intimation that he was succeeding came when
   - ☐ a. Watson heard Bell's voice over a wire.
   - ☐ b. the Emperor said "It talks!"
   - ☐ c. Bell heard a twang.
   - ☐ d. Bell spilled acid out of his batteries.

9. Deafness is
   - ☐ a. caused by a germ or virus.
   - ☐ b. often passed from parents to children.
   - ☐ c. mostly due to accidents.
   - ☐ d. never curable.

10. People began paying attention to the telephone
   - ☐ a. when it was installed in the Exposition buildings.
   - ☐ b. when the invention was announced.
   - ☐ c. after the Supreme Court decided in Bell's favor.
   - ☐ d. after important people praised it.

_____   _____   _____
Name   Date   Class

Reading Time: _____ _____ _____ _____ _____
                 Minutes   Seconds   Words per minute   Total number right   Percent

The Telephone and Its Inventor

CLOZE TEST: The following passage, taken from the selection you have just read, has words omitted from it. Fill in the blank without looking back at the passage. When finished, correct your answers by checking with the answer key on page 180.

A. Subject Matter Words Missing

In the nineteenth century, the _____ 1 of the telegraph made it possible to _____ 2 noises, signals, and even music over wires from one _____ 3 to another. However, the _____ 4 voice had never traveled this way. Many inventors tried to _____ 5 a way to send a voice over _____ 6, and in 1876 some of their efforts were crowned with _____ 7. Two American inventors, Alexander Graham Bell and Elisha Gray, succeeded at almost the same _____ 8. The United States Supreme Court _____ 9 had to decide which of the two was the _____ 10 inventor of the telephone.

B. Structure Words Missing

Bell never lost his interest _____ 1 helping the deaf. After all, it was _____ 2 of his work with them that he had begun his search _____ 3 a way to reproduce the human voice electrically. _____ 4 he had not tried to make speech visible _____ 5 the deaf, he might never have discovered _____ 6 telephone. Bell established a fund for the study _____ 7 deafness. His studies showed _____ 8 deafness was increasing in America, _____ 9 deaf people were kept in institutions _____ 10 they met and married one another.

Name _____   Date _____ Class _____

A. Number Right _____ Percent _____ B. Number Right _____ Percent _____

58

The Telephone and Its Inventor

VOCABULARY: The following words have been taken from the selection you have just read. Put an *X* in the box before the best meaning or synonym for the word as used in the selection.

1. **crowned**, page 55, col. 1, par. 1
"... some of their efforts were crowned with success."
☐ a. having received an honor
☐ b. having achieved success
☐ c. having gained power
☐ d. having gained royal recognition

2. **vibrations**, page 55, col. 2, par. 2
"... a way to reproduce the vibrations by electrical means."
☐ a. a trembling effect
☐ b. change of pitch
☐ c. musical sounds
☐ d. difficult patterns

3. **series**, page 55, col. 2, par. 2
"... spoken words are only a series of different vibrations."
☐ a. a succession of things
☐ b. a sum of terms
☐ c. different types
☐ d. a composition of things

4. **persuaded**, page 55, col. 2, par. 3
"... they persuaded some businessmen to help them financially."
☐ a. carefully suggested
☐ b. finally forced
☐ c. threatened with words
☐ d. strongly convinced

5. **exhibited**, page 56, col. 1, par. 2
"... the first telephone was exhibited at the Centennial Exposition of 1876"
☐ a. to be in competition
☐ b. to attract attention
☐ c. to attempt to show
☐ d. to expose to view

6. **curious**, page 56, col. 1, par. 2
"... table held a curious box with an unexciting appearance."
☐ a. ordinary and small
☐ b. strange or peculiar
☐ c. unattractive and old
☐ d. nicely painted

7. **exposition**, page 56, col. 1, par. 2
"There were many other things to see at the exposition."
☐ a. a point of view
☐ b. a show displaying products
☐ c. the act of explaining
☐ d. an open air show

8. **hitherto**, page 56, col. 1, par. 2
"The greatest marvel hitherto achieved by the electric telegraph."
☐ a. by accident
☐ b. with no purpose
☐ c. until now
☐ d. most definitely

9. **policy**, page 56, col. 1, par. 3
"This policy, he warned, was producing a deaf variety ..."
☐ a. a document or contract
☐ b. a type of shrewdness
☐ c. a setting forth
☐ d. a course of action

10. **advocated**, page 56, col. 1, par. 3
"He strongly advocated a policy where deaf people could be taught ..."
☐ a. to plead in favor of
☐ b. to fight for
☐ c. to develop the details
☐ d. to use half heartedly

An **advocate** is one who argues for a cause. The word **advocate** is made up of a prefix **ad** and the Latin word *vocare* which means *to call*. The prefix **ad** is a prefix of **direction** or **tendency**. An **advocate**, then, is one who calls to give evidence in a special direction.

_____   _____   _____
Name   Date   Class

_____   _____
Total Number Right   Percent

Set 3·C
A French Boy's
Adventures in Canada

Starting Time: Minutes_____ Seconds_____

Early one morning in the spring of 1652, three young men decided to go hunting. They left the little fort of Three Rivers, on the Saint Lawrence River, for the marshes of Lake St. Peter. On one side of the lake were the forest-covered hills. On the other side was the broad St. Lawrence, with miles of marshes. Wild ducks, geese, and other birds migrated there every year.

The three young men did not really know the dangers involved in leaving the fort at that time. Everyone else knew that the Iroquois Indians around the settlement had been lying in ambush for a long time. Every week some settler who worked his lands outside the protecting fence of the fort was set upon and killed. However, the boys, unaware, went happily along, boasting about how they would fight if the Indians attacked them. One boy stayed close to the forest, watching for Indians; the other two stayed by the river, looking for wild animals and birds to shoot. About a mile from the fort they met a herdsman. He warned them not to go too close to the hills because he had seen many Indians there.

When they had travelled some distance and shot a number of ducks, one boy said he had had enough. He decided he would go back to the fort. The second boy said that he would join him. However, the third boy, Pierre, laughed at the other two and continued hunting alone.

When Pierre had gone about nine miles from the fort, he came to a stream that was too deep to walk across, and he realized that he already had more birds than he could carry. He hid some of the birds in hollow trees and started back to the fort with a string of geese and ducks over his shoulder.

Finally, Pierre saw the roofs of the settlement above the river, gleaming in the last rays of sunlight. A great flock of ducks was swimming on the river and the sight of them reassured Pierre. He reasoned that if any people were nearby the ducks would have become frightened and would have flown away. Pierre decided not to miss this wonderful chance to shoot one or two more ducks. He moved quietly through the tall grass toward the water. Suddenly he stumbled over the bodies of his two friends. They had been stripped of their clothing and scalped.

Pierre tried to hide in the tall grass. He heard gun shots from the forest behind him, and fired back, but the Indians were too much for him. When he came to his senses, Pierre found himself being dragged back to the woods where the Iroquois showed him the scalps of his dead friends.

The Indians stripped Pierre of his clothes and tied him to a tree. Then they gathered around the fire for their evening meal. Suddenly an alarm was sounded: the French were coming. The Indians put the fire out immediately, and a number of Indians set out to see where their enemies were. The Indians soon returned with news which was evidently reassuring. A second fire was lit, and the meal continued.

Then Pierre's clothes were returned to him. When the young warriors offered Pierre some of their food, they saw that their rancid meat made him ill. Then they boiled some fresh meat in clean water and gave Pierre corn meal browned on burning sand with the meat. Since Pierre did not struggle or try to escape, he was untied. That night he slept between two Indians under a common blanket. In the morning they all set out for the Indian village.

The Indians shaved Pierre's head and decorated it with an Iroquois head-dress. They also taught him how to hold an oar and throw spears. Pierre reasoned that, since he had not been killed and scalped as his two friends had been, it might be because the Indians were impressed by the facts that he had gone on alone when his friends had turned back, and that he never seemed to be frightened of the Indians.

After several days of travelling, they arrived at a lake. The Iroquois went to a pool of water on the bank of the lake and threw hot stones into the pool until the water was steaming. Then each Iroquois took a bath, to clean himself before meeting his family.

The return of the Indians to their village was, as usual, a great occasion. The wives came to meet them. Then all the people of the village armed themselves with clubs and whips to torture the captives. The Indians formed two lines, through which the captives were forced to run. When it was Pierre's turn to run between the two lines of whippers, he was told quietly to run very fast so that he could not be hurt.

After Pierre had run through the line, a captive Huron woman, who had lived in the village for some time, took Pierre to her cabin. She gave him fresh clothes and food. Then he was taken to the Council Lodge of the Iroquois for judgment.

The wise men of the tribe sat around a fire, silently smoking their pipes. The old Huron woman came in and begged them to spare Pierre's life. The men listened and made signs of approval. Finally, the old woman was given permission to adopt Pierre as her son.

Pierre's new family dressed him in colored blankets and strings of wampum, which is made of shells and stones that are very highly polished. This wampum was used as money by the Indians.

So it was that Pierre came to live with the Iroquois Indians. They gave him a gun and he went hunting with them every day.

Although he was grateful for all these attentions, and happy to have made new friends, Pierre still hoped to return one day to his family at Three Rivers. He was finally allowed to return and, later in life, he became a fur-trader. His knowledge of the Indian customs and language helped him considerably in his explorations and commercial dealings. However, he was not always a successful man, because he was too independent to bow and scrape to governors and kings.

Finishing Time: Minutes_____ Seconds_____

A French Boy's Adventures in Canada

COMPREHENSION: Answer the questions without looking back at the passage. When finished, correct your answers by checking with the answer key on page 180. Find your words per minute by looking in the chart on page 185. Enter both scores on graphs provided at the end of this book.

1. The young hunters did not hesitate to leave the fort because
   □ a. they were very brave.
   □ b. they did not know how dangerous it was.
   □ c. they saw some ducks and geese to shoot.
   □ d. they were only going for the day.

2. When the Indians heard that the French were coming, they
   □ a. got their horses ready to fight.
   □ b. tried to dress Pierre like an Indian.
   □ c. put out the fire.
   □ d. showed Pierre the scalps of his dead friends.

3. When Pierre could not eat the meat, the Indians
   □ a. laughed at him.
   □ b. offered him a hot bath.
   □ c. put war-paint on his face.
   □ d. boiled him some fresh meat.

4. When they arrived at the village, Pierre was not tortured or killed because
   □ a. he had shown his courage.
   □ b. the old woman wanted to adopt him.
   □ c. everyone was too happy celebrating.
   □ d. the French did not attack.

5. In what century did this story take place?
   □ a. Sixteenth   □ c. Eighteenth
   □ b. Seventeenth   □ d. Nineteenth

6. Before the Iroquois met their families, they
   □ a. tried to show they had been brave.
   □ b. prepared their collection of scalps.
   □ c. threw hot stones into a pool.
   □ d. painted their faces.

7. From the way the Indians treated Pierre, it seemed they admired the trait of
   □ a. courage.   □ c. silence.
   □ b. curiosity.   □ d. hostility.

8. Wampum was different from plain shells and stones because
   □ a. the Indians put a special spell on it.
   □ b. the Indians decorated it with special paints.
   □ c. the Indians polished each piece for a long time.
   □ d. the Indians collected the wampum from the St. Lawrence.

9. Pierre realized the French were not going to attack when the Indians
   □ a. tied a rope around his waist.
   □ b. started to do a war dance.
   □ c. relit the fire and ate.
   □ d. displayed the scalps of his two friends.

10. This story shows that a European living with the Indians
   □ a. could never be happy.
   □ b. gradually forgot about his family.
   □ c. was never really trusted.
   □ d. could get along quite well with them.

Name _____   Date _____   Class _____

Reading Time: _____ _____   _____   _____   _____
               Minutes Seconds   Words per minute   Total no. right   Percent

62

A French Boy's Adventures in Canada

CLOZE TEST: The following passage, taken from the selection you have just read, has words omitted from it. Fill in the blank without looking back at the passage. When finished, correct your answers by checking with the answer key on page 180.

A. Subject Matter Words Missing

Although he was _____ 1 for all these attentions, and _____ 2 to have made new friends, Pierre still _____ 3 to return one day to his _____ 4 at Three Rivers. He was finally _____ 5 to return and, later in life, he _____ 6 a fur-trader. His knowledge of the _____ 7 customs and language helped him _____ 8 in his explorations and commercial dealings. However, he was not always a _____ 9 man, because he was too independent to _____ 10 and scrape to governors and kings.

B. Structure Words Missing

The wise men _____ 1 the tribe sat around a fire, silently smoking their pipes. _____ 2 old Huron woman came in and begged them _____ 3 spare Pierre's life. The men listened _____ 4 made signs of approval. Finally the old woman was given permission _____ 5 adopt Pierre _____ 6 her son. Pierre's new family dressed him _____ 7 colored blankets and strings of wampum, _____ 8 is made of shells and stones _____ 9 are very highly polished. This wampum was used as money _____ 10 the Indians.

_____   _____   _____
Name   Date   Class

_____   _____
A. Number Right   Percent   B. Number Right   Percent

63

A French Boy's Adventures in Canada

VOCABULARY: The following words have been taken from the selection you have just read. Put an X in the box before the best meaning or synonym for the word as used in the selection.

1. **migrated**, page 60, col. 1, par. 1
"Wild ducks, geese, and other birds migrated there every year."
☐ a. to settle down
☐ b. to go from one region to another
☐ c. to travel constantly
☐ d. to rove about

2. **unaware**, page 60, col. 1, par. 2
"However, the boys, unaware, went happily along ..."
☐ a. to deliberately ignore
☐ b. to be careless
☐ c. not to know
☐ d. to be indifferent

3. **string**, page 60, col. 2, par. 2
"... and started back to the fort with a string of geese ..."
☐ a. a connected series of things
☐ b. a long cord
☐ c. binding material
☐ d. a moving formation

4. **reassured**, page 60, col. 2, par. 3
"A great flock of ducks ... and the sight of them reassured Pierre."
☐ a. to make confident again
☐ b. to excite
☐ c. to confuse
☐ d. to cause wonder

5. **evidently**, page 61, col. 1, par. 2
"The Indians soon returned with news which was evidently reassuring."
☐ a. to suggest doubt
☐ b. to sense insecurity
☐ c. to present proof
☐ d. to tend toward clearness

6. **rancid**, page 61, col. 1, par. 3
"... they saw their rancid meat made him ill."
☐ a. unusual tasting
☐ b. foul smelling
☐ c. badly prepared
☐ d. quite rare

7. **common**, page 61, col. 1, par. 3
"That night he slept between two Indians under a common blanket."
☐ a. most unusual
☐ b. shared by all
☐ c. very ordinary
☐ d. plain looking

8. **reasoned**, page 61, col. 1, par. 4
"Pierre reasoned that, since he had not been killed ..."
☐ a. make a statement
☐ b. to be intelligent
☐ c. to have hope
☐ d. to decide by clear thinking

9. **approval**, page 61, col. 2, par. 2
"The men listened and made signs of approval."
☐ a. showing concern
☐ b. giving permission
☐ c. showing authority
☐ d. demanding discipline

10. **dealings**, page 61, col. 2, par. 5
"... helped him considerably in his explorations and commercial dealings."
☐ a. unfair transactions
☐ b. professional cards
☐ c. business affairs
☐ d. swapping and trading

The word **aware** means to have perception of knowledge. The prefix **un** means **not**. To be **unaware**, therefore, means not to have perception or knowledge. Frequently the words "I'm unaware" serve a better purpose than "I do not know." The syllable count is the same but the sound is less ordinary.

Name _____ Date _____ Class _____

Total Number Right _____ Percent _____

Set 4

Set 4·A
The Pleasures
of Eating

The first man who cooked his food, instead of eating it raw, lived so long ago that we have no idea who he was or where he lived. We do know, however, that for thousands of years, food was always eaten cold and raw. Perhaps the first cooked food was heated accidentally by a forest fire or by the molten lava from an erupting volcano. No doubt, when people first tasted food that had been cooked, they found it tasted better. However, even after this discovery, cooked food must have remained a rarity until man learned how to make and control fire.

Early peoples who lived in hot regions could depend on the heat of the sun to cook their food. For example, in the desert areas of the southwestern United States, the Indians cooked their food by placing it on a flat stone in the hot sun. They cooked pieces of meat and thin cakes of corn meal in this fashion.

We can surmise that the earliest kitchen utensil was a stick to which a piece of meat could be attached and held over a fire. Later this stick was replaced by an iron rod or spit which could be turned frequently to cook the meat on all sides.

Cooking food in water was impossible before man learned to make water containers that could not be destroyed by fire. The first cooking pots were reed or grass baskets in which soups and stews could be cooked. As early as 1600 B.C., the Egyptians had learned to make more permanent cooking pots out of sandstone. Many years later, the Eskimos learned to make similar pans.

The North American Indians adopted a different method of cooking their food. They placed their food in skin bags or birch bark kettles, then dropped hot stones in with the food. When the stones cooled off, the Indians replaced them with hot stones. The Indians continued to add fresh hot stones to the containers until the food was cooked.

Records left by the ancient Egyptians show that they knew how to cook food in many ways. Their frescoes (wall-paintings) portray people baking, boiling, roasting, frying and stewing food. The Egyptians also knew how to preserve meat by smoking and salting it.

The Bible tells us that the Jews were skilled cooks. The Book of Genesis, for instance, relates the story of Rebecca, who put food in a pan and placed it over burning charcoal. The Jews also knew the art of baking at an early point in their history. Carvings left by the ancient Jews show dough being put into a small round oven to be baked.

History reveals that early Greeks knew how to cook porridge and how to make flat, round loaves of bread from wheat and barley. They used olive oil as a cooking grease. Since food was scarce in the Greek peninsula, the Greeks expanded their territory in order to increase their food supply. From the people they conquered, the Greeks learned how to cook and enjoy many new foods.

The Romans were famous for their elaborate banquets. From all over their empire, they imported foods that they cooked over stone hearths or grilled over charcoal. The fact that Romans also baked their food is evident from the ovens found in the ruins of Pompeii.

In the troubled times of the Middle Ages, trade between countries dwindled. People lived on what they could grow in their gardens or bring back from the hunt, and the food they ate was simply prepared. Beans and turnips were the main vegetables eaten in Europe, and honey was used to sweeten food. The manuscripts of the Middle Ages tell us that boiling and broiling were the two most common methods of cooking. Bread was baked in the homes of rich people or in public bakeries, but the common man had no oven in his home. People killed their livestock, hoping to preserve it through the winter by salting it. However, salt was expensive and people did not always use enough of it to keep the meat from spoiling.

During the period of the Crusades (from the eleventh to the thirteenth centuries), many new foods were discovered by Europeans who traveled to the East. When the Crusaders returned to Europe, they wanted to continue eating the new things they had tried. As a result, trade developed again between Europe and Asia Minor.

It was not until the nineteenth century that the masses of people in Europe changed their ways of cooking. This change took place because the cast-iron cooking stove was invented. Until the stove came into use, fireplaces and spits had been in general use; sometimes a baking oven had been built into the sides of the fireplace. In northern Europe, stoves had been used for several centuries for heating. However, it was a long time before a stove was developed that would cook and bake, as well as heat.

Our methods of cooking have not changed very much in the last century, but we do have better equipment that makes cooking easier and more convenient. With modern standardized measures, we can follow recipes exactly and produce successful dishes more often.

All of man's history has been shaped by his search for food. Man's first occupation was that of hunter, and his first stone weapons were made for hunting. Man discovered that groups of men, banded together, could hunt animals more easily. As a consequence, men began to live together. Then, when men learned to grow plants for food, they settled in communities next to the fields. More people lived in the places where food grew the best. Progress has been greater in those parts of the world where there is more food to eat.

Many wars have been fought by poor, hungry countries which try to conquer rich countries for their food. Governments have fallen because the people of the country were hungry; starving people will follow any man who promises them food. Rulers who want to stay in power try to feed their people well, because, during times of famine, there are often revolutions.

Finishing Time: Minutes_____ Seconds_____

The Pleasures of Eating

COMPREHENSION: Answer the questions without looking back at the passage. When finished, correct your answers by checking with the answer key on page 180. Find your words per minute by looking in the chart on page 185. Enter both scores on graphs provided at the end of this book.

1. The first cooked food was probably cooked
   - ☐ a. on a fireplace.
   - ☐ b. by hot stones in a bag.
   - ☐ c. by a forest fire or volcano.
   - ☐ d. on a stick.

2. The first cooking pots were made of
   - ☐ a. metal.
   - ☐ b. clay.
   - ☐ c. reeds or grass.
   - ☐ d. stone.

3. Baking was probably known first to the
   - ☐ a. Jews.
   - ☐ b. Romans.
   - ☐ c. Crusaders of Europe.
   - ☐ d. people of the Middle Ages.

4. Cooking for many people was made easier by the
   - ☐ a. opening of trade routes.
   - ☐ b. control of fire.
   - ☐ c. use of water in pots.
   - ☐ d. invention of the stove.

5. Early people from hot countries often cooked their food by
   - ☐ a. dropping hot stones into a bag.
   - ☐ b. putting it on sun-heated stones.
   - ☐ c. removing the fire from the stones and putting the food on it.
   - ☐ d. digging a pit and letting the food cook under green leaves.

6. Cooking today is simpler for the housewife because
   - ☐ a. she can use recipes.
   - ☐ b. she can buy her food at the store.
   - ☐ c. she has better methods of cooking.
   - ☐ d. she has better equipment.

7. We can learn something about the eating habits of ancient people from
   - ☐ a. their writings.
   - ☐ b. their sculpture.
   - ☐ c. their paintings.
   - ☐ d. all of these.

8. The story of Rebecca, who cooked food over charcoal, is told in
   - ☐ a. Genesis.
   - ☐ b. The New Testament.
   - ☐ c. ancient Jewish carvings.
   - ☐ d. Exodus.

9. Revolutions often occur when
   - ☐ a. rulers offer plenty of food to the people.
   - ☐ b. people do not listen to the politicians.
   - ☐ c. governments have no food.
   - ☐ d. people do not have enough to eat.

10. During the Middle Ages, people preserved their food by
    - ☐ a. drying it.
    - ☐ b. smoking it.
    - ☐ c. salting it.
    - ☐ d. all of these.

Name _____ Date _____ Class _____

Reading Time: _____ _____ _____ _____ _____
              Minutes Seconds Words per minute Total number right Percent

The Pleasures of Eating

CLOZE TEST: The following passage, taken from the selection you have just read, has words omitted from it. Fill in the blank without looking back at the passage. When finished, correct your answers by checking with the answer key on page 180.

A. Subject Matter Words Missing

The North American Indians adopted a different _____ 1 of cooking their food. They _____ 2 their food in skin bags or birch bark _____ 3, then dropped hot stones in with the _____ 4. When the stones cooled off, the Indians _____ 5 them with hot stones. The Indians continued to _____ 6 fresh hot stones to the containers until the food was _____ 7. Records left by the ancient Egyptians show they _____ 8 how to cook food in many ways. Their frescoes (wall-paintings) portray _____ 9 baking, boiling, roasting, frying and _____ 10 food.

B. Structure Words Missing

History reveals _____ 1 early Greeks knew how to cook porridge and _____ 2 to make flat, round loaves of bread _____ 3 wheat and barley. They used olive oil _____ 4 a cooking grease. Since food was scarce in _____ 5 Greek peninsula, the Greeks expanded their territory _____ 6 order to increase their food supply. _____ 7 the people they conquered, the Greeks learned how _____ 8 cook and enjoy many new foods. _____ 9 Romans were famous _____ 10 their elaborate banquets.

_____ _____ _____
Name   Date   Class

_____ _____ _____ _____
A. Number Right   Percent   B. Number Right   Percent

The Pleasures of Eating

VOCABULARY: The following words have been taken from the selection you have just read. Put an X in the box before the best meaning or synonym for the word as used in the selection.

1. **erupting**, page 66, col. 1, par. 1
"... by the molten lava from an erupting volcano."
☐ a. to cause an upset
☐ b. to violently force out
☐ c. to break up
☐ d. to burn slowly

6. **expanded**, page 67, col. 1, par. 2
"... the Greeks expanded their territory in order to increase their food supply."
☐ a. to rebuild
☐ b. to enlarge
☐ c. to modernize
☐ d. to turn over

2. **rarity**, page 66, col. 1, par. 1
"... cooked food must have remained a rarity until man learned ..."
☐ a. uncommon or unusual
☐ b. not well done
☐ c. not well liked
☐ d. sought after

7. **dwindled**, page 67, col. 1, par. 4
"In the troubled times of the Middle Ages, trade between countries dwindled."
☐ a. to become greater
☐ b. to become complicated
☐ c. to become smaller
☐ d. to become devious

3. **surmise**, page 66, col. 1, par. 3
"We can surmise that the earliest kitchen utensil was a stick ..."
☐ a. to be certain
☐ b. to conjecture or guess
☐ c. to be general about
☐ d. to read about

8. **standardized**, page 67, col. 2, par. 2
"With modern standardized measures, we can follow recipes exactly ..."
☐ a. with rigid rules
☐ b. according to an approved basis
☐ c. recognized excellence
☐ d. a level of choice

4. **portray**, page 66, col. 2, par. 3
"Their frescoes portray people baking, ... frying and stewing food."
☐ a. to show historical facts
☐ b. to indicate an eating place
☐ c. to make a likeness of
☐ d. to print an illustration

9. **consequence**, page 67, col. 2, par. 3
"As a consequence men began to live together."
☐ a. as a reward
☐ b. as a compromise
☐ c. as a result
☐ d. as a remedy

5. **relates**, page 66, col. 2, par. 4
"The Book of Genesis, for instance, relates the story of Rebecca, ..."
☐ a. looks back upon
☐ b. is connected with
☐ c. has a record of
☐ d. tells the reader

10. **revolutions**, page 67, col. 2, par. 4
"... during times of famine, there are often revolutions."
☐ a. a feeling of moving
☐ b. a simple turn about
☐ c. a national celebration
☐ d. a rising up against authority

The prefix **re** can mean **withdrawal** or **backward motion**. The root word in **revolution** comes from *volo, I wish or will*. The suffix **tion** means **expressing action**. Revolutions, therefore, are acts of insurrection or rebellion.

Name _____   Date _____   Class _____

Total Number Right _____   Percent _____

70

Set 4·B
Rubber

Starting Time: Minutes_____ Seconds_____

Rubber is a very useful vegetable product. It is made from latex, a white liquid found in the stems and leaves of many plants. Latex is even found in milkweed and dandelions. However, not all latex contains rubber. And in some plants there is too little latex to use for making rubber.

More than nine-tenths of the world's supply of rubber comes from a tree known as the para rubber tree, which is native to the Amazon Valley in Brazil. There is another variety of rubber tree which is native to Central America. There is also a desert shrub which produces a rather large amount of rubber. And the Russians have even obtained rubber from a species of dandelion.

When Christopher Columbus made his first trip to the Americas, he saw Indians playing a game with rubber balls. Obviously, the Indians of South and Central America had discovered rubber long before the Europeans arrived.

Explorers reported that they saw the Indians make little statues, cups, and shoes out of latex. The Indians allowed the latex to dry in molds, which they made out of mud. When the latex was dry they removed it from the mold and smoked it over a fire. Smoking strengthened the latex and reduced its stickiness. Explorers also noticed that, in dances and processions, the Indians burned torches that were made with latex that was allowed to harden on the ends of sticks.

A Frenchman named Charles La Condamine introduced rubber to Europe. La Condamine was sent to South America to make scientific observations. When traveling in the Amazon Valley, he noticed many Indians collecting latex. He was interested to see how the Indians used the latex they collected. After making detailed observations, La Condamine sent samples of latex to Europe, along with a description of the ways in which the Indians used it. Before very long, Europeans found uses for latex too.

Latex was first used for waterproofing cloth. Melted rubber was spread on cloth and allowed to dry. The first experiments were not very satisfactory because the cloth became sticky in hot weather and cracked in cold weather.

However, more satisfactory methods were soon developed. In England, a man named Charles Mackintosh found a good method of making cloth for raincoats. Even today, many people call a raincoat a "mackintosh."

An Englishman named Sir Harry Wickham shipped seeds of the wild rubber tree to

71

England. After several unsuccessful attempts to grow rubber trees from the seeds, Wickham shipped about seventy thousand seeds to the Royal Botanical Gardens at Kew. The seeds were planted there and about two thousand of them produced plants. When the plants were about two months old, they were sent by boat to the Botanical Garden in Ceylon.

Another Englishman went to Brazil and collected more seeds, which he sent to Kew. Plants from these seeds were also sent to the East. From these trees came the millions of rubber trees in Ceylon, Java, Malaya, Borneo, Burma and parts of India.

An English chemist gave rubber its English name. He discovered that it could be used to rub out pencil marks. Since his rubber had come from India, he called it "India rubber."

After the rubber plantations were established in the East Indies, many experiments were made to discover the best ways of tapping the trees. At about the same time as the first rubber plantations were established, a disease killed most of the coffee trees growing in the East Indies. Many Dutch and English planters were left without a cash crop. The governments of England and Holland encouraged these planters to put in rubber trees instead of coffee trees.

More and more people began to buy automobiles, which need rubber tires. Soon the automobile industry was using most of the rubber produced. The rubber production from wild trees in South America declined because the plantation system was more economical. As the rubber business declined in South America, Brazil turned to the production of coffee. Now Brazil produces more coffee than any other country in the world.

Rubber plantations in the East Indies are of two main kinds—small family farms and large plantations. The small plantings are cared for and tapped by the family. These farmers usually grow rice and other food as well. They tap their rubber trees when the price of rubber is high enough to permit them to make a profit. About half of the world's rubber comes from such farms.

The big plantations are run by companies. Since many workers are needed, the companies generally provide them with housing, food, and medical care, in addition to their salaries. Most companies have research departments that carry out experiments to find better and cheaper ways of producing rubber. Usually, plantation rubber is of a higher quality than the rubber from small farms.

Rubber trees are grown from seeds. These seeds are planted in beds of specially prepared, rich soil so that they will come up quickly. When the plants are a few inches tall, they are set out in new beds. Those trees which do not develop well are removed, and the healthy trees are grafted so that they will produce a larger amount of latex.

When the trees are between five and six years old, they are ready to be tapped. This means cutting the bark in a certain way to allow the latex to flow into a cup, which is attached to the tree trunk. Some trees are tapped every day, but most trees are tapped every other day. Tapping goes on all year long, except for the period when the tree changes its leaves.

A tree produces a few spoonfuls of latex each time it is tapped. In a year, one young tree produces about three pounds of rubber. Well-grafted trees may produce ten pounds of rubber in a year, while some exceptional trees yield as much as twenty-five pounds in a year.

Finishing Time: Minutes_____ Seconds_____

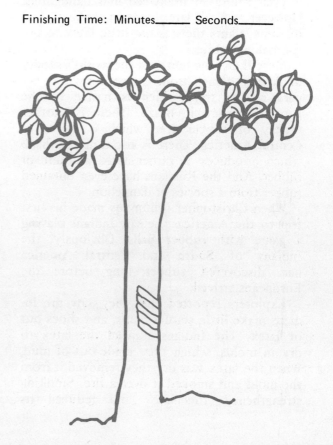

Rubber

COMPREHENSION: Answer the questions without looking back at the passage. When finished, correct your answers by checking with the answer key on page 180. Find your words per minute by looking in the chart on page 185. Enter both scores on graphs provided at the end of this book.

1. The para rubber tree is native to
   □ a. Brazil.
   □ b. Central America.
   □ c. Malaya.
   □ d. India.

2. Little rubber balls were first used by
   □ a. Indians.
   □ b. the French.
   □ c. the Spanish.
   □ d. the Indonesians.

3. Rubber was introduced to Europe by a
   □ a. Spaniard.
   □ b. Italian.
   □ c. Frenchman.
   □ d. Englishman.

4. Sir Harry Wickham was the Englishman who
   □ a. sent rubber tree seeds to England.
   □ b. operated a Brazilian rubber plantation.
   □ c. gave rubber its name.
   □ d. studied the Indians of Central America.

5. Rubber trees are usually tapped
   □ a. every day.
   □ b. every other day.
   □ c. twice a month.
   □ d. twice a year.

6. The English sent rubber trees to the East because
   □ a. the English did not like Brazil.
   □ b. the English controlled more land in the East.
   □ c. Brazil's trees were unhealthy.
   □ d. a milling method was developed.

7. Dutch and English planters in the East Indies were glad to plant rubber because
   □ a. the plants were shipped from Kew.
   □ b. the coffee plantations had been destroyed.
   □ c. they wanted to compete with Brazil.
   □ d. more profit is made.

8. Rubber from large plantations is of good quality because
   □ a. the small plantations are poor.
   □ b. the large companies have more money to spend on experiments.
   □ c. the large companies use a different milling process.
   □ d. the small plantations cannot give the workers so many advantages.

9. The industry which gave the greatest push to rubber was
   □ a. steel.   □ c. television.
   □ b. radio.   □ d. automobiles.

10. Will latex become out of date?
   □ a. No, because so many uses have been found for it.
   □ b. Yes, because of artificial rubber.
   □ c. No, because the plantations in Malaya are insured.
   □ d. Yes, because people are buying less.

Name _____   Date _____   Class _____

Reading Time: _____   _____   _____   _____   _____
              Minutes   Seconds   Words per minute   Total number right   Percent

73

Rubber

CLOZE TEST: The following passage, taken from the selection you have just read, has words omitted from it. Fill in the blank without looking back at the passage. When finished, correct your answers by checking with the answer key on page 180.

A. Subject Matter Words Missing

At about the same _____(1)_____ as the first rubber plantations were _____(2)_____, a disease killed most of the coffee trees _____(3)_____ in the East Indies. Many Dutch and English _____(4)_____ were left without a cash crop. The governments of England and Holland _____(5)_____ these planters to put in rubber trees instead of coffee _____(6)_____. More and more people began to buy _____(7)_____, which need rubber tires. Soon the automobile _____(8)_____ was using most of the rubber produced. The rubber production from _____(9)_____ trees in South America declined because the plantation system was more _____(10)_____.

B. Structure Words Missing

The big plantations are run _____(1)_____ companies. Since many workers are needed, _____(2)_____ companies generally provide them _____(3)_____ housing, food, and medical care, _____(4)_____ addition to their salaries. Most companies have research departments _____(5)_____ carry out experiments to find better _____(6)_____ cheaper ways of producing rubber. Usually, plantation rubber is _____(7)_____ a higher quality than the rubber _____(8)_____ small farms. Rubber trees are grown from seeds. These seeds are planted _____(9)_____ beds of specially prepared, rich soil _____(10)_____ that they will come up quickly.

Name _____   Date _____   Class _____

A. Number Right _____   Percent _____   B. Number Right _____   Percent _____

Rubber

VOCABULARY: The following words have been taken from the selection you have just read. Put an *X* in the box before the best meaning or synonym for the word as used in the selection.

1. **species**, page 71, col. 1, par. 2
   "... obtained rubber from a species of dandelion."
   □ a. a rare growth
   □ b. a particular classification
   □ c. a difficult growth to classify
   □ d. a category of green plants

2. **mold**, page 71, col. 1, par. 4
   "When the latex was dry they removed it from the mold ..."
   □ a. a growth of fungus
   □ b. a pile of loose earth
   □ c. a hollow form for shaping
   □ d. a distinctive form

3. **observations**, page 71, col. 2, par. 2
   "... to make scientific observations."
   □ a. to follow rules
   □ b. to notice or perceive
   □ c. to remark about
   □ d. to be prepared for

4. **tapping**, page 72, col. 1, par. 4
   "... to discover the best ways of tapping the trees."
   □ a. striking lightly
   □ b. obtaining a special drink
   □ c. drawing off any liquid
   □ d. keeping time

5. **economical**, page 72, col. 1, par. 5
   "... declined because the plantation system was more economical."
   □ a. budgeting too rigorously
   □ b. careful use of resources
   □ c. avoiding waste or extravagance
   □ d. being frugal to a fault

6. **declined**, page 72, col. 1, par. 5
   "As the rubber business declined in South America, ..."
   □ a. to be last
   □ b. a failing or gradual loss
   □ c. to be on an incline
   □ d. to withhold consent

7. **research**, page 72, col. 1, par. 7
   "Most companies have research departments that carry out experiments ..."
   □ a. a valueless inquiry
   □ b. an exploration
   □ c. a systematic investigation
   □ d. an expensive adventure

8. **experiments**, page 72, col. 1, par. 7
   "... carry out experiments to find better and cheaper ways ..."
   □ a. a test or trial
   □ b. an inexpensive test
   □ c. a long operation
   □ d. a difficult process

9. **grafted**, page 72, col. 2, par. 2
   "... and the healthy trees are grafted ..."
   □ a. inserting one part into another
   □ b. performing an illegal act
   □ c. becoming nourished
   □ d. attempting an experiment

10. **exceptional**, page 72, col. 2, par. 4
    "... may produce ten pounds of rubber in a year, while some exceptional trees ..."
    □ a. taller and heavier
    □ b. difficult to grow
    □ c. hard to find
    □ d. very unusual

The verb **to observe** comes from the Latin *observare, to watch, comply with or observe*. The suffix **tion** added to the word **observe** produces a noun. The addition of **al** to **observation** gives us an adjective which means **pertaining to observation**. Finally, **tory** added to the root word gives us **a place in which to observe**.

Name _____   Date _____   Class _____

Total Number Right _____   Percent _____

Set 4·C
A Roof
over Our Heads

Starting Time: Minutes_____ Seconds_____

Man has three basic needs: food, clothing and shelter. If a man lives in a warm climate, clothing is not absolutely necessary. However, man cannot live without food, and, he has little chance of survival without shelter. Mankind needs shelter to protect him from the weather, wild animals, insects, and his enemies.

Long before man learned how to build houses, he looked for natural shelters, as the animals did. He found that he could protect himself by climbing up into trees or by crouching under the overhanging edges of cliffs, or by crawling into caves. The first shelters or homes actually built by man were very simple. For his building materials, he used what he could find easily around him: rocks, tree branches, dried grasses, animal skins. It was a long time, however, before man began to build permanent shelters because, until man learned to farm, he lived by hunting. And, in order to follow game, he had to be able to move from one hunting ground to another. Thus, the first man-made shelters were those that could be easily transported.

The first permanent shelters were probably built twenty to forty thousand years ago by fish-eating people who lived in one place as long as the fish supply lasted. Fish-eaters could stay in one place for several years.

However, once man learned to farm, he could live longer in one place. Thus, he was able to build a permanent home. Once again, he built his home with the materials he found at hand. In Egypt, for example, wood was scarce, so most houses were built of bricks made of dried mud, with a roof supported by palm tree trunks.

When the Norsemen came from Scandinavia to northern Europe, they found many forests, so they built homes with a framework of heavy tree trunks and they filled the space between the trunks with clay. The Eskimos, on the other hand, lived in a land where there was little or no wood. They learned to adapt their homes perfectly to their surroundings. In the winter time, when everything was covered with snow and ice, the Eskimos built their homes with blocks of ice. When the warm weather came and melted the ice, the Eskimos lived in a tent made of animal skins.

The weather is man's worst natural enemy. He has to protect himself from extremes of heat and cold and from storms, wind and rain.

Where the weather is hot and dry, the house is generally made of clay brick. The windows are small and high up, so that the heat stays outside. There is often a flat roof, where people can find a cool place to sleep. In hot, humid areas, on the other hand, people need to be protected from the rain, as well as the heat. In such places, houses are built with wide, overhanging roofs, balconies or verandas.

Where there are torrential rains, houses are either built on piles to keep them off the ground, or they have steep thatched roofs to drain off the rain. People living in the Congo River region have found that steep, heavily-thatched roofs drain off the jungle rains more quickly. Other people in Africa have found that a roof of broad leaves sheds rain quickly.

In Borneo, houses are built on high posts to protect people from dampness. And there are tribes in Malaya who build their homes in the forked branches of trees, and climb up to their houses on bamboo ladders.

In northern countries, people build houses to protect themselves from cold and snow. Their houses are built of sturdy materials, and the roofs are steep, so that the snow will slide off. There are also overhanging eaves to keep the snow from piling up next to the house. And, in northern Siberia, where snowfall is extremely heavy, the roofs even have a funnel-shaped platform to protect the chimneys from drifting snow.

Protection from danger has also influenced the type of house man builds. When enemies threatened him, man made his house as inaccessible as possible. The tree-dwellers of the Philippines protect themselves by living high above the ground. When danger threatens, they remove the ladders leading to their homes. The cliff dwellers of the American Southwest built their homes high up on the sides of cliffs, where access was very difficult.

Nomad tribes must move from place to place, taking care of flocks of sheep that are always in need of fresh grass. Their houses must be simple and easy to transport. The nomads of central Asia have developed a house made of a framework of poles covered with felt. The house is round because the framework is curved. The poles are fastened together at the top with a wooden ring, and there is a hole at the top to let the smoke out.

In Europe there are very few wooden houses being built today. This is partly because wood is no longer as plentiful as it once was, and partly because wooden houses are quite inflammable. On the other hand, there are many wooden houses in America. This is because the first settlers wanted to build houses quickly and inexpensively. Since the country was covered in many places with forests, some trees had to be cut down to make room for houses.

Houses in many cities used to be made of wood. However, since the houses were very close together, fire could easily spread from one house to another. There were disastrous fires in some cities, such as the great fire of London in 1666. When the burned-out cities were rebuilt, wood was still used for the frames and the roofs, but stones or bricks were used for walls.

There are so many people living in some cities that it is often very difficult to find a place to live, and if one does find a place it is often too small. And many of the houses are too old and uncomfortable. Just as in prehistoric times, finding a good place to live continues to be one of man's most urgent problems.

Finishing Time: Minutes_____ Seconds_____

A Roof over Our Heads

COMPREHENSION: Answer the questions without looking back at the passage. When finished, correct your answers by checking with the answer key on page 180. Find your words per minute by looking in the chart on page 185. Enter both scores on graphs provided at the end of this book.

1. The first people to have permanent shelters were probably
   - ☐ a. hunters.
   - ☐ b. farmers.
   - ☐ c. fishermen.
   - ☐ d. none of these.

2. The nomad tribes of central Asia live in
   - ☐ a. tents.
   - ☐ b. round houses of felt.
   - ☐ c. small houses of clay.
   - ☐ d. tree houses.

3. When danger threatens, the tree-dwellers of the Philippines
   - ☐ a. remove their ladders.
   - ☐ b. pull up the bridge over their moat.
   - ☐ c. wind up the ropes leading to their homes.
   - ☐ d. bombard the enemy from above.

4. In Borneo, because of the dampness, houses are built
   - ☐ a. on high posts.
   - ☐ b. in forks of trees.
   - ☐ c. on rock platforms.
   - ☐ d. high on the cliffsides.

5. There are more wooden houses in America than in Europe because
   - ☐ a. there was more wood in America.
   - ☐ b. people can fireproof their wooden houses in America.
   - ☐ c. stone was not available in America.
   - ☐ d. many people live in the same house in America.

6. Man's most urgent need, in building a house, is protection from
   - ☐ a. enemies.
   - ☐ b. the weather.
   - ☐ c. earthquakes.
   - ☐ d. floods.

7. A house with a steep sloping roof is more likely to be found
   - ☐ a. in the desert.
   - ☐ b. near the coast.
   - ☐ c. in a windy country.
   - ☐ d. in a rainy country.

8. Houses with roofs of bread leaves can be found in
   - ☐ a. Borneo.
   - ☐ b. Africa.
   - ☐ c. the Philippines.
   - ☐ d. none of these.

9. The Norsemen who came to Northern Europe built their houses with
   - ☐ a. rocks.
   - ☐ b. wooden roofs and stone walls.
   - ☐ c. wood.
   - ☐ d. wooden walls and thatched roofs.

10. Nowadays, we want our houses to be well-built and also
    - ☐ a. cheap.
    - ☐ b. expensive.
    - ☐ c. beautiful.
    - ☐ d. comfortable.

Name _____   Date _____   Class _____

Reading Time: _____ _____   _____   _____   _____
               Minutes   Seconds   Words per minute   Total number right   Percent

A Roof over Our Heads

CLOZE TEST: The following passage, taken from the selection you have just read, has words omitted from it. Fill in the blank without looking back at the passage. When finished, correct your answers by checking with the answer key on page 180.

A. Subject Matter Words Missing

Long before man learned how to _____ 1 _____ houses, he looked for _____ 2 _____ shelters, as the animals did. He found that he could _____ 3 _____ himself by climbing up into trees or by crouching under the _____ 4 _____ edges of cliffs, or by crawling into _____ 5 _____. The first shelters or homes actually built by man were very _____ 6 _____. For his building materials, he used what he could find _____ 7 _____ around him: rocks, tree branches, dried grasses, animal skins. It was a long _____ 8 _____, however, before man began to build _____ 9 _____ shelters because, until man learned to farm, he lived by _____ 10 _____.

B. Structure Words Missing

Houses in many cities used _____ 1 _____ be made of wood. However, _____ 2 _____ the houses were very close together, fire could easily spread _____ 3 _____ one house to another. There were disastrous fires in some cities, _____ 4 _____ as the great fire of London in 1666. _____ 5 _____ the burned-out cities were rebuilt, wood was still used _____ 6 _____ the frames and the roofs, _____ 7 _____ stones or bricks were used for walls. There are _____ 8 _____ many people living in some cities that it is _____ 9 _____ very difficult to find a place to live, and _____ 10 _____ one does find a place it is often too small.

_____ _____ _____
Name   Date   Class

A. Number Right _____ Percent _____   B. Number Right _____ Percent _____

A Roof over Our Heads

VOCABULARY: The following words have been taken from the selection you have just read. Put an *X* in the box before the best meaning or synonym for the word as used in the selection.

1. **survival**, page 76, col. 1, par. 1
   "However, man ... has little chance of survival without shelter."
   □ a. not being hurt
   □ b. remaining alive
   □ c. protecting himself
   □ d. getting along

2. **crouching**, page 76, col. 1, par. 2
   "He found that he could protect himself ... by crouching under ..."
   □ a. a lying down position
   □ b. a kneeling position
   □ c. a stooping position
   □ d. a standing position

3. **adapt**, page 76, col. 2, par. 2
   "They learned to adapt their homes perfectly to their surroundings."
   □ a. to build a rain barrier
   □ b. to make suitable to requirements
   □ c. to change the adornments
   □ d. to fit with necessities

4. **torrential**, page 77, col. 1, par. 2
   "Where there are torrential rains, houses are either built on piles to keep them off the ground, ..."
   □ a. light drizzle
   □ b. only occasional
   □ c. excessive pouring
   □ d. mildly overwhelming

5. **eaves**, page 77, col. 1, par. 4
   "There are also overhanging eaves to keep the snow from piling up ..."
   □ a. slate shingles
   □ b. a porch roof
   □ c. narrow gutters
   □ d. a border or edge

6. **inaccessible**, page 77, col. 1, par. 5
   "When enemies threatened him, man made his house as inaccessible ..."
   □ a. to be far away
   □ b. to be barricaded
   □ c. to be unapproachable
   □ d. to be vulnerable

7. **inflammable**, page 77, col. 1, par. 7
   "... and partly because wooden houses are quite inflammable."
   □ a. fire proofed
   □ b. easily fire proofed
   □ c. capable of being set on fire
   □ d. equipped to repel flames

8. **inexpensively**, page 77, col. 2, par. 1
   "... the first settlers wanted to build houses quickly and inexpensively."
   □ a. very cheaply
   □ b. without conveniences
   □ c. lacking in detail
   □ d. without care

9. **disastrous**, page 77, col. 2, par. 2
   "There were disastrous fires in some cities, such as the great fire of London ..."
   □ a. dangerous but controlled
   □ b. extremely serious
   □ c. probably set
   □ d. never uncontrolled

10. **urgent**, page 77, col. 2, par. 3
    "... a good place to live continues to be one of man's most urgent problems."
    □ a. extremely old
    □ b. very pressing
    □ c. occasionally upsetting
    □ d. quite adequate

The meaning of **inflammable** is often interpreted as not easily ignited because **flammable** means easily ignited. So does **inflammable**! The prefix **in** means **in** or **on**, **flame** means **a state of blazing combustion** and the suffix **able** means, **can be**. Hence, **inflammable**, properly looked at, defines itself.

_____   _____   _____
Name   Date   Class

_____ _____
Total Number Right   Percent

80

Set 5·A
Going
Up

During the Middle Ages, thinkers outlined ideas for building machines that could travel in the air. However, no such machines were ever built at that time. In the seventeenth century, an Italian priest designed a flying machine composed of a wicker basket attached to four thin metal balls. He thought that if all the air were taken out of the balls the machine would be light enough to float in the air. We now realize, however, that these empty balls would have been crushed by atmospheric pressure. In the eighteenth century, a Scottish professor suggested that animal bladders filled with hydrogen might float in the air. However, this idea, too, remained untried.

In 1783, the Montgolfier brothers, in France, built a balloon that successfully carried a man into the air. The brothers had noticed that smoke rises and floats in the air, and so they tried filling paper bags with smoke. When this proved successful, they tried the same experiment with cloth bags. They soon discovered smoke rises when the air around it is cooler. However, as soon as the smoke cools, it stops rising. Consequently, they made a little fire of charcoal on a pan underneath the bag. This arrangement kept the air under the bag warm for some time.

After three months of experimentation, the Montgolfier brothers sent some animals up in a balloon. For this occasion, King Louis XVI came to the town of Annonay where the Montgolfiers lived. The brothers put a duck, a rooster, and a sheep in a basket attached to the bag. Then they sent the whole thing into the air. The bag stayed up for eight minutes, and landed safely. Plans were quickly made for a man to go up.

The king was willing to provide for the experiment a criminal who had been sentenced to death. However, the king's historian said that he would be honored to go himself. A month later the balloon was ready. Under the balloon they erected a platform large enough for a man, a fire pan, and damp straw that could burn slowly to provide the necessary heat and smoke.

The new experiment worked. The king's historian stayed about 80 feet up in the air for four and a half minutes. A month later, the same historian and a colleague went up 500 feet and stayed there twenty-five minutes, floating over Paris. Not long after, a bigger balloon carried seven passengers 3,000 feet up over Lyons.

Despite their apparent success, these balloons had certain disadvantages. For one

82

thing, the fire was always a possible source of danger because it might ignite the balloon.

Some physicists, realizing this, found a way of making hydrogen-filled balloons. First, they varnished fine silk so that no hydrogen could pass through it. Then they had to obtain enough hydrogen to fill the silk balloon. When the first hydrogen balloon was finally completed and sent up, it rose to 3,000 feet above Paris. It stayed in view for an hour and came down in a field fifteen miles away. There it was promptly torn into pieces by some peasants who were afraid of it. Some peasants thought it was an evil spirit. Others thought that it was the moon, which had fallen down to crush the earth. To quell these misapprehensions, the king issued a proclamation describing balloons, telling people not to be afraid of them, and ordering everyone not to damage them.

In December, 1783, two French scientists went up in a hydrogen balloon. They traveled a distance of twenty-five miles and stayed up almost two hours. When the balloon landed, one of the men stepped out and the other man quickly shot up in the balloon to a height of 9,000 feet! He found the air up there very cold and very thin. He did, however, return safely to earth.

An American doctor, in 1784, made the first scientific records of air pressure at high altitudes. Soon after that, two Frenchmen flew across the English Channel in a hydrogen balloon. It took them two hours to cross from Dover to Calais. However, the balloon leaked, and some gas was lost. The men almost fell into the water, but they threw out their ballast and most of their clothes in order to make a safe landing on ground.

In 1793, President George Washington watched a balloon ascent in Philadelphia. During the next hundred years balloonists, like acrobats, were popular at fairs and celebrations. One man dropped leaflets from a balloon—copies of poems he had written about the joys of flying. Another man made a practice of letting his balloon burst, and then using it as a parachute to float slowly down to earth.

In 1870, the Prussian armies surrounded Paris. For four months the Parisians kept in touch with the outside by means of balloons and carrier pigeons. Quite a lot of mail and messages were carried by balloons. Balloons also aided over 100 people, including many political leaders, to escape from Paris.

After this war, balloon corps were established in the armies of many large countries. During the First World War, they were used for observation, especially for the spotting of submarines.

During the twentieth century, balloons have been used for the exploration of the upper atmosphere and stratosphere. Before the era of rockets and space-ships, men went up in balloons to a height of fourteen miles. Weather forecasters find balloons most useful in finding out what the weather is at different places and difference levels of the atmosphere. The balloons send back the recordings of the instruments they carry by way of small short-wave radios. Such observations help the forecasters predict what the weather is going to be.

Although balloons are not easy to steer, and can only travel as fast as they are pushed by the wind, they have served an important function by introducing men to the pleasures and problems of flight. Through the use of balloons it became evident that it was indeed possible for man to travel in the air.

Finishing Time: Minutes_____ Seconds_____

Going Up

COMPREHENSION: Answer the questions without looking back at the passage. When finished, correct your answers by checking with the answer key on page 181. Find your words per minute by looking in the chart on page 185. Enter both scores on graphs provided at the end of this book.

1. Man did not actually go up in balloons until
   - ☐ a. the Middle Ages.
   - ☐ b. the seventeenth century.
   - ☐ c. the eighteenth century.
   - ☐ d. the nineteenth century.

2. To stay up, the first successful balloons used
   - ☐ a. no air or gas.
   - ☐ b. warm air.
   - ☐ c. hydrogen.
   - ☐ d. molybdenum.

3. Hydrogen was useful for balloons because
   - ☐ a. it precluded the use of fire.
   - ☐ b. it was cheap.
   - ☐ c. it had already been used successfully.
   - ☐ d. it lasted for a shorter time, but carried the balloon higher.

4. When a balloon came down in the fields near Paris, the peasants were
   - ☐ a. amused.
   - ☐ b. curious.
   - ☐ c. happy.
   - ☐ d. afraid.

5. One of the most important uses of balloons is in
   - ☐ a. transport.
   - ☐ b. circuses.
   - ☐ c. weather forecasting.
   - ☐ d. radio sending.

6. To float, balloons must be filled with
   - ☐ a. astrogen.
   - ☐ b. a gas under pressure.
   - ☐ c. a gas lighter than air.
   - ☐ d. smoke.

7. The Montgolfiers' greatest problem was
   - ☐ a. finding enough money.
   - ☐ b. finding people to go up.
   - ☐ c. getting the approval of the authorities.
   - ☐ d. finding a way to keep the balloon in the air.

8. Balloons can go higher if
   - ☐ a. they are made of silk cloth.
   - ☐ b. they are filled with more smoke.
   - ☐ c. they carry lighter loads.
   - ☐ d. the wind is blowing from the west.

9. Balloons were popular in the nineteenth century because
   - ☐ a. they were used for entertainment.
   - ☐ b. they were not considered dangerous.
   - ☐ c. they were used for scientific observations.
   - ☐ d. they were not expensive to make.

10. Perhaps the greatest importance of balloons was that
   - ☐ a. they entertained many people.
   - ☐ b. they provided escape during wartime.
   - ☐ c. they showed man could fly.
   - ☐ d. they speeded up travel.

Name _____   Date _____   Class _____

Reading Time: _____ _____   _____   _____ _____
              Minutes Seconds Words per minute Total number right Percent

Going Up

CLOZE TEST: The following passage, taken from the selection you have just read, has words omitted from it. Fill in the blank without looking back at the passage. When finished, correct your answers by checking with the answer key on page 181.

A. Subject Matter Words Missing

An American doctor, in 1784, _____1_____ the first scientific records of air pressure at _____2_____ altitudes. Soon after that, two Frenchmen _____3_____ across the English Channel in a hydrogen balloon. It _____4_____ them two hours to cross from Dover to Calais. However, the _____5_____ leaked, and some gas was lost. The men almost _____6_____ into the water, but they _____7_____ out their ballast and most of their _____8_____ in order to make a _____9_____ landing on ground. In 1793, President George Washington watched a balloon _____10_____ in Philadelphia.

B. Structure Words Missing

The king was willing _____1_____ provide _____2_____ the experiment a criminal who had been sentenced to death. However, the king's historian said _____3_____ he would be honored to go himself. _____4_____ month later the balloon was ready. _____5_____ the balloon they erected a platform large _____6_____ for a man, a fire pan, and damp straw _____7_____ could burn slowly to provide _____8_____ necessary heat and smoke. The Montgolfier brothers kept a bucket of water, and a few sponges handy, _____9_____ _____10_____ case the fire got too big.

_____ _____ _____
Name   Date   Class

_____ _____ _____ _____
A. Number Right   Percent   B. Number Right   Percent

Going Up

VOCABULARY: The following words have been taken from the selection you have just read. Put an X in the box before the best meaning or synonym for the word as used in the selection.

1. **composed**, page 82, col. 1, par. 1
"... a flying machine composed of a wicker basket attached to ..."
☐ a. to compile in an orderly way
☐ b. to make by uniting parts
☐ c. to put together tranquilly
☐ d. to attach carefully

2. **atmospheric**, page 82, col. 1, par. 1
"... these empty balls would have been crushed by atmospheric pressure."
☐ a. pertaining to weather
☐ b. pertaining to environment
☐ c. pertaining to weight or pressure
☐ d. pertaining to the atmosphere

3. **despite**, page 82, col. 2, par. 4
"Despite their apparent success, these balloons had certain disadvantages."
☐ a. as a result of
☐ b. in accordance with
☐ c. not withstanding
☐ d. in defiance of

4. **ignite**, page 82, col. 2, par. 4
"... the fire was always a possible source of danger ... it might ignite the balloon."
☐ a. to overheat
☐ b. to set on fire
☐ c. to deflate
☐ d. to overinflate

5. **source**, page 83, col. 1, par. 1
"... the fire was always a possible source of danger ..."
☐ a. an important part
☐ b. a weak condition
☐ c. a total cause
☐ d. a beginning point

6. **quell**, page 33, col. 1, par. 2
"To quell these misapprehensions, the king issued a proclamation ..."
☐ a. to make important
☐ b. to establish firmly
☐ c. to put an end to
☐ d. to bring out in the open

7. **misapprehensions**, page 83, col. 1, par. 2
"To quell these misapprehensions, the king issued a proclamation ..."
☐ a. ignorant comments
☐ b. strong feelings of disappointment
☐ c. poor evaluations
☐ d. incorrect interpretations

8. **acrobats**, page 83, col. 1, par. 5
"... acrobats were popular at fairs and celebrations."
☐ a. traveling performers
☐ b. performers of magic tricks
☐ c. those skilled in balance
☐ d. those skilled in animal acts

9. **era**, page 83, col. 2, par. 3
"Before the era of rockets and space-ships, ..."
☐ a. a distinctive period of time
☐ b. a time denoting mistakes
☐ c. a short space of time
☐ d. a specific date

10. **forecasters**, page 83, col. 2, par. 3
"Such observations help the forecasters predict ..."
☐ a. those who look into the future
☐ b. those who conjecture beforehand
☐ c. those who foretell accurately
☐ d. those who guess inaccurately

The prefix **mis** may mean **mistaken** or **wrong**, or it may simply negate a word. In the case of **misapprehensions** it means **mistaken**. **Apprehend** can mean **to anticipate**. **Apprehension** means **anticipation of adversity**. Finally, the suffix **ions** denotes a **state or condition**. Don't anticipate the worst!

Name _____   Date _____   Class _____

Total Number Right _____   Percent _____

86

Starting Time: Minutes_____ Seconds_____

The South American country of Bolivia has a highly varied climate which ranges from hot and moist in the east to high and cool in the west. In fact, the one missing element is a sea breeze, since Bolivia has no coastline.

The population of Bolivia is about three and a half million. Three-fourths of the people live in the mountainous regions, where the altitude varies from 8,000 to over 13,000 feet. The highest mountains are over 21,000 feet high.

About one-tenth of the total Bolivian population is white. Some of these white citizens are descendants of the Spanish conquerors who came to South America with Pizarro in the sixteenth century. Other white citizens migrated to Bolivia from Europe and the United States because of their interest in trade. The white people in Bolivia control the government and the industries.

About one-fourth of the Bolivians are mixed Indian and white. They usually work as shopkeepers or government employees. More than half of the Bolivians are full-blooded Indians. They are the descendants of the peoples who made up the Inca Empire. The Inca rulers professed to have come from a race of gods living on an island of the sun in Lake Titicaca. This lake is the largest in South America and one of the highest lakes in the world.

When the Spanish soldiers conquered the Incas, they imposed their own government on the country. They also tried to force the people to practice Roman Catholicism and to speak Spanish. However, even today, most of the Indians still speak their own languages.

Today, the Indians of Bolivia live in much the same way as their ancestors lived before the coming of the Spaniards. Most of them are farmers. They plough their land with metal-tipped sticks, just as their ancestors did. The women walk behind the men as they plough, breaking up the clods of earth. Using these archaic methods, the Indians grow their two chief foods—a grain called Quinoa and potatoes. Potatoes were first exported to Europe from this part of South America.

Almost as important as food to the Indians is an intoxicating drink called chicha, which is made from corn and coca leaves. The Indians also chew the coca leaves to give themselves energy. Chewing these leaves keeps the people from feeling too hungry, thirsty, or cold.

Most of the Indians' household goods and clothes are made by hand at home. The women weave the brightly-colored cloth on handlooms. The Indians also are skillful at making pottery. Their baked clay pots are well-made, but they are not as beautiful as the pots their ancestors made centuries ago.

Many of the Bolivian Indians work in the mines, because mining is the most important industry in Bolivia. Some gold and silver are mined there, but the most important mining product is tin. Bolivia is the world's third largest producer of tin, and this metal makes up three-fourths of all Bolivia's exports. Other minerals, such as tungsten, are also mined there. Most of these mines are located on the high plateaus.

The eastern slopes of the Andes are quite different from the high plateaus. They are a fertile region, with thick forests. Many fine woods, such as ebony and mahogany, grow there. However, since there are very few roads in this region, it is not very highly developed. The two primary means of transportation are river boats and porters. Heavy loads are carried by mules or llamas. Llamas are fairly large animals which are very sure-footed on the mountain slopes. They can travel long distances with very little food or water. The Indians weave the wool of the llamas into a coarse, heavy cloth. Finer cloth is woven from the skin of two similar animals—the vicuña and the alpaca. All three of these animals are so useful to the Indians that some historians believe the Indians came to live in the high country because these animals lived there.

East of the hill region are the great plains that stretch toward Brazil. These plains are warm and have a good rainfall. Tropical plants, such as coffee, sugar, tobacco and cotton, can be grown there. Close to the Brazilian border, the plains are fertile, but very sparsely populated. It is difficult to keep in touch with other places from these plains, because there are few rivers and almost no railroads. Some Indian tribes in this area live by hunting, fishing, cattle-raising, or gardening.

A serious problem for Bolivia is the transport of food from the warm regions, where it is grown, to the mountains, where most of the people live. Airlines are the most convenient solution to this problem, but they are expensive.

La Paz, the capital of Bolivia, is the country's largest city. Nearly all the foreigners in Bolivia live there, but most of its inhabitants are Indians. La Paz lies in a valley under one of the highest peaks of the Andes. The surrounding region is barren and food is scarce there.

Lake Titicaca is sixty miles northwest of La Paz. Boats carry people and goods across the water. The steamers used on the lake have to be brought across the mountains in pieces, then reassembled on the shores of the lake. The Indians who live near the lake use roundish boats made of the reeds that grow along the lake shores. The sails are made of reeds too. People and animals can be carried in these boats, which are quite strong.

Bolivia has one of the oldest universities in the western hemisphere. It is 400 years old. However, many Bolivians still cannot read and write. Some schooling is given by the mine owners in the mining camps.

Under the Incas, Bolivia was rich and well-governed. The Spanish invasion upset this society. Since Bolivia gained its independence, about a hundred years ago, there have been several wars over boundaries. Bolivia has been slow in developing, but its rich resources promise a more brilliant future in it.

Finishing Time: Minutes_____ Seconds_____

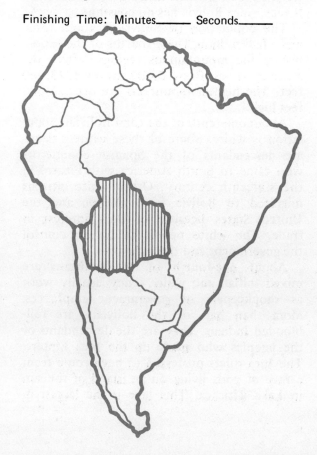

High Up in the Tropics

COMPREHENSION: Answer the questions without looking back at the passage. When finished, correct your answers by checking with the answer key on page 181. Find your words per minute by looking in the chart on page 185. Enter both scores on graphs provided at the end of this book.

1. Bolivia's climate varies from
   □ a. warm coastal plains to a high, cool plateau.
   □ b. warm coastal plains to high, cool mountains.
   □ c. hot moist plains to high, cool mountains.
   □ d. cool inland plains to warm mountain valleys.

2. Since the Spanish conquest, the Spanish language has been
   □ a. spoken by no one in Bolivia.
   □ b. the official language of Bolivia.
   □ c. spoken by most of the native population.
   □ d. changed by the church in Bolivia.

3. Coca leaves are popular because
   □ a. they make people drunk easily.
   □ b. they make people forget they are hungry or tired.
   □ c. they are forbidden by the authorities.
   □ d. they can be kept in clay pots for a long time.

4. The most important industry in Bolivia is
   □ a. making clothes.   □ c. mining.
   □ b. growing potatoes. □ d. pottery.

5. The greatest hope for Bolivia's future lies in
   □ a. her mineral resources.
   □ b. her undeveloped agricultural areas.
   □ c. her schools and universities.
   □ d. her system of roads.

6. Bolivia's development has been slow in the eastern Andes region, because
   □ a. not enough tin has been mined.
   □ b. there are not enough roads.
   □ c. the Indians are illiterate.
   □ d. the money earned from the mines has not been used in the country.

7. The Indians plough their fields with
   □ a. wooden ploughs.
   □ b. tin ploughs.
   □ c. inexpensive machines.
   □ d. metal-tipped sticks.

8. The Inca rulers professed to come from
   □ a. the highest mountain peak in Bolivia.
   □ b. an island on Lake Titicaca.
   □ c. another part of South America.
   □ d. the famous jungle village of Coronoka.

9. Existence was possible in the high mountains centuries ago because of
   □ a. the green valleys that could be used for farming.
   □ b. the llamas and vicuñas.
   □ c. the healthy climate.
   □ d. the tin mines.

10. People have come to Bolivia from the United States and Europe mostly
   □ a. to make good business profits.
   □ b. to hunt llamas and vicuñas.
   □ c. to help educate the Indians.
   □ d. to spread revolutionary propaganda.

Name	Date	Class

Reading Time:				
Minutes	Seconds	Words per minute	Total number right	Percent

High Up in the Tropics

CLOZE TEST: The following passage, taken from the selection you have just read, has words omitted from it. Fill in the blank without looking back at the passage. When finished, correct your answers by checking with the answer key on page 181.

A. Subject Matter Words Missing

About one-tenth of the _____1_____ Bolivian population is white. Some of these white citizens are _____2_____ of the Spanish conquerors who _____3_____ to South America with Pizarro in the sixteenth century. Other _____4_____ citizens migrated to Bolivia from Europe and the United States because of their _____5_____ in trade. The white people in Bolivia _____6_____ the government and the industries. About one-fourth of the Bolivians are _____7_____ Indian and white. They _____8_____ work as shopkeepers or government employees. More than half of the Bolivians are _____9_____ Indians. They are the descendants of the _____10_____ who made up the Inca Empire.

B. Structure Words Missing

Almost as important _____1_____ food to the Indians is an intoxicating drink called chicha, _____2_____ is made from corn and coca leaves. The Indians _____3_____ chew the coca leaves to give themselves energy. Chewing these leaves keeps _____4_____ people from feeling too hungry, thirsty, _____5_____ cold. Most of the Indians' household goods and clothes are made _____6_____ hand at home. The women weave the brightly-colored cloth _____7_____ handlooms. The Indians also are skillful _____8_____ making pottery. Their baked clay pots are well-made, _____9_____ they are not as beautiful _____10_____ the pots their ancestors made centuries ago.

Name _____ Date _____ Class _____

A. Number Right _____ Percent _____ B. Number Right _____ Percent _____

High Up in the Tropics

VOCABULARY: The following words have been taken from the selection you have just read. Put an X in the box before the best meaning or synonym for the word as used in the selection.

1. **element**, page 87, col. 1, par. 1
"In fact, the one missing element is a sea breeze, since Bolivia has no coastline."
☐ a. an uncompounded substance
☐ b. a component part of a whole
☐ c. a simple substance
☐ d. a sphere or environment

2. **descendants**, page 87, col. 1, par. 3
"Some of these white citizens are descendants of the Spanish conquerors ... "
☐ a. those who were defeated
☐ b. those who were cousins
☐ c. a group of admirers
☐ d. a continuing line of relations

3. **professed**, page 87, col. 1, par. 4
"The Inca rulers professed to have come from a race of gods ..."
☐ a. to lay claim to
☐ b. to declare as an expert
☐ c. to know specifically
☐ d. to declare as a religious belief

4. **imposed**, page 87, col. 2, par. 2
"... they imposed their own government on the country."
☐ a. to point out the value of
☐ b. to establish as compulsory
☐ c. to introduce the parts of
☐ d. to include details of

5. **plough**, page 87, col. 2, par. 3
"They plough their land with metal-tipped sticks, just as their ancestors did."
☐ a. to plant
☐ b. to break open for planting
☐ c. to landscape
☐ d. to develop

6. **clods**, page 87, col. 2, par. 3
"The women walk ... breaking up the clods of earth."
☐ a. large sections
☐ b. clogs of dirt
☐ c. lumps of clay or earth
☐ d. blockages in the earth

7. **intoxicating**, page 87, col. 2, par. 4
"Almost as important as food to the Indians is an intoxicating drink ..."
☐ a. especially delicious
☐ b. often sickening
☐ c. stimulating or exciting
☐ d. very depressing

8. **primary**, page 88, col. 1, par. 3
"The two primary means of transportation are river boats and porters."
☐ a. first in origin
☐ b. most effective
☐ c. first in importance
☐ d. most inexpensive

9. **sparsely**, page 88, col. 1, par. 4
"Close to the Brazilian border, the plains are fertile, but very sparsely populated."
☐ a. uncrowded areas
☐ b. overcrowded and poor
☐ c. poorly developed
☐ d. very richly populated

10. **barren**, page 87, col. 2, par. 1
"The surrounding region is barren and food is scarce there."
☐ a. to be unfruitful
☐ b. to be fertile
☐ c. to be very distant
☐ d. to be underdeveloped

The word **intoxication** is, and has always been, very much in the news. The basic meaning comes from the Latin *toxicum* which means *poison* or the Greek *toxikòn*, pertaining to *the poison used on arrows*. The medieval Latin *intoxicātus* means *poisoned* or *having taken poison in*. A state of **intoxication**, today, generally means, having "imbibed the poison," liquor, to excess.

_____   _____   _____
Name   Date   Class

_____   _____
Total Number Right   Percent

Set 5·C
Beauty
on the Wing

Starting Time: Minutes_____ Seconds_____

One of the loveliest sights in the world is a multicolored butterfly, gracefully gliding through the air. Some poets have called butterflies and moths "flying flowers" or "living jewels." Yet these little insects must go through many changes to become such lovely creatures.

Together, butterflies and moths form one order of insects. Generally, butterflies are seen in the daytime while moths are seen as the evening sky darkens. Butterflies' bodies are usually thinner than moths'; and butterflies have thin antennae (or "feelers") with tips like little knobs, while moths have feathery or threadlike antennae.

There are over eighty thousand kinds of butterflies and moths, and they are found in any part of the world where flowering plants grow. There are naturally more moths and butterflies in tropical countries, but a few are found north of the Arctic circle.

Certain kinds of butterflies and moths migrate from one place to another in different seasons. Some butterflies spend the summer in Europe and the winter in Africa or southern Asia. Once in a while ships may sight them far out at sea. And some butterflies have been seen a thousand miles from land.

The bodies of butterflies and moths are divided into three parts: a head, a thorax, and an abdomen. While some do not eat at all, those who do have a long, flexible tube that can penetrate the deep centers of flowers and suck up the nectar. Sometimes these tubes are a foot long. Some moths have little tooth-like projections at the end of their tubes. With these they can "saw" through the skins of fruits to drink the juice. The antennae of butterflies and moths are useful not only for feeling, but also for smelling and, perhaps, hearing.

The legs and wings of butterflies and moths are attached to the thorax, which is smaller than the abdomen. They have six legs, as do other insects; and their wings are covered with a large number of very small scales. If too many of these scales are brushed off, the butterflies cannot fly any more. The shape and arrangement of the scales affect the color of the wings, because light can be reflected from the scales in many different ways.

The wingspread of these insects varies from an eighth of an inch to twelve inches. Some of the males have glands on their wings which contain smells attractive to females. Although females do not have such perfume glands, many do have unpleasant odors. Scientists surmise that these unpleasant smells prevent birds and animals from eating the female butterflies.

Butterflies and moths pass through four life stages, or periods: the egg, the larva, the pupa, and the adult. The females lay large numbers of eggs, only a few of which hatch into living caterpillars (as the young butterfly-worms are called). Eggs are laid on or near plants which the young worms can eat. The young spend most of their time eating. Then, when they get too big for their skins, they shed them and take on new skins. Some caterpillars are very hairy, which prevents birds from eating them. Others are colored so that they are difficult to see among the leaves. In spite of these protective devices, many are eaten by birds or other insects. There are even some flies which lay eggs in the bodies of the caterpillar so that the fly grubs can eat the tissues of the caterpillar. Without these natural enemies, there would soon be so many caterpillars that considerable damage would be done to gardens and forests.

When the larva, or caterpillar, is fully grown, it enters a quiet stage called the pupa stage. Moths spin a covering of thread to protect themselves against the weather and certain kinds of enemies. Silkworms, of course, are the most useful moths at this stage. A butterfly-worm becomes an exposed pupa, or chrysalis, and hangs from a branch or a leaf, or attaches itself to some other surface.

After the pupa stage has lasted for some time—in cold countries, this period corresponds to the winter season—the time finally comes for the chrysalis or cocoon to break open. The butterfly or moth emerges slowly, looking very damp and weak. It rests for some time, drying its wings and moving them in preparation for flight. Then it flies off to look for flowers.

As is the case with some caterpillars, some adult moths and butterflies have the advantage of resembling leaves, twigs, or bark. It is sometimes very difficult for the human eye to discern the difference between a leaf and an insect. Other butterflies have different means of protection: one kind tastes bad to birds, and another kind looks so much like the bad-tasting kind that birds will not eat it either.

Although butterflies are generally liked, their caterpillars often do great damage by eating the leaves of trees and plants. The larvae of certain small moths cause damage, too, by feeding on woolen clothing.

However, caterpillars can also be useful. Some take pollen from one flower to another, which makes it possible for seeds to form. Others eat aphids, those tiny insects that destroy the tender leaves of garden plants. Still other caterpillars are used in certain parts of the world for food.

Some people make very interesting and valuable collections of butterflies and moths from different parts of the world. Butterflies can be kept for years in glass cases exposed to the light, but moths must be kept in dark cabinets. Their colors fade if the wings are exposed to the light for very long.

School children sometimes enjoy collecting the pupas before they hatch. If the pupa is taken with the branch or leaf to which it is attached, it can be kept in a jar until the time comes for the adult to emerge. Then the children can watch it unfold its wings and prepare for flight. Caterpillars can be collected before they "go to sleep" in their cocoons. They can also be kept in jars, but they must be provided with plenty of food.

Finishing Time: Minutes_____ Seconds_____

Beauty on the Wing

COMPREHENSION: Answer the questions without looking back at the passage. When finished, correct your answers by checking with the answer key on page 181. Find your words per minute by looking in the chart on page 185. Enter both scores on graphs provided at the end of this book.

1. Butterflies and moths have differently-shaped
   ☐ a. heads.
   ☐ b. legs.
   ☐ c. antennae.
   ☐ d. abdomens.

2. All butterflies
   ☐ a. migrate.
   ☐ b. stay in the locale where they hatched.
   ☐ c. eat from long tubes.
   ☐ d. emerge from an exposed chrysallis.

3. How many life stages have moths?
   ☐ a. More than butterflies
   ☐ b. Fewer than butterflies
   ☐ c. As many as butterflies
   ☐ d. The number varies

4. Do adult butterflies eat leaves?
   ☐ a. Sometimes
   ☐ b. Never
   ☐ c. Usually
   ☐ d. Rarely

5. Some caterpillars are protected by their
   ☐ a. color.
   ☐ b. antennae.
   ☐ c. scales.
   ☐ d. size.

6. The second stage in a butterfly's life is called
   ☐ a. pupa.
   ☐ b. chrysalis.
   ☐ c. egg.
   ☐ d. larva.

7. Butterflies live in large numbers in the tropics because
   ☐ a. there is lots of heat.
   ☐ b. there are many flowers.
   ☐ c. there is a lot of sunshine.
   ☐ d. there are many big trees.

8. Which term does not refer to part of a butterfly's body?
   ☐ a. Abdomen
   ☐ b. Wings
   ☐ c. Thorax
   ☐ d. Head

9. Butterflies are generally considered
   ☐ a. useful.
   ☐ b. tasty.
   ☐ c. necessary.
   ☐ d. pretty.

10. Some moths have little toothlike projections at the end of their tubes in order
    ☐ a. to penetrate deep into the flower center.
    ☐ b. to protect themselves from birds.
    ☐ c. to saw through the skins of fruits.
    ☐ d. to cut through the cocoon.

Name _____   Date _____   Class _____

Reading Time: _____ _____ _____ _____ _____
              Minutes   Seconds   Words per minute   Total no. right   Percent

94

Beauty on the Wing

CLOZE TEST: The following passage, taken from the selection you have just read, has words omitted from it. Fill in the blank without looking back at the passage. When finished, correct your answers by checking with the answer key on page 181.

A. Subject Matter Words Missing

When the larva, or _____1_____, is fully grown, it enters a _____2_____ stage called the pupa stage. Moths _____3_____ a covering of thread to _____4_____ themselves against the weather and certain kinds of _____5_____. Silkworms are, of course, the most _____6_____ moths at this stage. A butterfly-worm _____7_____ an exposed pupa, or chrysalis, and _____8_____ from a branch or a leaf, or _____9_____ itself to some other _____10_____.

B. Structure Words Missing

Butterflies and moths pass _____1_____ four life stages, or periods: the egg, _____2_____ larva, the pupa and the adult. The females lay large numbers of eggs, _____3_____ a few of which hatch _____4_____ living caterpillars (as the young butterfly-worms are called.) Eggs are laid _____5_____ or near plants which the young worms can eat. The young spend _____6_____ of their time eating. Then, _____7_____ they get too big _____8_____ their skins, they shed them _____9_____ take on new skins. Some caterpillars are very hairy, which prevents birds _____10_____ eating them.

Name _____   Date _____   Class _____

A. Number Right _____   Percent _____   B. Number Right _____   Percent _____

95

Beauty on the Wing

VOCABULARY: The following words have been taken from the selection you have just read. Put an *X* in the box before the best meaning or synonym for the word as used in the selection.

1. **flexible**, page 92, col. 2, par. 1
   "While some do not eat at all, those who do have a long, flexible tube ..."
   □ a. to be unsteady
   □ b. to be muscular
   □ c. to easily adapt
   □ d. to be strong

2. **penetrate**, page 92, col. 2, par. 1
   "... have a long, flexible tube that can penetrate the deep centers ..."
   □ a. to damage
   □ b. to enter into
   □ c. to see into
   □ d. to discover

3. **projections**, page 92, col. 2, par. 1
   "Some moths have little tooth-like projections at the end of their tubes."
   □ a. to defend against
   □ b. to have protruding parts
   □ c. to have favorable conditions
   □ d. to drive forward

4. **scales**, page 92, col. 2, par. 2
   "If too many of these scales are brushed off, the butterflies cannot fly any more."
   □ a. flake-like layers
   □ b. wing shape
   □ c. wing defect
   □ d. sounds of moving wings

5. **reflected**, page 92, col. 2, par. 2
   "... because light can be reflected from the scales ..."
   □ a. thrown back from a surface
   □ b. pointed in one direction
   □ c. made colorful
   □ d. made less powerful

6. **devices**, page 93, col. 1, par. 2
   "In spite of these protective devices, many are eaten by birds ..."
   □ a. types of schemes
   □ b. kinds of defects
   □ c. particular types of apparatus
   □ d. miscellaneous materials

7. **stage**, page 93, col. 1, par. 3
   "When the larva, or caterpillar, is fully grown, it enters a quiet stage ..."
   □ a. the setting of an event
   □ b. an arrangement of layers
   □ c. a particular category
   □ d. a developmental step

8. **exposed**, page 93, col. 1, par. 3
   "A butterfly becomes an exposed pupa ..."
   □ a. to bring to light
   □ b. to be sensitive
   □ c. to be alive
   □ d. to be unprotected

9. **emerges**, page 93, col. 1, par. 4
   "The butterfly or moth emerges slowly, looking very damp and weak."
   □ a. to be evasive
   □ b. to come into sight
   □ c. to spurt out
   □ d. to scratch out

10. **discern**, page 93, col. 1, par. 5
    "... to discern the difference between a leaf and an insect."
    □ a. to make an attempt
    □ b. to look carelessly
    □ c. to perceive by sight
    □ d. to discover accurately

A suffix is a letter or group of letters added to the end of a word. This addition changes the meaning of the word. Let's look at the word **flexible**. The root word is **flex** and comes from the Latin *flexus, to bend*. The addition of the suffix **ible** which means **that can be** gives us the complete meaning, capable of being bent.

Name _____   Date _____   Class _____

Total Number Right _____   Percent _____

Set 6

Set 6·A
The History
of Books

Starting Time: Minutes_____ Seconds_____

The first books were quite different from the books of today. They were made of baked clay tablets. Some of these tablets have been found that were used in Mesopotamia about fifty-five hundred years ago. The people of that time used symbols to represent their language. When the clay was soft, the symbols were written in the clay. After the tablets were baked, the clay hardened and the messages were permanently preserved. Most of the tablets that have been found are business records, such as deeds to certain lands in the area.

The Egyptians found a material that was more convenient to write on than clay. They used the bark of the papyrus, a grassy plant that grows wild in the Nile Valley. They pasted layers of this bark together to make long sheets—sometimes over a hundred feet long. A wooden roller was attached to each end of the sheet so that a small portion could be read, then the papyrus could be rolled up a little to reveal a new portion of writing. Because this method was employed, the Egyptian writing was done in columns, reading from top to bottom.

For centuries this type of book was used in Greece, Egypt, China, and Rome. The Romans made roll books of vellum, a soft parchment made from the skins of young animals such as lambs, kids or calves. About 300 A.D. a new type of book was developed: three or four sheets of vellum were folded and sewn together. Then the ends were cut so that the pages could be turned.

The Chinese began printing books during the Middle Ages, long before the Europeans. Their printing type was made of baked clay and their books were made of paper—another Chinese invention. The Chinese books looked very much like our modern books. However, the Chinese had little or no contact with Europe at that time, so it is not clear whether or not the Europeans learned about printing from the Chinese.

The first known inventor of printing in Europe was Johannes Gutenberg of Germany. The first book printed in his workshop was a Latin Bible. A few copies of this first book still exists. They are now over five hundred years old. The Gutenberg Bible was printed on a hand press with type made of lead. Most of the copies were printed on paper, but a few were printed on vellum. The books are about 12 inches wide and 16½ inches long.

Men who had been trained in Gutenberg's workshop soon established themselves as independent printers. By 1500, about fifty

98

years after the first Bible was printed, more than 30,000 books had been printed. The Bible was still the most popular book. Other church books were also printed, as were Greek and Latin classics, history books, and astronomy books.

The tools of the first printers were simple and could be moved about easily. At the end of the fifteenth century there were more than a thousand printers in Europe. Since many people could not read Latin and Greek, books were soon printed in various languages. The printers also began to make the books smaller, so that they could be handled more easily. Furthermore, the printers began to make their books more elaborate, adding pictures and ornamental letters at the beginning of chapters. Gradually the letters of the type were made smaller, finer and more delicate. The letters began to look less like manuscript letters, and, eventually, the form of the letters was simplified to the point where they were well-adapted to the metal of the type.

Sometimes books were illustrated with woodcuts. Blocks of wood were carved so that the white parts of the picture were below the surface of the wood. When the surface was inked and stamped onto paper, the dark part of the picture was reproduced. The first attempts, of course, were rather crude, but eventually the block printers were making meticulous and artistic illustrations. Florence, in Italy and Lyons, in France, became famous for their illustrated books.

In the seventeenth century, great numbers of religious pamphlets were printed. These pamphlets were not always neat or artistic because the writers were only interested in spreading their ideas quickly, and the readers did not consider the appearance of the book important. The art of metal engraving was developed about this time and enabled printers to illustrate their books with pictures of very fine, delicate lines. The use of an engraving on the first page of a book became popular. The quality of the paper improved too.

By 1800, hand printers could not supply enough books to satisfy the demand. Books were not printed fast enough when hand-made paper and wooden hand presses were used. Fortunately, about this time, many machines were invented that aided in the mass production of such products as cotton and woolen cloth. The invention of new types of printing machines and paper machines followed on the heels of these inventions and helped to speed up the production of books. The paper machine produced paper in rolls instead of sheets; and the iron handpress enabled the printer to use larger pieces of paper on which more text could be printed in less time. Finally, the linotype was invented, a machine which could cast an entire line of type at one time.

In the twentieth century, many books have been produced in paperback editions. Although these books do not last as long as books with cloth or leather bindings, they are much cheaper. Thus, many poor people, who could not afford books before, can now buy them. Today books are available to everyone because they are no longer expensive, they do not take long to produce, and, consequently, they are no longer rare. Because of this progress in book production, more and more people are learning to read. More and more people are now writing books, as well as reading them, so that the literature of the world is being constantly enriched.

Finishing Time: Minutes_____ Seconds_____

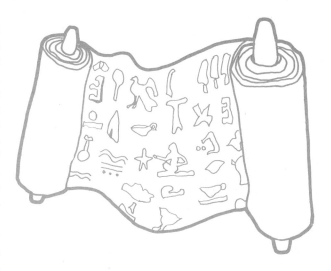

The History of Books

COMPREHENSION: Answer the questions without looking back at the passage. When finished, correct your answers by checking with the answer key on page 181. Find your words per minute by looking in the chart on page 185. Enter both scores on graphs provided at the end of this book.

1. The oldest books found were made of
   □ a. clay.
   □ b. wood.
   □ c. stone.
   □ d. papyrus.

2. The oldest books known were found in
   □ a. Europe.
   □ b. Africa.
   □ c. Mesopotamia.
   □ d. China.

3. The first printed books were made by the
   □ a. Chinese.
   □ b. Egyptians.
   □ c. Germans.
   □ d. French.

4. Engravings are made on
   □ a. clay.
   □ b. wood.
   □ c. metal.
   □ d. paper.

5. The Romans made a new kind of book out of
   □ a. bull skins.
   □ b. the bark of certain trees.
   □ c. papyrus.
   □ d. vellum.

6. The Gutenberg Bible was about
   □ a. 1½ feet wide.
   □ b. 16 inches wide.
   □ c. 12 inches wide.
   □ d. 7 inches wide.

7. The religious pamphlets of the seventeenth century were
   □ a. beautifully illustrated.
   □ b. carelessly made.
   □ c. smaller than previous books.
   □ d. the first books printed by machine.

8. About 1800, when machines were developed,
   □ a. hand printing became completely out of date.
   □ b. books became more expensive.
   □ c. more books could be produced.
   □ d. the quality of printing improved.

9. The tools of the first printers were
   □ a. easy to carry around.
   □ b. too heavy to be moved.
   □ c. complicated and light.
   □ d. simple but cumbersome.

10. Printing was speeded up when
   □ a. paper was made in sheets instead of rolls.
   □ b. paper was made in rolls instead of sheets.
   □ c. the quality of paper was improved.
   □ d. the raw materials for paper became more readily available.

Name _____   Date _____   Class _____

Reading Time: _____   _____   _____   _____   _____
               Minutes   Seconds   Words per minute   Total number right   Percent

The History of Books

CLOZE TEST: The following passage, taken from the selection you have just read, has words omitted from it. Fill in the blank without looking back at the passage. When finished, correct your answers by checking with the answer key on page 181.

A. Subject Matter Words Missing

The first books were quite _____1_____ from the books of today. They were made of _____2_____ clay tablets. Some of these tablets have been _____3_____ that were used in Mesopotamia about fifty-five hundred years ago. The _____4_____ of that time used symbols to represent their _____5_____. When the clay was soft, the symbols were _____6_____ in the clay. After the tablets were _____7_____, the clay hardened and the messages were _____8_____ preserved. Most of the _____9_____ that have been found are business records, such as deeds to certain _____10_____ in the area.

B. Structure Words Missing

The Egyptians found a material that was _____1_____ convenient to write on _____2_____ clay. They used the bark of the papyrus, _____3_____ grassy plant that grows wild _____4_____ the Nile Valley. They pasted layers _____5_____ this bark together to make long sheets—sometimes _____6_____ a hundred feet long. A wooden roller was attached _____7_____ each end of the sheet so that a small portion could be read, _____8_____ the papyrus could be rolled _____9_____ a little to reveal a new portion _____10_____ writing.

Name _____   Date _____ Class _____

A. Number Right _____   Percent _____   B. Number Right _____   Percent _____

The History of Books

VOCABULARY: The following words have been taken from the selection you have just read. Put an X in the box before the best meaning or synonym for the word as used in the selection.

1. **represent**, page 98, col. 1, par. 1
"The people of that time used symbols to represent their language."
☐ a. to supplement
☐ b. to cover up for
☐ c. to stand in the place of
☐ d. to make up for

2. **portion**, page 98, col. 1, par. 2
"... small portion could be read ..."
☐ a. a part of the whole
☐ b. a printed selection
☐ c. a separated part
☐ d. the first section

3. **invention**, page 98, col. 2, par. 2
"... their books were made of paper—another Chinese invention."
☐ a. artistic talent
☐ b. domestic skill
☐ c. expensive product
☐ d. created device

4. **independent**, page 98, col. 2, par. 4
"... soon established themselves as independent printers."
☐ a. free thinking
☐ b. not relying upon others
☐ c. self governing
☐ d. free from influence

5. **delicate**, page 99, col. 1, par. 2
"Gradually the letters of the type were made smaller, finer, and more delicate."
☐ a. to be too fragile
☐ b. to be remarkably accurate
☐ c. to be a luxury
☐ d. to be technically exquisite

6. **illustrated**, page 99, col. 1, par. 3
"Sometimes books were illustrated with woodcuts."
☐ a. to be provided with pictures
☐ b. to be clarified by comparison
☐ c. to be made famous
☐ d. to be duplicated

7. **reproduced**, page 99, col. 1, par. 3
"When the surface was inked ... the dark part of the picture was reproduced."
☐ a. poorly traced
☐ b. blotted out
☐ c. exactly copied
☐ d. somewhat imitated

8. **crude**, page 99, col. 1, par. 3
"The first attempts, of course, were rather crude ..."
☐ a. rough and unpolished
☐ b. newly made
☐ c. easily understood
☐ d. lacking parts

9. **available**, page 99, col. 2, par. 2
"Today books are available to everyone because they are no longer expensive,..."
☐ a. just as important
☐ b. offered to
☐ c. not as valuable
☐ d. easily found for use

10. **enriched**, page 99, col. 2, par. 2
"... the literature of the world is being constantly enriched."
☐ a. to make more expensive
☐ b. to increase in quality
☐ c. to induce wealth
☐ d. to improve production

The word **illustrated** comes from the Latin *illustratus, to enlighten.* If we change the suffixes we can show the slight variation on the basic meaning of a word. **Illustration** — that which illustrates. **Illustrative** — serving to illustrate. **Illustrator** — one who illustrates.

Name _____   Date _____   Class _____

Total Number Right _____   Percent _____

Set 6·B
A Time
of Revolutions

Starting Time: Minutes_____ Seconds_____

Each generation of men has believed that it was living at one of the most crucial moments in the history of the world. Naturally, each generation does not deserve such a label. However, this generation does seem to be facing many critical moments that were never even imagined in former years. In fact, we are living at a time of three revolutions which may change man's life in the world tremendously, if mankind itself survives. These revolutions are in the fields of science, warfare, and societies.

Every day we read of new wonders of science. When burnt, a piece of wood big enough to fill a tablespoon can give enough heat to boil three tablespoons full of water. However, a tablespoonful of uranium can give us, through atomic energy, enough heat to boil a million gallons of water.

Some day we may be able to fly planes and heat houses by means of atomic fuel. Factories may run without any workers, or, with only a few workers to oversee the machines which do everything once done by hand. The salt water of the sea can be changed into fresh water that can irrigate the deserts and transform them into fertile lands of plenty. Doctors have developed procedures to replace very ill people's internal

organs, such as the heart or kidney, just as they replace amputated arms and legs with artificial arms and legs.

Man seems to be reaching a point he has always dreamed of, when he will be the master of the world around him. It even seems possible that man may learn to control the weather. Blocks of frozen carbon dioxide ("dry ice") have been dropped from planes into clouds to induce the clouds to drop their rain immediately instead of carrying the rain elsewhere.

The revolution in warfare makes use of some of these new scientific inventions. However, we are already beginning to wonder what the results of this revolution in warfare will be.

In World War II, between 1939 and 1945, all of the countries fighting used up about six million tons of the high explosive called TNT. Then, in 1945, the United States dropped a bomb that had the force of 20,000 tons of TNT. One bomb tested not long ago in Russia was as powerful as 58 million tons of TNT.

The 1945 bomb was the first atomic bomb. It killed 70,000 people when it was dropped, and many thousands died later from the bomb's effects. Many of these later victims died as a result of radiation burns, even when they were quite distant from the impact point of the bomb. Many other people died from eating food which was affected by the radioactive "fallout" after the explosion. Other people became ill long after the bomb fell from the radioactivity in the air after the explosion.

In spite of the horrors of the bomb, each country today is so afraid of the other countries' atomic power that there are now enough atomic bombs in the world to kill the entire population ten or twenty times over. And countries that had no such bombs a few years ago are busy making them now, in order to feel more "protected."

Obviously, the atomic bomb has changed the whole concept of victory and defeat in war. In the past, a tribe or country that won a war became richer and more powerful. Now, however, if an atomic war started, it would not be long before many, or most, of the people on both sides were killed or hopelessly burned. Furthermore, there would be victims among the non-fighting nations, since radioactive waves know no national boundaries. As former U.S. President Eisenhower put it: "With modern weapons there can be no victory for anyone."

In the late eighteenth century and during the nineteenth, a number of wars were fought for liberty and independence. The American Revolution ended with the United States becoming independent of Great Britain. The French Revolution established a republic in that country. A series of revolutions in Latin America resulted in the independence of a whole group of countries from their European masters.

Now the same sort of thing is happening in many places in Africa and Asia. Peoples who have never felt free to make their own decisions are trying to establish free national societies. However, in some places which are politically free, the economy of the country is still controlled from the outside.

After the Second World War, a number of independent African countries were made from former colonies which had belonged to other nations. In some places independence was gained more easily than in others, where it took years of struggle and promises to become free. In other places it has not yet been achieved. It is very difficult for the countries that have profited by colonies for years and years to give up the flow of profits they are accustomed to and to reorganize their economy along different lines. However, it is evident that efforts to hold on to colonies can no longer be really successful. The example of the success of the European and American revolutions in the past is too strong for that. All people feel they have just as much right to national existence as those who have enjoyed it for so long.

Here another difficulty arises. The nations of Europe and America have found that no country can produce all its needs without trading. More and more trade agreements are necessary. Thus, the nations have grouped themselves together in associations and organizations. They have even created one super-organization—the United Nations—to deal with problems affecting the peace and security of the world. However, all the countries of the world are not members of the U.N. For instance, some of the countries in the U.N. did not want the Chinese Communists to become members. And, among the countries that are members, some are close allies of the United States, while others are allied with Russia.

Will we succeed in forgetting our differences and establishing a world where the nations can cooperate and put their discoveries and inventions to use for the good of everyone? Only time will tell.

Finishing Time: Minutes_____ Seconds_____

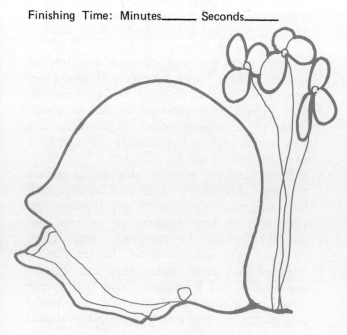

104

A Time of Revolutions

COMPREHENSION: Answer the questions without looking back at the passage. When finished, correct your answers by checking with the answer key on page 181. Find your words per minute by looking in the chart on page 185. Enter both scores on graphs provided at the end of this book.

1. The first atomic bomb was dropped in
   ☐ a. 1943.   ☐ c. 1945.
   ☐ b. 1944.   ☐ d. 1946.

2. The idea of victory and defeat in war has been changed because
   ☐ a. countries can no longer become richer or more powerful.
   ☐ b. both sides now would lose more than they gained.
   ☐ c. modern weapons make it possible for a small country to defeat a big one.
   ☐ d. the people are not interested in war.

3. The United Nations is composed of
   ☐ a. all the countries of the world.
   ☐ b. most of the countries of the world.
   ☐ c. the U.S., the Soviet Union, and their allies.
   ☐ d. all the free countries of the world.

4. A recently tested atomic bomb in Russia was as powerful as
   ☐ a. 70,000 tons of TNT.
   ☐ b. 20,000 tons of TNT.
   ☐ c. 58 million tons of TNT.
   ☐ d. 70 million tons of TNT.

5. The UN was established
   ☐ a. to make the U.S. more powerful.
   ☐ b. to keep Chinese Communists out of world politics.
   ☐ c. to help maintain world peace and security.
   ☐ d. to save colonies that were disappearing.

6. The writer of the text seems to be trying to be
   ☐ a. favorable to China.
   ☐ b. favorable to the U.S.
   ☐ c. favorable to Russia.
   ☐ d. favorable to no one in particular.

7. Former U.S. President Eisenhower stated that, with modern weapons,
   ☐ a. there can be no victory for anyone.
   ☐ b. future wars will be impossible.
   ☐ c. all countries have an equal opportunity for victory.
   ☐ d. victory will be swift.

8. Most of Africa became independent
   ☐ a. after the First World War.
   ☐ b. before the Second World War.
   ☐ c. after the Second World War.
   ☐ d. in the past five years.

9. What is dropped from planes to induce rain?
   ☐ a. Frozen carbon dioxide
   ☐ b. Frozen carbon tetrachloride
   ☐ c. Blocks of ice
   ☐ d. Blocks of TNT

10. This is the critical moment in history because
    ☐ a. some countries are still not free.
    ☐ b. man is trying to control the weather.
    ☐ c. man now has the power to kill everyone.
    ☐ d. man must decide how to use his power.

Name _____   Date _____   Class _____

Reading Time: _____ _____ _____ _____ _____
              Minutes Seconds Words per minute Total number right Percent

105

A Time of Revolutions

CLOZE TEST: The following passage, taken from the selection you have just read, has words omitted from it. Fill in the blank without looking back at the passage. When finished, correct your answers by checking with the answer key on page 181.

A. Subject Matter Words Missing

Some day we may be _____ 1 to fly planes and heat houses by means of _____ 2 fuel. Factories may run without any workers, or, with only a few workers to _____ 3 the machines which do everything once done by _____ 4. The salt water of the sea can be changed into fresh water that can _____ 5 the deserts and transform them into _____ 6 lands of plenty. Doctors have developed procedures to replace very ill people's _____ 7 organs, such as the heart or the kidney, just as they _____ 8 amputated arms and legs with _____ 9 arms and legs. Man seems to be reaching a point he has always dreamed of, when he will be the _____ 10 of the world around him.

B. Structure Words Missing

More and more trade agreements are necessary. _____ 1, the nations have grouped themselves together _____ 2 associations and organizations. They have _____ 3 created one super-organization—the United Nations— to deal _____ 4 problems affecting the peace and security of the world. _____ 5, all the countries of the world are _____ 6 members of the U.N. For instance, some of the countries _____ 7 the U.N. did not want the Chinese Communists to become members. And, _____ 8 the countries that are members, _____ 9 are close allies of the United States, _____ 10 others are allied with Russia.

Name _____   Date _____   Class _____

A. Number Right _____ Percent _____   B. Number Right _____ Percent _____

106

A Time of Revolutions

VOCABULARY: The following words have been taken from the selection you have just read. Put an *X* in the box before the best meaning or synonym for the word as used in the selection.

1. **crucial**, page 103, col. 1, par. 1
   "... living at one of the most crucial moments in the history of the world."
   ☐ a. most decisive
   ☐ b. most valuable
   ☐ c. most exciting
   ☐ d. most depressing

2. **critical**, page 103, col. 1, par. 1
   "... to be facing many critical moments that were never even imagined ..."
   ☐ a. pertaining to crisis
   ☐ b. times of harsh judgment
   ☐ c. occupied with criticism
   ☐ d. times of truth

3. **oversee**, page 103, col. 1, par. 3
   "... a few workers to oversee the machines which do everything ..."
   ☐ a. to direct or manage
   ☐ b. to look beyond
   ☐ c. to be better than
   ☐ d. to exceed in quality

4. **transform**, page 103, col. 1, par. 3
   "... irrigate the deserts and transform them into fertile lands of plenty."
   ☐ a. to change the energy quality
   ☐ b. to change in appearance or nature
   ☐ c. to overcome
   ☐ d. to produce a new substance

5. **induce**, page 103, col. 2, par. 2
   "Blocks ... have been dropped from planes into clouds to induce ..."
   ☐ a. to gradually destroy
   ☐ b. to make lighter
   ☐ c. to change the position
   ☐ d. to bring about or cause

6. **impact**, page 103, col. 2, par. 4
   "... even when they were quite distant from the impact point of the bomb."
   ☐ a. a serious step
   ☐ b. a geographical point
   ☐ c. a point of contact
   ☐ d. a close fixation

7. **concept**, page 104, col. 1, par. 3
   "... has changed the whole concept of victory and defeat in war."
   ☐ a. that which is contrived
   ☐ b. a faulty judgment
   ☐ c. a general notion
   ☐ d. a complex idea

8. **boundaries**, page 104, col. 1, par. 3
   "... since radioactive waves know no national boundaries."
   ☐ a. a military area
   ☐ b. lines that cannot be seen
   ☐ c. something that sets limits
   ☐ d. unimportant details

9. **security**, page 104, col. 2, par. 2
   "... problems affecting the peace and security of the world."
   ☐ a. to be above risks
   ☐ b. to be free from apprehension
   ☐ c. to be free from danger
   ☐ d. to be over confident

10. **allied**, page 104, col. 2, par. 2
    "... some are close allies of the U.S., while others are allied with Russia."
    ☐ a. to be involved with
    ☐ b. to be joined by treaty
    ☐ c. to be a lesser partner of
    ☐ d. to be guarded by

The word **induce** means to lead or move by persuasion or influence. In Latin, *inducere* means *to lead in, bring in or persuade.* This word is composed of the Latin word *ducere, to lead* and the prefix **in** which in this case, means **in.**

Name _____ Date _____ Class _____

Total Number Right _____ Percent _____

Set 6·C
Telling
the Time

Starting Time: Minutes_____ Seconds_____

Men who lived thousands of years ago guessed at the time of day by watching the sun as it moved across the sky. They tried to judge how much daylight remained by comparing the distance between the sun and the horizon.

Eventually, men noticed that the length and position of shadows changed at different times of day. They found it was easier to tell the exact time by looking at the shadows, rather than by looking at the sky. The sundial utilized this fact. And even today sundials can still be found in various gardens, because of their ornamental, rather than their utilitarian, function. As men began to develop the sundial, they found that the shadow of a piece of metal on a circle of stone could indicate at a glance how far the day had progressed.

Before metal sundials were made, there were simpler sundials. For example, some men stuck a pole into the ground and arranged stones around it to mark the positions of the pole's shadow during the day. In some places, huge stone columns were used. The obelisks of Egypt are examples of this type sundial.

The sundial proved a convenient timepiece in sunny weather. However, another type of timepiece was necessary for cloudy weather and night time. One such timepiece consisted of a piece of rope with knots tied in it at regular intervals. The rope was made of a slow-burning grass. After the grass was set on fire, the passage of time was evident from the number of knots that had been burned through.

A sand glass was another common measurer of time. Two glass bulbs, mounted one over the other in a frame, were connected by a very small opening. The top bulb was filled with sand, which dropped slowly into the bottom bulb. When the sand had completely run out, the glass was turned upside down and the sand began flowing back. These sand glasses were often called "hour glasses" because it took an hour for the sand to pass from one bulb to another.

In the English House of Commons, a two-minute sand glass is still used to measure the time allowed the members to assemble for a vote. Three minute sand glasses are used in many homes to time the boiling of eggs. In the English colonies of America, during the seventeenth century, Puritan preachers used two-hour sand glasses to measure the length of their sermons.

The real ancestor of modern clocks was the water clock, which has existed for thousands of years. One example of the water clock is a coconut shell which is pierced with holes and set in a pail of water so that it will fill up with water and sink within a certain time interval.

In China, an early water clock was composed of two bowls. Water trickled from one bowl to another. To tell the time more precisely, one or two more bowls were added. The water flowed steadily into the last bowl. When the last bowl was full, it was emptied into the first bowl to keep the clock going.

The Greeks developed a water clock which was connected to a flute. The flute was used to sound the hours. The Greeks developed another water clock in which the rising water moved a pointer which indicated the hours. This indicator was similar to the hour hand on a modern clock.

The King of Persia gave the French King Charlemagne a clock which has become quite famous. On the face of the clock were twelve little doors, corresponding to the twelve hours. As the water rose, it opened the doors, one by one. As each door opened, little balls fell out onto a brass drum. In that way, the hour could be heard by anyone in the room. At twelve o'clock, twelve toy knights on horseback came out and marched around the clock face, closing all the doors.

In the Middle Ages a clock was invented which used weights as well as water. As the water rose, the rising float allowed a weight to drop. The dropping of this weight turned a spindle to which the hour hand was attached. Eventually a waterless clock was invented which worked by means of weights alone. To keep the weight falling at the same speed, instead of faster and faster, a system of wheels was invented which utilized extra weights to act as brakes. The pendulum was soon developed to control the speed of the wheels effectively.

In modern clocks and watches, springs have replaced the weights of the Middle Ages, but the principle remains the same. Nowadays, electricity is often used to replace the spring as the force that makes the clock run.

Watches, which are really small clocks, were first made during the sixteenth century. The earliest watches were made of heavy iron, and people wore them hanging from their belts. Little by little, watches were made smaller so that they could be carried more easily. The invention of machinery for the mass production of the parts of clocks and watches was an important step in making clocks and watches available to the general public. In some watches, small pieces of precious stones, such as rubies or sapphires, are used at the points on which the pivots of the wheels turn. Since these stones are very hard, they do not wear down easily under the friction of the moving wheels. Thus a watch utilizing such stones will keep accurate time over a much longer period than other watches.

Some modern watches can measure very small fractions of time. These watches are useful in timing athletic events. When a button is pressed on the watch, a special second hand begins to move. This type of watch enables us to tell exactly how long it takes a runner, for example, to cover a certain distance. Doctors and nurses use watches with second hands to count a patient's pulse. It would be difficult to imagine the world of today without clocks and watches.

Finishing Time: Minutes_____ Seconds_____

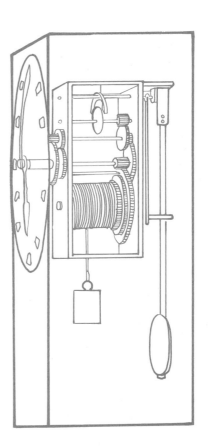

COMPREHENSION: Answer the questions without looking back at the passage. When finished, correct your answers by checking with the answer key on page 181. Find your words per minute by looking in the chart on page 185. Enter both scores on graphs provided at the end of this book.

1. The earliest clocks used
   □ a. the sun.
   □ b. water.
   □ c. candles.
   □ d. ropes.

2. Sand glasses were often called
   □ a. obelisks.
   □ b. hour glasses.
   □ c. sermon glasses.
   □ d. egg glasses.

3. The real ancestor of modern clocks was the
   □ a. sand glass.
   □ b. rope clock.
   □ c. water clock.
   □ d. sundial.

4. To regulate the speed of the falling weight, clockmakers used
   □ a. a brass drum.
   □ b. a spindle.
   □ c. water.
   □ d. a pendulum.

5. The weights of early clocks have been replaced by
   □ a. springs.
   □ b. hands.
   □ c. pendulums.
   □ d. wires.

6. The Greeks developed a water clock which was connected to
   □ a. a flute.
   □ b. twelve knights.
   □ c. a brass drum.
   □ d. a coconut shell.

7. One example of time-telling by the sun is
   □ a. a marked candle.
   □ b. the obelisks.
   □ c. the punctured coconut shell.
   □ d. King Charlemagne's time-piece.

8. In electric clocks, the electricity replaces
   □ a. the pivot.
   □ b. the pendulum.
   □ c. the spring.
   □ d. the weights.

9. Rubies and sapphires keep watches working longer because
   □ a. they are very hard.
   □ b. they are more expensive than other pivot points.
   □ c. they are very resonant.
   □ d. they have a smooth surface.

10. Sundials are still found today because
    □ a. some people cannot afford a clock.
    □ b. they are more accurate than other clocks.
    □ c. they have an ornamental value.
    □ d. of their historical equilibrium.

Name _____   Date _____   Class _____

Reading Time: _____ _____ _____ _____ _____
              Minutes Seconds Words per minute Total number right Percent

Telling the Time

CLOZE TEST: The following passage, taken from the selection you have just read, has words omitted from it. Fill in the blank without looking back at the passage. When finished, correct your answers by checking with the answer key on page 181.

A. Subject Matter Words Missing

A sand glass was another _____ 1 measurer of time. Two _____ 2 bulbs, mounted one over the other in a frame, were _____ 3 by a very small opening. The top bulb was _____ 4 with sand, which dropped _____ 5 into the bottom bulb. When the sand had _____ 6 run out, the glass was _____ 7 upside down and the _____ 8 began flowing back. These sandglasses were often called "hour glasses" because it took an _____ 9 for the sand to pass from one _____ 10 to the other.

B. Structure Words Missing

In the English House _____ 1 Commons, a two-minute sand glass is _____ 2 used to measure the time allowed _____ 3 members to assemble _____ 4 a vote. Three-minute sand glasses are used _____ 5 many homes to time the boiling of eggs. _____ 6 the English colonies of America, _____ 7 the seventeenth century, Puritan preachers used two-hour sand glasses _____ 8 measure the length of their sermons. The real ancestor of modern clocks was the water clock, _____ 9 has existed for thousands _____ 10 years.

Name _____   Date _____   Class _____

A. Number Right _____   Percent _____   B. Number Right _____   Percent _____

111

Telling the Time

VOCABULARY: The following words have been taken from the selection you have just read. Put an X in the box before the best meaning or synonym for the word as used in the selection.

1. **utilized**, page 108, col. 1, par. 2
"The sundial utilized this fact."
☐ a. to perform a service
☐ b. to put to use
☐ c. to pertain to
☐ d. to find fruitless

2. **consisted**, page 108, col. 2, par. 1
"One such timepiece consisted of a piece of rope with knots ..."
☐ a. to be made up of
☐ b. to contain
☐ c. to tend to look like
☐ d. to function like

3. **intervals**, page 108, col. 2, par. 1
"... timepiece consisted of a piece of rope with knots tied in it at regular intervals."
☐ a. a time lapse
☐ b. pauses in music
☐ c. big, uneven pauses
☐ d. a space between objects

4. **ancestor**, page 108, col. 2, par. 4
"The real ancestor of modern clocks was the water clock, which has existed for thousands of years."
☐ a. a predecessor
☐ b. a successor
☐ c. a similar object
☐ d. completely authentic

5. **precisely**, page 109, col. 1, par. 2
"To tell the time precisely, one or two more bowls were added."
☐ a. nearly automatically
☐ b. very exactly
☐ c. quite distinctly
☐ d. as nearly as possible

6. **corresponding**, page 109, col. 1, par. 4
"On the face ... were twelve little doors, corresponding to the twelve hours."
☐ a. to be communicating
☐ b. to be in harmony
☐ c. to be in agreement
☐ d. to be paralleling each other

7. **principle**, page 109, col. 1, par. 6
"... springs have replaced the weights ... but the principle remains the same."
☐ a. by some authority
☐ b. important construction
☐ c. a strict rule
☐ d. a similar characteristic

8. **precious**, page 109, col. 2, par. 1
"In some watches, small pieces of precious stones ..."
☐ a. good looking
☐ b. of great value
☐ c. very important
☐ d. easily purchased

9. **pivots**, page 109, col. 2, par. 1
"... are used at the points on which the pivots of the wheels turn."
☐ a. short pins or rods
☐ b. the spokes
☐ c. the end of something
☐ d. the middle section

10. **friction**, page 109, col. 2, par. 1
"... they do not wear down easily under the friction of the moving wheels."
☐ a. great intensity
☐ b. constant regularity
☐ c. clashing or conflicting
☐ d. rubbing one thing against another

We are familiar with the word **respond** as one used quite frequently. The word *respondere* means *to answer*. The addition of the prefix **cor** which means **together** gives us **correspond**. Whether using **correspondent** or **correspondence** we are dealing with words that imply communication.

_____   _____   _____
Name   Date   Class

_____   _____
Total Number Right   Percent

112

Set 7·A
Useful
Companions

Starting Time: Minutes _____ Seconds _____

Next to the development of agriculture, the most progressive step taken by primitive man was probably the domestication of animals. Animals helped man in his work and assured him of a meat supply. Once man began to raise his own animals, he did not have to go out and hunt for his meat. And, since he did not have to move from one place to another hunting for food, man was able to settle down and live in one place. This was one of the first foundations upon which civilization was built.

Very little is known about the early history of domestic animals. We do know that there was a time when all domestic animals were born wild and tamed one by one. We can also be fairly certain that the dog was the first animal to be tamed. One legend has it that, when animals were created, a gulf opened up between Adam and the animals, and the dog leaped across the gulf to be by man's side.

It is not surprising that the earliest domestic animals were those which could help maintain the food supply. Dogs have always been man's greatest helpers in hunting. Cattle, sheep, goats and pigs furnished meat, milk, or both. Domestic birds, notably chickens, provided food and eggs. The goose was probably the first bird to be domesticated, and the duck was probably tamed soon after. Both geese and ducks were common pets in ancient Egypt.

Beasts of burden were domesticated later than the food-producing farm animals. The ass and the camel were probably man's first beasts of burden, while wild horses were not tamed until a later date. The mule is another domesticated animal which has served man for thousands of years. The mule is a hybrid animal, produced by crossing an ass with a horse.

The elephant is a beast of burden which cannot be strictly called a domestic animal, since it rarely breeds in captivity. However, elephants have been tamed and put to use for many centuries. Other beasts of burden are the water-buffalo and the llama. In India, the natives can make the bad-tempered water-buffalo work, but the white man cannot control the animal. In the mountains of South America, the llama has carried the Indian's burdens for untold centuries. From earliest times, the dog's keen nose has sniffed out game, and his speed in retrieving game has prevented animals from escaping. Although cats have the same abilities, they have never been used in hunting to the extent that dogs have. In Persia and India, however, the cheetah or hunting leopard, a member of the cat family, has been trained for centuries to stalk game. And hunting with cheetahs is still a royal sport in some places today.

In ancient Egypt, cats were domesticated about 1600 B.C. because Egypt was a grain-producing country, and the cats protected the places where grain was stored against rats and mice. Many traps and poisons have been invented to destroy mice, but the cat is still the best destroyer of these pests. In fact, in England, the government keeps about 2000 cats on its payroll explicitly for killing mice. However, tame cats were rare in Europe until after 1000 A.D., because many superstitious Europeans considered the cat an evil spirit. In fact, the devil was often pictured as a black cat.

Domestic animals can usually be classified as (1) hunting animals, (2) beasts of burden, and (3) food producers. Some animals fit into all three of these classifications. The dog, for example, is a hunter in all parts of the world, a sled-puller in northern countries, and a source of food in China. Dogs also serve other useful purposes. They protect property, guide the blind, and save people from danger. Many instances have been recorded of dogs saving people from burning buildings or from deep water. And, in the Alps, St. Bernard dogs have saved the lives of hundreds of people lost in the mountains.

The reindeer is another animal that fits all three of the above classifications. The reindeer, in fact, meets nearly all the needs of certain wandering tribes in the far north. The reindeer carries burdens, pulls sleds, and provides milk and meat. The contents of the reindeer's stomach is cooked as a vegetable; and reindeer skins are used to make leather clothes, which are sewn with thread made from reindeer tendons. Finally, the reindeer's horns and bones can be made into tools and household utensils. The camel is similarly important to the nomads of Africa and Asia.

Two insects have been domesticated by man: the honey bee and the silkworm. The bee produces both honey and beeswax. For thousands of years, man considered honey especially valuable because it was the main sweetener for his food. Honey was a common food in ancient Egypt. The breeding of silkworms is still an important industry in Japan and China.

To many people, a domestic animal is a pet. Pets are kept for companionship and to satisfy people's desire to take care of something. Many primitive people believed that certain animals had supernatural qualities. The ancient Egyptians, for example, worshipped a cat god. Some animals that are considered supernatural are harmful. For instance, in India, cobras have killed thousands of people who refused to destroy them because of their supernatural qualities.

Domestication has often produced variations in animals which would not have allowed them to survive under natural conditions. There are, for example, lop-eared rabbits with twenty-three-inch ears and sheep with such enormous tails that herdsmen make carts to support them. Such changes show that selection and evolution can be controlled, to a certain extent, by man. In fact, changes are continually taking place in all living things, and new varieites are constantly developing. Some of these varieties, which are better adapted to existing conditions than others, multiply and replace older varieties of animals. However, such changes take place very slowly, taking centuries to be completed.

Finishing Time: Minutes_____ Seconds _____

COMPREHENSION: Answer the questions without looking back at the passage. When finished, correct your answers by checking with the answer key on page 182. Find your words per minute by looking in the chart on page 185. Enter both scores on graphs provided at the end of this book.

1. The first animal to be tamed was probably
   □ a. the sheep.
   □ b. the pig.
   □ c. the cat.
   □ d. the dog.

2. The earliest domestic animals were those that could
   □ a. carry burdens.
   □ b. maintain the food supply.
   □ c. provide eggs as well as meat.
   □ d. allow men to live in one place.

3. A well-known hybrid animal is the
   □ a. ass.
   □ b. mule.
   □ c. goat.
   □ d. llama.

4. As destroyers of rats and mice, cats
   □ a. are almost as good as modern poisons.
   □ b. were widely used up to the nineteenth century.
   □ c. are still the best means.
   □ d. were neglected for a long time.

5. The dog can be called all but one of the following:
   □ a. beast of burden.
   □ b. protector of man.
   □ c. food for man.
   □ d. supernatural creature.

6. The elephant cannot be strictly called a domestic animal because
   □ a. it cannot be easily tamed.
   □ b. it is accustomed to a jungle environment.
   □ c. it does not often produce babies in captivity.
   □ d. it is so much larger than other domesticated animals.

7. The usefulness of the camel is similar to that of the
   □ a. pigeon.   □ c. cat.
   □ b. reindeer.   □ d. horse.

8. A beast of burden which is difficult to control because of its bad temper is
   □ a. the yak.
   □ b. the water-buffalo.
   □ c. the llama.
   □ d. the camel.

9. In England, about how many cats are on the government payroll?
   □ a. 2000   □ c. 500
   □ b. 200   □ d. 3000

10. Strange varieties of domestic animals show that
    □ a. nature does queer things without man's help.
    □ b. man can influence nature completely.
    □ c. the process of change and selection is always going on.
    □ d. Darwin did not know all the answers.

Name _____   Date _____   Class _____

Reading Time: _____   _____   _____   _____   _____
               Minutes   Seconds   Words per minute   Total number right   Percent

116

Useful Companions

CLOZE TEST: The following passage, taken from the selection you have just read, has words omitted from it. Fill in the blank without looking back at the passage. When finished, correct your answers by checking with the answer key on page 182.

A. Subject Matter Words Missing

Beasts of burden were _____1_____ later than the food-producing farm animals. The ass and the camel were probably _____2_____ first beasts of burden, while wild horses were not _____3_____ until a later date. The mule is another domesticated _____4_____ which has served man for thousands of years. The mule is a _____5_____ animal, produced by crossing an ass with a horse. The elephant is a _____6_____ of burden which cannot be strictly _____7_____ a domestic animal, since it rarely breeds in _____8_____. However, elephants have been _____9_____ and put to use for many _____10_____.

B. Structure Words Missing

In the mountains _____1_____ South America, the llama has carried the Indian's burdens _____2_____ untold centuries. From earliest times, _____3_____ dog's keen nose has sniffed _____4_____ game, and his speed in retrieving game has prevented animals _____5_____ escaping. Although cats have the same abilities, they have _____6_____ been used in hunting _____7_____ the extent that dogs have. In Persia and India, _____8_____, the cheetah or hunting leopard, a member of the cat family, has been trained _____9_____ centuries to stalk game. And hunting with cheetahs is _____10_____ a royal sport in some places today.

_____ Name

_____ Date   _____ Class

_____ A. Number Right   _____ Percent   _____ B. Number Right   _____ Percent

117

Useful Companions

VOCABULARY: The following words have been taken from the selection you have just read. Put an *X* in the box before the best meaning or synonym for the word as used in the selection.

1. **domestication**, page 114, col. 1, par. 1
   "... step taken by primitive man was probably the domestication of animals."
   □ a. taming for household use
   □ b. training for hunting
   □ c. breeding for show
   □ d. using for protection

2. **foundations**, page 114, col. 1, par. 1
   "This was one of the first foundations upon which civilization was built."
   □ a. to be an institution
   □ b. to be original
   □ c. to be an old establishment
   □ d. to be the basis of a thing

3. **gulf**, page 114, col. 1, par. 2
   "... animals were created, a gulf opened up between Adam and the animals ..."
   □ a. a deep passage
   □ b. a wide separation
   □ c. a bad feeling
   □ d. a body of warm water

4. **maintain**, page 114, col. 1, par. 3
   "... domestic animals were those which could help maintain the food supply."
   □ a. to keep guard over
   □ b. to keep in existence
   □ c. to be a principal force
   □ d. to be the mainstay of

5. **stalk**, page 114, col. 2, par. 3
   "... a member of the cat family, has been trained for centuries to stalk game."
   □ a. to capture
   □ b. to walk stiffly
   □ c. to pursue stealthily
   □ d. to attack

6. **explicitly**, page 115, col. 1, par. 2
   "... the government keeps about 2000 cats on its payroll explicitly for killing."
   □ a. necessarily and quickly
   □ b. clearly and specifically
   □ c. almost unavoidably
   □ d. skillfully and neatly

7. **classifications**, page 115, col. 1, par. 3
   "Some animals fit into all three of these classifications."
   □ a. types of origins
   □ b. listings and titles
   □ c. types of ranks
   □ d. groups with similar qualities

8. **burdens**, page 115, col. 1, par. 4
   "The reindeer carries burdens, ..."
   □ a. heavy loads
   □ b. small packages
   □ c. excessive cargo
   □ d. similar animals

9. **supernatural**, page 115, col. 2, par. 1
   "... who refused to destroy them because of their supernatural qualities."
   □ a. to be very strong
   □ b. to be beyond what is natural
   □ c. to be religious
   □ d. to be destructive

10. **variations**, page 115, col. 1, par. 2
    "Domestication has often produced variations in animals ..."
    □ a. physical defects
    □ b. rates of change
    □ c. changes or differences
    □ d. traits of inbreeding

The root meaning of **domestication** comes from the Latin *domesticus* which means *belonging to the household*. *Domesticus* gets its meaning from *domus* which means *house*. That which is **domesticable** is capable of being **domesticated**. We most frequently use this word with reference to animals.

_____   _____   _____
Name   Date   Class

_____   _____
Total Number Right   Percent

118

Starting Time: Minutes _____ Seconds _____

For years, children in the industrial areas of Europe and America seldom left their smoky cities to see the beauties of the countryside. Not that the woods and fields were always far away, but they were too far from the city to permit people to make a round trip between morning and nightfall. What's more, factory workers did not have enough money to send their children on country holidays away from home.

In 1907, a young German schoolmaster had an idea which changed this state of affairs. He decided to turn his little schoolhouse into a dormitory for the summer holidays. Anyone who brought his sleeping bag and cooking equipment along could stay there for a very small amount of money. The idea was a success. A few years later, the schoolhouse was far too small to hold the many young people who wanted to stay there. Consequently, a dormitory was set up in an old castle nearby. This was the first Youth Hostel.

Today, young students and workers of every country can meet in the hostels and get to know each other. Some spend a week or more in the same hostel, seeing the surrounding sights and meeting the people of the area. Other youths go on foot or by bicycle from place to place, spending a night or two in one hostel, then going on to the next.

When young people arrive at a hostel, they have only to show their card of membership in a hostel organization in their own country. This card will permit them to use the facilities of hostels all over the world for a minimum price.

Often, at the evening meal, a group of boys and girls of different ages, from various parts of the country or the world, will happen to meet at the same hostel. They may put their provisions together and prepare a dinner with a wide variety of dishes on the menu. Such a meal would certainly be more interesting and plentiful than the meal that one or two students alone could prepare.

Sometimes an informal program will be organized after the meal, with dances, songs, or short talks followed by a question period. One can learn a lot of things about other places, just by meeting people who come from those places. Hence, a few weeks spent "hosteling" can be just as useful a part of one's education as classes in school.

Since the end of World War II, hostels have been opened in Africa and Asia. Today, there are thousands of centers in 62 countries

119

on five continents. These hostels have facilities for more than 250,000 young people, who can travel to different parts of their own country or the world, without spending a lot of money. There will soon be over two million members of the Youth Hostels organization all over the world. Consequently, more hostels are constantly being opened.

In today's world, where so much depends on understanding between nations, hostels are extremely important. They are more than convenient places for young travelers to spend the night, because they also give people the opportunity to meet and learn about each other. All too often, people have wrong ideas about other countries, because they have never known natives of the countries personally. A first-hand contact with youths of other lands can be worth far more than lectures or books when it comes to creating better understanding.

Many groups of young people volunteer to serve at a work camp, without pay, during their summer holidays. There they spend several weeks or months working eight hours a day. In their free time they see the country, meet the people, and have discussions about world problems and problems of the region where they are working. At the same time, those young people working in a foreign country can learn the language of the people who work with them.

In Peru, for example, a thousand university students responded enthusiastically to their President's appeal that they spend two months of their vacation working in isolated villages in the Andes Mountains. Many of these students have thus become aware of conditions in their country of which they were unaware before. The Peruvian students have since been joined by a small group of volunteers from Europe and the United States.

These students teach the people of the Andes how to read and write, how to take care of their water supply, and how to better care for their farms and animals. They also give medical and dental care to the villagers. They may even build community buildings, such as schools, or repair roads, bridges, and houses in places where the people cannot afford to do such things themselves.

Such volunteer groups do not work only in the "poor" areas of Latin America, Africa and Asia, but also in the "rich" countries of Europe and America. Even the most fortunate countries have large numbers of people who have not been able to find decent jobs or housing. When the volunteer workers come to a community, building community centers and playgrounds, organizing clubs and games for the children and young people, the formerly hopeless and discouraged members of the community see that all is not lost. Because of the work of volunteers, many small communities are learning that they can and should solve their problems themselves. They are discovering that they have the right to ask certain things of the local or national governments. Some villagers discover, for the first time, the joys and advantages of working together and pooling their resources to build things the community needs.

The fact that someone is interested enough to come to such villages and help them often works wonders. The people of the community become interested in helping themselves. They become less discouraged when they realize that they themselves can help make a better future. Even after the volunteers have gone, the villagers often keep in touch with their new friends.

Finishing Time: Minutes_____ Seconds _____

120

Education Out of School

COMPREHENSION: Answer the questions without looking back at the passage. When finished, correct your answers by checking with the answer key on page 182. Find your words per minute by looking in the chart on page 185. Enter both scores on graphs provided at the end of this book.

1. The first youth hostel was opened in
    ☐ a. Germany.   ☐ c. Austria.
    ☐ b. America.   ☐ d. England.

2. The price of hostels is low because
    ☐ a. people bring their own equipment.
    ☐ b. the hostels are in old buildings.
    ☐ c. a ruined castle does not cost anything.
    ☐ d. hostels receive money from the government.

3. All the hostels in the world have room for about
    ☐ a. 10,000.   c. 250,000.
    ☐ b. 150,000.   d. 2,000,000.

4. According to the text, young people can stay in a hostel if they
    ☐ a. arrive early enough.
    ☐ b. have enough equipment.
    ☐ c. have a card of membership in the hostel where they are staying.
    ☐ d. have a card of membership in the hostels of their country.

5. The writer considers hostels important, mainly because they
    ☐ a. are convenient places to spend the night.
    ☐ b. do not cost very much.
    ☐ c. get different kinds of people to meet each other.
    ☐ d. have proved their usefulness in international understanding.

6. Work camps are popular because
    ☐ a. they are often in far-away places.
    ☐ b. they are for students as well as workers.
    ☐ c. young people like to do volunteer work.
    ☐ d. the work is not too hard.

7. The work done in a camp is usually for the good of
    ☐ a. a government.   ☐ c. a city.
    ☐ b. a community.   ☐ d. a family.

8. After campers have worked in a place, the inhabitants
    ☐ a. try to get another work camp.
    ☐ b. organize clubs and games.
    ☐ c. often continue to work together.
    ☐ d. are able to solve their own problems.

9. There are work camps in the United States because
    ☐ a. all young Americans cannot afford to travel far away.
    ☐ b. everyone does not know a foreign language.
    ☐ c. the government does not always take care of the poor.
    ☐ d. even in rich countries there are poor areas.

10. One may learn most about people of other countries by
    ☐ a. reading books and magazines.
    ☐ b. meeting the people personally.
    ☐ c. writing letters to them.
    ☐ d. going to a work camp.

Name _____ Date _____ Class _____

Reading Time: _____ _____ _____ _____ _____
             Minutes Seconds Words per minute Total number right Percent

Education Out of School

CLOZE TEST: The following passage, taken from the selection you have just read, has words omitted from it. Fill in the blank without looking back at the passage. When finished, correct your answers by checking with the answer key on page 182.

A. Subject Matter Words Missing

Today young students and _____ of every country can meet in the hostels and get to _____ each other. Some spend a week or more in the _____ hostel, seeing the surrounding sights and _____ the people of the area. Other youths go on foot or by _____ from place to place, _____ a night or two in one hostel, then going on to the next. When _____ people arrive at a hostel, they have only to _____ their card of membership in a hostel organization in their own _____. This card will permit them to use the facilities of hostels all over the world for a _____ price.

B. Structure Words Missing

Such volunteer groups do _____ work only in the "poor" areas _____ Latin America, Africa and Asia, but _____ in the "rich" countries of Europe and America. _____ the most fortunate countries have large numbers _____ people who have not been able to find decent jobs _____ housing. When the volunteer workers come to _____ community, building community centers and playgrounds, organizing clubs _____ games for the children and young people, _____ formerly hopeless and discouraged members of the community see that all is _____ lost.

Name _____   Date _____   Class _____

A. Number Right _____   Percent _____   B. Number Right _____   Percent _____

Education Out of School

VOCABULARY: The following words have been taken from the selection you have just read. Put an X in the box before the best meaning or synonym for the word as used in the selection.

1. **minimum**, page 119, col. 2, par. 2
   "This card will permit them to use the facilities ... for a minimum price."
   □ a. the least amount allowable
   □ b. the average price
   □ c. the fairest price
   □ d. the price according to country

2. **provisions**, page 119, col. 2, par. 3
   "They may put their provisions together and prepare a dinner ..."
   □ a. arrangements or preparations
   □ b. basic requirements
   □ c. supplies or stock of things
   □ d. products easily prepared

3. **informal**, page 119, col. 2, par. 4
   "Sometimes an informal program will be organized after the meal, with dances, ..."
   □ a. not customary
   □ b. casual or offhand
   □ c. very informative
   □ d. overly proper

4. **personally**, page 120, col. 1, par. 2
   "... they have never known natives of the country personally."
   □ a. in an emotional way
   □ b. face to face
   □ c. as a representative
   □ d. only socially

5. **volunteer**, page 120, col. 1, par. 3
   "Many groups of young people volunteer to serve at a work camp, without pay, ..."
   □ a. to offer oneself freely
   □ b. to enroll in an organization
   □ c. to gather together
   □ d. to make an error

6. **enthusiastically**, page 120, col. 1, par. 4
   "...university students responded enthusiastically to their President's appeal ..."
   □ a. with a sense of duty
   □ b. in a negative way
   □ c. rather half-heartedly
   □ d. with lively interest

7. **isolated**, page 120, col. 1, par. 4
   "... that they spend two months of their vacation working in isolated villages ..."
   □ a. poorly developed
   □ b. mostly agricultural
   □ c. set apart from
   □ d. not well populated

8. **fortunate**, page 120, col. 2, par. 1
   "Even the most fortunate countries have large numbers of people ..."
   □ a. having favorable circumstances
   □ b. having good natural resources
   □ c. having good contacts
   □ d. having no problems

9. **resources**, page 120, col. 2, par. 1
   "... the joys and advantages of working together and pooling their resources ..."
   □ a. stored up riches
   □ b. building equipment
   □ c. original ideas
   □ d. abilities and materials

10. **discouraged**, page 120, col. 2, par. 2
    "They become less discouraged when they realize ..."
    □ a. dull and sulky
    □ b. sad and depressed
    □ c. afraid and overcome
    □ d. worried and sick

Discourage is a word which begins with a Latin prefix. **Dis** means **apart, assunder or away**. The root *corage* means *courage*. If the suffix **ment** is added to **discourage** the word becomes a noun.

Name _____   Date _____   Class _____

Total Number Right _____   Percent _____

Set 7·C
The
Whale

The largest animal that ever lived on land or in water still exists. Not even the giant dinosaurs were as large as some whales. One sulphur-bottom whale caught in the Antarctic was 110 feet long, and weighed between 90 and 100 tons.

Whales can grow to such enormous size because their bodies are supported by the water. An animal that lives on land can only grow to a size that his legs can support, while a bird's size is limited by its wing size. A whale has none of these difficulties.

Millions of years ago, whales lived on land and walked on four legs. Today, whales still have small bones that are the remains of their hind legs, but these bones can only be seen on the inside of the whale. No one knows why whales left the land to live in the water. However, scientists can surmise that when the whales changed their environment, their bodies underwent a change—taking on a more fish-like appearance. This new form offered less resistance to the water, enabling the whales to swim faster.

Despite their fish-like form, whales are not fish. A whale will drown, just as a man will, if it stays under water too long. When a whale is under water, it closes its nostrils tightly and holds its breath. The air in its lungs becomes very hot and full of water vapour. When the whale rises to the surface and exhales, its hot breath produces a column of water vapor that rises high in the air. A man produces the same effect when he exhales warm air on a cold morning.

Whales are classified as mammals because they bear their young, rather than laying eggs, and because the mother whales give the babies milk. Like other mammals, whales have warm blood. Their blood stays at the same temperature, even when they move from hot to cold water. They keep warm in cold water because they have a thick layer of fat just under their skins. This fat is called blubber, and it is thicker on whales that spend their lives in cold water. Almost all land mammals, except man, have hair on their bodies to keep them warm, but whales, which have very few hairs, are kept warm by their fat.

A baby whale's size at birth depends on the size of its mother. For example, a sulphur whale measuring 80 feet gave birth to a 25 foot baby that weighed 8 tons. Another whale, 60 feet long, gave birth to a 22 foot baby.

Whales do not bear young more often than every two years. The births are usually

124

single births, but there have been instances of whale twins. Mother whales show a great deal of affection for their young. If the baby whale is killed, the mother will stay close to it for a long time. The young grow very rapidly during their first three or four years. And, although no one is certain how long a whale lives, the normal life span is probably less than 100 years.

There are two main groups of whales: those with teeth and those without teeth. Whales that have no teeth have bristles in their mouths to strain their food. When a whale of this kind eats, he opens his mouth and swims into a mass of shrimp or small fish. As he closes his mouth, he pushes the water out with his tongue (which weighs almost a ton). The food stays on the bristles. These whales feed at or near the surface of the water.

The other group of whales have teeth to catch the slippery fish they eat. They have larger throats than the toothless whales, because they eat larger fish.

The huge sulphur-bottom whales, mentioned previously, are of the bristle or bateen type. The biggest whales with teeth are the sperm whales, which grow to a length of 70 feet. The *spermaceti* they contain is a waxy substance that was once used for making candles. When a sperm whale is sick, it gives off ambergris, another waxy substance, that is sometimes found floating in the sea. Ambergris is used as a base for expensive perfumes.

At one time whale oil was used as lamp fuel, but this use declined with the introduction of kerosene as a lamp fuel. However, whale oil is still used in making soap, for oiling machinery, for treating leather, in making margarine, and in the manufacture of glycerine for explosives. Sperm oil, the highest quality whale oil, is often used for lubricating sewing machines and watches.

A century ago, whale bristles were used to make stiffening for ladies' corsets and ribs for umbrellas. Today, they are used to make brushes, mattress stuffing, and other useful items. Whale meat is eaten by cattle and poultry, as well as by people. To some people it has a taste similar to beef. Finally, the carcass of the whale is used to make fertilizer.

Whaling used to be hard and dangerous work. A ship went on a long voyage to find whales. When one was sighted, some of the men grabbed their harpoons and jumped into a small boat. They rowed the boat out to where the whale was and harpooned it. It usually took several hours of hard struggle before the whale was conquered and could be towed back to the ship. During this struggle the whale might easily overturn the small boat unless the men were careful to keep the boat out of the whale's way.

Today, a whaling ship is a sort of factory. Modern harpoons are shot from guns, and some are electrified to kill the whale instantly. Airplanes radio the location of a herd of whales to a ship. Fast motor boats are used to chase the whales. And steam winches are used to haul the whales aboard ship. In fact, modern whalers are so efficient that whales are in danger of becoming extinct.

Finishing Time: Minutes _____ Seconds _____

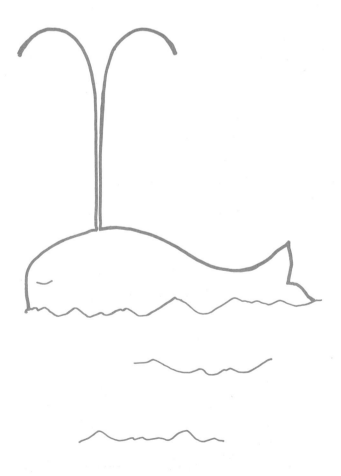

125

The Whale

COMPREHENSION: Answer the questions without looking back at the passage. When finished, correct your answers by checking with the answer key on page 182. Find your words per minute by looking in the chart on page 185. Enter both scores on graphs provided at the end of this book.

1. Whales
   - ☐ a. used to be fish.
   - ☐ b. are fish now, but have not always been.
   - ☐ c. have never been fish.
   - ☐ d. have always been fish.

2. The blood temperature of a whale
   - ☐ a. varies in hot water.
   - ☐ b. grows colder as the blubber accumulates.
   - ☐ c. remains the same.
   - ☐ d. grows warmer as the whale grows older.

3. When whales spout, they let out a column of
   - ☐ a. hot water.
   - ☐ b. cold water.
   - ☐ c. water vapor.
   - ☐ d. invisible air.

4. Whales may reach a length of
   - ☐ a. 70 feet.
   - ☐ b. 80 feet.
   - ☐ c. 90 feet.
   - ☐ d. 110 feet.

5. Ambergris is used in making
   - ☐ a. perfume.
   - ☐ b. glycerine.
   - ☐ c. leather.
   - ☐ d. margarine.

6. Whale eggs
   - ☐ a. are seldom found on land.
   - ☐ b. are of varying sizes.
   - ☐ c. are not edible.
   - ☐ d. are non-existent.

7. Whales would find living on land difficult now because
   - ☐ a. they cannot breathe air.
   - ☐ b. there are no fish on land.
   - ☐ c. they have too much blubber.
   - ☐ d. they are too big.

8. When a baby whale is killed, its mother usually
   - ☐ a. dies soon afterwards.
   - ☐ b. calls loudly to other whales.
   - ☐ c. stays in the same area.
   - ☐ d. swims away rapidly.

9. When a whale is swimming under water, it closes its
   - ☐ a. bristles.
   - ☐ b. nostrils.
   - ☐ c. mouth.
   - ☐ d. eyes.

10. A bateen type whale
   - ☐ a. has bristles.
   - ☐ b. has teeth.
   - ☐ c. has spermeceti.
   - ☐ d. has several nostrils.

Name _____ Date _____ Class _____

Reading Time: _____ _____ _____ _____ _____
              Minutes   Seconds   Words per minute   Total number right   Percent

126

The Whale

CLOZE TEST: The following passage, taken from the selection you have just read, has words omitted from it. Fill in the blank without looking back at the passage. When finished, correct your answers by checking with the answer key on page 182.

A. Subject Matter Words Missing

A baby whale's size at birth _____ 1 _____ on the size of its mother. For _____ 2 _____, a sulphur whale measuring 80 feet gave birth to a 25 foot _____ 3 _____ that weighed 8 tons. Another whale, 60 feet long, _____ 4 _____ birth to a 22 foot baby. Whales do not _____ 5 _____ young more often than every two years. The births are _____ 6 _____ single births, but there have been _____ 7 _____ of whale twins. Mother whales show a great deal of _____ 8 _____ for their young. If a baby whale is _____ 9 _____, the mother will stay close to it for a _____ 10 _____ time.

B. Structure Words Missing

There are two main groups _____ 1 _____ whales: those with teeth and those _____ 2 _____ teeth. Whales that have no teeth _____ 3 _____ bristles in their mouths _____ 4 _____ strain their food. When a whale _____ 5 _____ this kind eats, he opens _____ 6 _____ mouth and swims into a mass of shrimp _____ 7 _____ small fish. As he closes his mouth, he pushes the water out _____ 8 _____ his tongue (which weighs _____ 9 _____ a ton). The food stays _____ 10 _____ the bristles.

Name _____   Date _____   Class _____

A. Number Right _____   Percent _____   B. Number Right _____   Percent _____

The Whale

VOCABULARY: The following words have been taken from the selection you have just read. Put an *X* in the box before the best meaning or synonym for the word as used in the selection.

1. **environment**, page 124, col. 1, par. 3
   "... when the whales changed their environment, their bodies underwent ..."
   ☐ a. eating habits
   ☐ b. daily routine
   ☐ c. the surroundings
   ☐ d. swimming routine

2. **resistance**, page 124, col. 1, par. 3
   "This new form offered less resistance to the water, ..."
   ☐ a. making a stand
   ☐ b. causing aggravation
   ☐ c. minor distress
   ☐ d. power of withstanding

3. **classified**, page 124, col. 2, par. 2
   "Whales are classified as mammals because they bear their young ..."
   ☐ a. to share cultural characteristics
   ☐ b. to be listed secretly
   ☐ c. to be divided
   ☐ d. to be placed according to category

4. **instances**, page 124, col. 2, par. 4
   "The births are usually single births, but there have been instances of whale twins."
   ☐ a. sudden births
   ☐ b. a case or example
   ☐ c. small accounts
   ☐ d. urgent news

5. **previously**, page 125, col. 1, par. 4
   "The huge sulphur-bottom whales, mentioned previously, ..."
   ☐ a. only casually
   ☐ b. with reservation
   ☐ c. mentioned earlier
   ☐ d. at first

6. **base**, page 125, col. 1, par. 4
   "Ambergris is used as a base for expensive perfumes."
   ☐ a. chief ingredient
   ☐ b. safety area
   ☐ c. main form
   ☐ d. fundamental quality

7. **lubricating**, page 125, col. 1, par. 5
   "Sperm oil, ... is often used for lubricating sewing machines and watches."
   ☐ a. checking and repairing
   ☐ b. placing in categories
   ☐ c. preventing errors in
   ☐ d. oiling for smooth running

8. **carcass**, page 125, col. 1, par. 6
   "Finally, the carcass of the whale is used to make fertilizer."
   ☐ a. internal organs only
   ☐ b. remains of an animal body
   ☐ c. a specific part of the skin
   ☐ d. the lower part of an animal

9. **conquered**, page 125, col. 2, par. 1
   "... took several hours of hard struggle before the whale was conquered ..."
   ☐ a. to be subjugated
   ☐ b. to be mistreated
   ☐ c. to defeat or subdue
   ☐ d. to be taken alive

10. **efficient**, page 125, col. 2, par. 2
    "... whalers are so efficient that whales are in danger of becoming extinct."
    ☐ a. having great capability
    ☐ b. having uncontrolled power
    ☐ c. very dangerous
    ☐ d. overly mechanical

Often simple words prove interesting because they can be changed by affixes. The word **base** is a root word from the Latin *bassus* meaning *low.* Add the prefix **de** and we have **debase**, meaning to degrade. Add the suffix **ness** to **base** and the word means a state or quality of being base or low.

Name _____   Date _____   Class _____

Total Number Right _____   Percent _____

128

Set 8

Set 8·A
How Nice
to be Clean

Starting Time: Minutes_____ Seconds_____

Long before recorded history, our ancestors were bathing for pleasure and health. Man has found many interesting ways to take his bath. The earliest records often mention the use of rivers for bathing. The Bible speaks of the healing waters of the River Jordan. Egyptian history mentions bathing in the Nile. And the Hindus have believed for centuries that the Ganges River has the power to clean the soul, as well as the body.

Several thousand years ago, the inhabitants of the island of Crete, in the eastern Mediterranean, built baths with running water. The early Jews took ceremonial baths on certain occasions, making use of oils and ointments. The Jews also had a custom of bathing the feet of all strangers that came within their gates. This friendly custom is still practiced in parts of Palestine.

Swimming was popular among the Greeks of antiquity. By the third century before Christ, almost every Greek city of a certain size had at least one public bath. The wealthy classes had private baths and pools, some of which were beautifully decorated.

Many of the public baths that the Romans built utilized natural mineral springs. Since most of these springs were naturally warm, the Romans took advantage of this free hot water. By the time of the Roman Emperors, these baths were often housed in large, marble buildings. The baths built by the Emperor Caracalla, in the center of Rome, covered about one square mile and could hold sixteen thousand people.

The Roman baths were as richly ornamented as a palace. The floors were of marble and mosaic, and statues lined the walls. There were rooms in which the Romans could eat, read scrolls, and even watch plays. The baths included swimming pools, warm baths, steam baths and hot air baths.

While public baths kept the Romans clean, they also helped to undermine their character. Men would spend the entire day relaxing lazily in these beautiful buildings. In fact, a famous Roman philosopher, Seneca, said the Romans were not satisfied unless their baths were ornamented with precious stones. While the men were being massaged and rubbed with perfumes and oils, they discussed their favorite games and gladiators. Sometimes wealthy bathers had the whole tub or pool filled with wines or perfumes. Many of the Roman women bathed in milk: the Emperor's wife kept five hundred donkeys to carry the milk for her bath!

As a result of all this bath-oriented frivolity, the early fathers of the Christian church forbade Christians to bathe for pleasure. They were permitted to bathe only for hygienic reasons.

During the early Middle Ages, people were not very concerned about keeping clean. However, ceremonial baths were taken on certain occasions. For example, a bath was part of the ceremony of making one's self pure and clean before becoming a knight.

When the Crusaders invaded Palestine, they were surprised to find that it was part of the Mohammedan religion to bathe each day before praying. The Crusaders were so impressed by this cleanliness that, when they returned to Europe, they tried to make the bathing habit more widespread. This effort, however, was not very successful.

No one knows exactly when the soap which we associate with bathing came into general use. The Romans had no soap. They used sand and skin scrapers to clean themselves. It is probable that soap originated when the wood ashes containing lye combined with the fat from the animal carcasses burned on the sacrificial altars of the ancient Hebrews.

During the Middle Ages, any baths that existed were presided over by the barber. In Germany, the barber was also in charge of leeches, which were used to suck sick people's blood and, supposedly, rid them of their illness.

In the seventeenth and eighteenth centuries, many people considered bathing unhealthy. Instead of taking baths, men and women used powder, paint and perfume to try and hide the uncleanliness of their bodies. The great castles of the kings were without bathing facilities.

It was not until about a hundred years ago that people began to realize the importance of bathing. In Europe and America, the people began to bathe regularly. However, in many places bathing is still considered a bit of a luxury. In many European hotels, for example, a guest often has to pay extra for the use of a bath tub. It is in the United States that the greatest number of homes have private baths. There is also a large number of public baths and swimming pools in America.

Next to the people of the United States, the Japanese probably have the most progressive attitude toward bathing. Every Japanese home has its circular wooden tub. In the older villages it is usually placed outdoors, filled with very hot water, and used by all the members of the family in turn. Personal privacy is not considered necessary. In the urban public baths, both men and women bathe together.

All baths do not use a tub or shower. Hot air baths, for example, are taken in a room heated by a furnace. The hot, dry air makes the bather perspire. After he is perspiring freely, he is given a shower and rubbed hard with a towel.

In a Turkish bath, one goes through a series of rooms of different degrees of heat. It is a long process and is often combined with massages and periods of rest and sleep. Turkish baths are often taken to reduce weight.

In northern Europe, bathers first go into a room filled with hot steam. When they are quite hot, they plunge into a pool of cold water or roll in the snow outside. The American Indians used a similar bath as a treatment for pneumonia.

Many people take baths as a medical treatment. Some of the natural hot springs used by the Romans are still helping Europeans treat certain diseases. Mud baths are also popular.

Finishing Time: Minutes_____ Seconds_____

How Nice to be Clean

COMPREHENSION: Answer the questions without looking back at the passage. When finished, correct your answers by checking with the answer key on page 182. Find your words per minute by looking in the chart on page 185. Enter both scores on graphs provided at the end of this book.

1. The Jews in Palestine used to bathe
   - ☐ a. the soul as well as the body.
   - ☐ b. the feet of strangers.
   - ☐ c. themselves every day.
   - ☐ d. in public baths.

2. According to the text, natural mineral springs were used by the
   - ☐ a. Greeks.
   - ☐ b. Cretans.
   - ☐ c. Jews.
   - ☐ d. Romans.

3. The baths of Caracalla could hold
   - ☐ a. 5,000.
   - ☐ b. 8,000.
   - ☐ c. 10,000.
   - ☐ d. 16,000.

4. The Romans' baths had the disadvantage of making the Romans
   - ☐ a. ill.
   - ☐ b. overly fond of luxury.
   - ☐ c. poorer.
   - ☐ d. cleaner.

5. The custom of bathing was brought back to Europe by the
   - ☐ a. Romans.
   - ☐ b. Greeks.
   - ☐ c. Crusaders.
   - ☐ d. Mohammedans.

6. In the seventeenth century, people
   - ☐ a. took ceremonial baths every year.
   - ☐ b. bathed only in rivers.
   - ☐ c. used powder and perfume instead of baths.
   - ☐ d. discovered the usefulness of natural springs.

7. The great castles of European kings contained
   - ☐ a. no bathing facilities.
   - ☐ b. marble baths with many decorations.
   - ☐ c. wooden tubs for bathing.
   - ☐ d. a steam bath as well as a hot water bath.

8. It was part of the Mohammedan religion
   - ☐ a. to take baths using sand.
   - ☐ b. to take steam baths.
   - ☐ c. to bathe daily before praying.
   - ☐ d. to bathe after daily prayers.

9. Soap was probably invented as a result of
   - ☐ a. the search for more effective perfumes.
   - ☐ b. the long time it took to scrape one's self clean.
   - ☐ c. a combination of oils and perfumes with animal fat.
   - ☐ d. ancient Hebrew ceremonies.

10. Compared to the Emperor of Rome, King Louis XIV was
    - ☐ a. dirtier.
    - ☐ b. cleaner.
    - ☐ c. a fanatic about cleanliness.
    - ☐ d. less fond of ornament.

Name _____   Date _____   Class _____

Reading Time: _____ _____   _____   _____ _____
              Minutes Seconds   Words per minute   Total number right Percent

132

How Nice to be Clean

CLOZE TEST: The following passage, taken from the selection you have just read, has words omitted from it. Fill in the blank without looking back at the passage. When finished, correct your answers by checking with the answer key on page 182.

A. Subject Matter Words Missing

In the seventeenth and eighteenth centuries, _____1_____ people considered bathing unhealthy. Instead of _____2_____ baths, men and women used _____3_____, paint, and perfume to try and hide the _____4_____ of their bodies. The _____5_____ castles of the kings were without bathing _____6_____. It was not until about a hundred _____7_____ ago that people began to _____8_____ the importance of bathing. In Europe and America, the _____9_____ began to bathe _____10_____.

B. Structure Words Missing

No one knows exactly _____1_____ the soap which we associate _____2_____ bathing came into general use. The Romans had _____3_____ soap. They used sand _____4_____ skin scrapers to clean themselves. It is probable that soap originated _____5_____ the wood ashes containing lye combined _____6_____ the fat _____7_____ the animal carcasses burned _____8_____ the sacrificial altars _____9_____ the ancient Hebrews. During the Middle Ages, any baths were presided _____10_____ by the barber.

Name		Date	Class
A. Number Right	Percent	B. Number Right	Percent

How Nice to be Clean

VOCABULARY: The following words have been taken from the selection you have just read. Put an *X* in the box before the best meaning or synonym for the word as used in the selection.

1. **antiquity**, page 130, col. 1, par. 3
"Swimming was popular among the Greeks of antiquity."
☐ a. a period of ease
☐ b. ancient or olden times
☐ c. a wealthy period of history
☐ d. a prominent time

2. **undermine**, page 130, col. 2, par. 3
"... they also helped to undermine their character."
☐ a. to permanently destroy
☐ b. to cause anxiety
☐ c. to make bitter
☐ d. to gradually weaken

3. **frivolity**, page 131, col. 1, par. 1
"As a result of all this bath-oriented frivolity, ..."
☐ a. of little or no importance
☐ b. of genuine worth
☐ c. of some importance
☐ d. of serious value

4. **hygienic**, page 131, col. 1, par. 1
"They were permitted to bathe only for hygienic reasons."
☐ a. to be sanitary
☐ b. to be helpful
☐ c. to be uncomplicated
☐ d. to be religious

5. **widespread**, page 131, col. 1, par. 3
"... they tried to make the bathing habit more widespread."
☐ a. with regard to space
☐ b. very exclusive
☐ c. frequent in many places
☐ d. easily engaged in

6. **associate**, page 131, col. 1, par. 4
"No one knows exactly when the soap which we associate with bathing ..."
☐ a. make an attachment
☐ b. usually label
☐ c. join or connect
☐ d. assume or guess

7. **probable**, page 131, col. 1, par. 4
"It is probable that soap originated ..."
☐ a. rather unlikely
☐ b. definitely established
☐ c. not important
☐ d. likely to be true

8. **presided**, page 131, col. 1, par. 5
"... any baths that existed were presided over by the barber."
☐ a. to be the owner of
☐ b. to occupy a place of authority
☐ c. to be an expert
☐ d. to be a protector

9. **facilities**, page 131, col. 1, par. 6
"The great castles ... were without bathing facilities."
☐ a. expensive bathing chambers
☐ b. the means provided for bathing
☐ c. some reproductions
☐ d. artificial accommodations

10. **progressive**, page 131, col. 1, par. 8
"... Japanese probably have the most progressive attitude toward bathing ..."
☐ a. newest and best
☐ b. quite professional
☐ c. very ongoing
☐ d. somewhat restrained

Facility is a word which is most easily changed by adding suffixes. The Latin *facilitas* gets its meaning from *facilis* which means *easy to do*. By adding **ate**, **facilitate** meaning to make easier, is formed. The act or process of **facilitating** is the definition of the word **facilitation**.

Name _____   Date _____   Class _____

Total Number Right _____   Percent _____

Starting Time: Minutes_____ Seconds_____

Every day, the news of the world is relayed to people by over 300 million copies of daily papers, over 400 million radio sets, and over 150 million television sets. Additional news is shown by motion pictures, in theaters and cinemas all over the world. As more people learn what the important events of the day are, fewer are still concerned exclusively with the events of their own household. As the English writer John Donne put it, nearly four hundred years ago, "no man is an island." This idea is more appropriate today than it was when Donne lived. In short, wherever he lives, a man belongs to some society; and we are becoming more and more aware that whatever happens in one particular society affects, somehow, the life and destiny of all humanity.

Newspapers have been published in the modern world for about four hundred years. Most of the newspapers printed today are read in Europe and North America. However, soon they may be read in all parts of the world, thanks to the new inventions that are changing the techniques of newspaper publishing.

Electronics and automation have made it possible to produce pictures and text far more quickly than before. Photographic reproduction eliminates the need for type and printing presses. And fewer specialists, such as type-setters, are needed to produce a paper or magazine by the photo-offset method. Therefore, the publishing of newspapers and magazines becomes more economical. Furthermore, photo-copies can be sent over great distances now by means of television channels and satellites such as Telstar. Thus, pictures can be brought to the public more quickly than previously.

Machines that prepare printed texts for photo-copies are being used a great deal today. Thousands of letters and figures of different sizes and thicknesses can now be arranged on a black glass disc that is only eight inches in diameter, to be printed in negative form (white on a black background). The disc on the machine turns constantly at the rate of ten revolutions a second. A beam of light from a stroboscopic lamp shines on the desired letters and figures for about two-millionths of a second. Then the image of the letters and figures that were illuminated is projected onto a film through lenses. The section of film is large enough to hold the equivalent of a page of text. There is a keyboard in front of the machine that is similar to the keyboard of a typewriter, and the machine operator has only to strike the proper keys for the image of the corresponding letters to be immediately transferred to the film. The negative image on the film can quickly be transferred onto paper. This method makes it as easy to reproduce photographs and illustrations as it is to reproduce the text itself.

Film, being light and small, can be sent rapidly to other places and used to print copies of the text where they are needed. Film images can also be projected easily on a movie or television screen.

Television broadcasts are limited to an area that is within sight of the sending station or its relay. Although television relays are often placed on hills and mountains so that they can cover a wider region, they still cannot cover more land than one could see from the same hilltop on a clear day. However, the rays also go out into the atmosphere, and if there is a relay station on a satellite that revolves around the earth, it can transmit the pictures to any point on the earth from which the satellite is visible. Three satellites permanently revolving over the equator transmit any television program to any part of the earth. This makes it possible for world editions of newspapers to give the news in all countries at the same time. Some day it may be possible for a subscriber to a televised newspaper to press a button and see a newspaper page on his television screen. He could also decide when he wants the page to turn, and, by dialing different numbers such as those on a telephone dial, he could choose the language or the edition of the paper he wants to read.

It seems strange to think that, even today, methods of the past are not entirely useless. For example, sometimes press agencies that use radio and Telstar use carrier pigeons to send messages between offices in large cities because the pigeons are not bothered by traffic problems.

It may be some time before television sets become common in the average homes in Africa and Asia. However, radio is already rapidly becoming accessible to thousands of people in these areas. And, now that good radios are being made with transistors, and their price is gradually dropping because of mass production, it may not be too long before radios become commonplace in areas which have no newspapers. Transistors make it possible for people to carry small radios wherever they go, without need of electric current. Even television sets are now operating on transistors, and the pocket TV may soon be as widespread as the pocket radio.

Now that scientific progress is making it possible to send the news to all the inhabitants of the earth, it will be important to consider what news is going to be sent to them. No matter what criteria are used in making the decision, a decision must be made, since no one would have time to read or listen to an account of everything there is going on in the world!

People who have time to read several papers can already compare different reports of the same event. When an event has political significance, each paper reports it from the point of view of its own political beliefs or preferences. Ideally, of course, the expression of editorial opinion should be limited to the editorial page, and the news articles should be objective—telling the facts as completely as possible, without trying to give them a particular interpretation, or without otherwise trying to influence the reader's opinion. However, reporters and editors are only human, and if they have strong political beliefs it is almost impossible for them to hide them. If editors believe their point of view is best for the readers of their paper, what's to stop them from using the paper to try to influence public opinion? And if, some day, a world newspaper becomes a reality, will it be the most powerful press agencies that will choose the news to be sent out to all countries?

Finishing Time: Minutes_____ Seconds_____

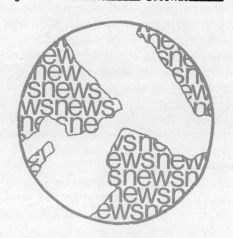

Informing the World

COMPREHENSION: Answer the questions without looking back at the passage. When finished, correct your answers by checking with the answer key on page 182. Find your words per minute by looking in the chart on page 185. Enter both scores on graphs provided at the end of this book.

1. The expression "no man is an island" means that
   - ☐ a. no man lives surrounded by water.
   - ☐ b. every man is in some way alone.
   - ☐ c. no man can live the life of a hermit.
   - ☐ c. every man belongs to some society.

2. Newspapers have been published for about
   - ☐ a. 100 years.
   - ☐ b. 200 years.
   - ☐ c. 300 years.
   - ☐ d. 400 years.

3. Thousands of letters and figures can be arranged on a disc
   - ☐ a. one foot in diameter.
   - ☐ b. two inches in diameter.
   - ☐ c. eight inches in diameter.
   - ☐ d. eighteen inches in diameter.

4. The transferring of newspaper texts to film
   - ☐ a. is rapid but comparatively costly.
   - ☐ b. is rapid and comparatively inexpensive.
   - ☐ c. requires more specialists.
   - ☐ d. none of these.

5. Transistors are particularly useful because
   - ☐ a. they are common even in Africa and Asia.
   - ☐ b. they are used in small radio and TV sets.
   - ☐ c. they do not work by electricity.
   - ☐ d. they are more sensitive to radio waves.

6. In the future, the people of Africa and Asia will
   - ☐ a. know more about world events.
   - ☐ b. know all about world events.
   - ☐ c. have a large number of daily papers.
   - ☐ d. be able to see all the events.

7. Television relays are often placed on a hilltop
   - ☐ a. so that they can reach a satellite.
   - ☐ b. so that the rays meet less static interference.
   - ☐ c. so that they can cover a wider region.
   - ☐ d. so that they will not be affected by changes in the weather.

8. Compared to today's newspaper, the newspaper of the future will be
   - ☐ a. better.
   - ☐ b. cheaper.
   - ☐ c. more widely available.
   - ☐ d. less full of the editors' opinions.

9. Any television program could be transmitted to any part of the world by
   - ☐ a. Telstar.
   - ☐ b. three satellites revolving around the equator.
   - ☐ c. two satellites moving north-west.
   - ☐ d. electromagnetic processes.

10. Today, methods of the past have
    - ☐ a. not become entirely useless.
    - ☐ b. become entirely useless.
    - ☐ c. remained as useful as ever.
    - ☐ d. none of these.

Name _____ Date _____ Class _____

Reading Time: _____ _____ _____ _____ _____
              Minutes   Seconds   Words per minute   Total number right Percent

Informing the World

CLOZE TEST: The following passage, taken from the selection you have just read, has words omitted from it. Fill in the blank without looking back at the passage. When finished, correct your answers by checking with the answer key on page 182.

A. Subject Matter Words Missing

Television broadcasts are _____ 1 _____ to an area that is within sight of the _____ 2 _____ station or its relay. Although television relays are often _____ 3 _____ on hills and mountains so that they can cover a _____ 4 _____ region, they still cannot cover more land than one could _____ 5 _____ from the same hilltop on a _____ 6 _____ day. However, the rays also go out into the _____ 7 _____, and if there is a relay station on a _____ 8 _____ that revolves around the earth, it can transmit the _____ 9 _____ to any point on the earth from which the satellite is _____ 10 _____.

B. Structure Words Missing

Every day the news _____ 1 _____ the world is relayed to people _____ 2 _____ over 300 million copies of daily papers, over 400 million radio sets, _____ 3 _____ over 150 million television sets. Additional news is shown _____ 4 _____ motion pictures, in theaters and cinemas _____ 5 _____ over the world. As more people learn _____ 6 _____ the important events of the day are, fewer are still concerned exclusively _____ 7 _____ the events of their own household. _____ 8 _____ the English writer John Donne put it, nearly four hundred years _____ 9 _____, "no man is an island." This idea is more appropriate today _____ 10 _____ it was when Donne lived.

Name _____ Date _____ Class _____

A. Number Right _____ Percent _____ B. Number Right _____ Percent _____

Informing the World

VOCABULARY: The following words have been taken from the selection you have just read. Put an *X* in the box before the best meaning or synonym for the word as used in the selection.

1. **exclusively**, page 135, col. 1, par. 1
"... fewer are still concerned exclusively with the events of their own household."
☐ a. to be nervous
☐ b. to be the only consideration
☐ c. to be serious
☐ d. to be tense

2. **appropriate**, page 135, col. 1, par. 1
"This idea is more appropriate today than it was when Donne lived."
☐ a. difficult to use
☐ b. actually legal
☐ c. favored or liked
☐ d. suitable or fitting

3. **eliminates**, page 135, col. 1, par. 3
"Photographic reproduction eliminates the need for type ..."
☐ a. makes less demanding
☐ b. gets rid of
☐ c. removes part of
☐ d. makes shorter

4. **equivalent**, page 135, col. 1, par. 2
"... is large enough to hold the equivalent of a page of text."
☐ a. matching amount
☐ b. exact details
☐ c. to closest copy
☐ d. to duplicate of

5. **relay**, page 136, col. 1, par. 3
"... that is within sight of the sending station or its relay."
☐ a. a less effective station
☐ b. a stopping off station
☐ c. a helping station
☐ d. a supply station

6. **subscriber**, page 136, col. 1, par. 3
"Some day it may be possible for a subscriber to a televised newspaper ..."
☐ a. one who approves of
☐ b. one who receives and pays for
☐ c. one who understands
☐ d. one who works for

7. **edition**, page 136, col. 1, par. 3
"... he could choose the language or the edition of the paper ..."
☐ a. type of print
☐ b. numbered copy
☐ c. particular issue
☐ d. kind of selection

8. **accessible**, page 136, col. 1, par. 5
"However, radio is already rapidly becoming accessible to thousands ..."
☐ a. less expensive
☐ b. more approachable
☐ c. not authorized
☐ d. most obtainable

9. **significance**, page 136, col. 2, par. 3
"When an event has political significance, ..."
☐ a. to have complications
☐ b. to have undertones
☐ c. to have importance
☐ d. to have parts

10. **preferences**, page 136, col. 2, par. 3
"... political beliefs or preferences."
☐ a. complete certainties
☐ b. simple statements
☐ c. favored choices
☐ d. complete advantages

Subscribers are those who promise, as by signing an agreement, to give or pay (a sum of money) as a contribution, payment or share. The prefix **sub** means **under**, freely used as an attribute. A **scribe** is a **penman** or **one who writes**. The Latin word *scriba* means *writer*. A **subscriber** is under an obligation "to put his money where his signature is."

_____   _____   _____
Name   Date   Class

_____   _____
Total Number Right   Percent

Set 8·C
The
Secluded Life

Starting Time: Minutes_____ Seconds_____

During the Middle Ages, abbeys were very important. In fact, each abbey was a small town in itself. The monks, with their own fields, grain mills, flocks and herds, were able to produce almost everything they needed to live.

The buildings of the abbey were grouped around the church. A covered walk, called a cloister, stretched across the open courtyard. This walk enabled the monks to go from one building to another without being exposed to rain, sun and inclement weather. Each abbey had a dining hall, a school, an infirmary, outbuildings, and a guest house.

The monks obeyed the orders of their Abbot, the chosen head of the abbey. The monks were not allowed to own anything, not even the clothes they wore. Neither were they allowed to marry.

There were regulations in the abbey covering every hour of the day. The monks spent seven hours a day working with their hands at some useful task. Those monks who could not work in the fields were given books or manuscripts to copy for the monastery library. Two hours of each day were given over to reading or study. And, finally, the monks had to attend seven services in the church daily.

The monk of the Middle Ages had a very busy life. At six in the morning he left his bed in the dormitory, which was often icy cold in winter. He washed in the stone washroom, attended early morning prayers, and then ate breakfast with the other monks in the dining hall, or refectory.

After breakfast the entire community met in the chapter house. After the meeting, during which the business of the abbey was discussed, each monk went about his daily occupations. Some went to the fields, while others went to the vegetable garden or the kitchen or the library.

In the writing room, one monk kept the daily records, or chronicle, of the abbey. Three other monks copied legal documents, such as leases of the lands belonging to the abbey. The more artistic and scholarly monks copied the illuminated manuscripts. In this way the great literature of the past was preserved. Many of these illuminated manuscripts can be seen today in museums. Even after several hundred years, the colors of the designs are often surprisingly clear and bright.

The monks often made their own paper. Unlike the paper used today, it was made from the skins of sheep and goats. This kind of paper was called parchment. One special kind of parchment, made from the skins of new-born lambs or kids, was called vellum.

The monks were not allowed the society of women, but they had many contacts with the outside world. The abbey gave hospitality to rich and poor alike. When a stranger knocked at the gate of the abbey, he was welcomed by the porter or gate keeper. The porter then sent for the Abbot. Since hospitality was a very important part of monastery life, the Abbot left whatever he was doing to go and greet the stranger.

After being greeted by the Abbot, the guest was taken care of by another monk. This monk first saw to the visitor's horse or carriage (if he were not travelling by foot). The guest was then housed according to his rank in society. Those of noble birth were not lodged in the same place with the poor. The very poor were even given money at the end of their stay to enable them to continue their journey. There was ample room to receive these guests without upsetting the routine of the Abbey's 400 monks.

As time went on, villages grew up about the Abbeys. The Abbots were usually the landlords of the villages, and of much of the surrounding country as well. Since the tenants of the abbey were not always content, the monks who worked in the writing room were kept busy with legal matters.

The abbeys gave protection to the villages surrounding them. In return for this protection, the abbey demanded certain privileges. The villagers were not always happy to do the things demanded of them by the abbeys. The Abbey of St. Albans in England was attacked by the townsmen in 1314 because they wanted to grind their own corn instead of having to bring it to the abbey mills.

As the centuries went by, life in many of the monasteries grew less strict. Many people felt that the monks lived too comfortably and that the great abbots were too independent, since they were free of all control by the bishops and were responsible only to the Pope.

The abbots had private apartments inside the abbeys. Some of them received great sums of money in taxes and other contributions. However, the expenses of the abbey were often very heavy, especially when many visitors of high rank had to be entertained.

Some of the abbots lived like rich lords—riding around on mules with beautiful trappings; hunting as the feudal lords did, on horseback or with hawks; and eating their meals on silver plates. Other abbots continued to live very simply.

As the discipline in the abbeys grew less strict, reformers started new orders of monks. The aim of these new orders was a return to the simple, austere life; and their formation was a protest against the rather easy life of some abbeys. The life of the new orders was even more strictly regulated than the life had been in the early monasteries. In the Carthusian monasteries, each monk lives alone. He has almost no contact with his fellow monks, and his life is spent in meditation and prayer. The food he eats is of the simplest, and the buildings he works in, though attractive, are without ornamentation.

Today, there are still many abbeys in Spain and Italy, some in France, and very few in England. The English abbeys were largely destroyed for their wealth by King Henry VIII. Although a few have been restored, the great influence of the abbeys is gone forever.

Finishing Time: Minutes_____ Seconds_____

The Secluded Life

COMPREHENSION: Answer the questions without looking back at the passage. When finished, correct your answers by checking with the answer key on page 182. Find your words per minute by looking in the chart on page 185. Enter both scores on graphs provided at the end of this book.

1. In the first abbeys, the monks spent their time
   □ a. meditating.
   □ b. working.
   □ c. farming and writing.
   □ d. meditating and working.

2. Vellum is a special kind of parchment because
   □ a. it was treated with special oils.
   □ b. it was made from the skin of new-born kids or goats.
   □ c. it was made from a particular breed of lamb.
   □ d. it was not made from skins as other parchment was.

3. If a visitor knocked at the abbey, the monks
   □ a. received him if he was rich.
   □ b. gave him money.
   □ c. received him, no matter who he was.
   □ d. lodged him in the communal guest room.

4. The abbeys
   □ a. had no right to possess property.
   □ b. lived on money from Rome.
   □ c. owned land and collected rents.
   □ d. were controlled by the towns.

5. Today, there are abbeys
   □ a. in very few places.
   □ b. in more countries than before.
   □ c. in Catholic countries such as Spain and Italy.
   □ d. mostly in England and America.

6. The monks' life was
   □ a. comfortable but well-disciplined.
   □ b. austere and well-regulated.
   □ c. austere but rather free.
   □ d. spent entirely in meditation.

7. How many contacts did the monks have with the world outside the abbey?
   □ a. None.
   □ b. Very few
   □ c. Few
   □ d. Many

8. The relations between the abbeys and the towns built around them were similar to the relations between
   □ a. friends.
   □ b. master and servant.
   □ c. rivals.
   □ d. priest and parishioner.

9. The Abbey at St. Albans was attacked because the people
   □ a. wanted to grind their own corn.
   □ b. felt the abbot was too rich.
   □ c. thought the regulations had become too lax.
   □ d. believed the monks had too much contact with the outside world.

10. The main difference between the older abbeys and the newer, reformed ones is that:
    □ a. the older ones had older buildings.
    □ b. the newer ones are richer.
    □ c. the older ones were better organized.
    □ d. the newer ones have more austere regulations.

Name _____ Date _____ Class _____

Reading Time: _____ _____ _____ _____ _____
           Minutes   Seconds   Words per minute   Total number right   Percent

The Secluded Life

CLOZE TEST: The following passage, taken from the selection you have just read, has words omitted from it. Fill in the blank without looking back at the passage. When finished, correct your answers by checking with the answer key on page 182.

A. Subject Matter Words Missing

In the writing _____ 1, one monk kept the daily _____ 2, or chronicle, of the abbey. Three other monks _____ 3 legal documents, such as leases of the _____ 4 belonging to the abbey. The more artistic and _____ 5 monks copied the illuminated manuscripts. In this way the _____ 6 literature of the past was _____ 7. Many of these illuminated manuscripts can be seen _____ 8 in museums. Even after several hundred _____ 9, the colors of the designs are often surprisingly clear and _____ 10.

B. Structure Words Missing

The monks were _____ 1 allowed the society of women, _____ 2 they had many contacts _____ 3 the outside world. The abbey gave hospitality to rich and poor _____ 4. When a stranger knocked _____ 5 the gate of the abbey, he was welcomed _____ 6 the porter or gate keeper. The porter then sent _____ 7 the Abbot. Since hospitality was _____ 8 very important part of monastery life, _____ 9 Abbot left whatever he was doing _____ 10 go and greet the stranger.

Name _____ Date _____ Class _____

A. Number Right _____ Percent _____ B. Number Right _____ Percent _____

The Secluded Life

VOCABULARY: The following words have been taken from the selection you have just read. Put an X in the box before the best meaning or synonym for the word as used in the selection.

1. **inclement**, page 140, col. 1, par. 2
"... without being exposed to rain, sun and inclement weather."
☐ a. rather desirable
☐ b. very uncompassionate
☐ c. being severe or harsh
☐ d. seeming unpredictable

2. **manuscripts**, page 140, col. 1, par. 4
"... who could not work in the fields were given books or manuscripts ..."
☐ a. religious speeches
☐ b. original writings
☐ c. magazines
☐ d. newspapers

3. **society**, page 141, col. 1, par. 2
"... monks were not allowed the society of women, but they had many contacts ..."
☐ a. wealthy friends
☐ b. a helping hand
☐ c. companionship
☐ d. a social class

4. **hospitality**, page 141, col. 1, par. 2
"Since hospitality was a very important part of monastery life ..."
☐ a. instruction for pupils
☐ b. medical attention
☐ c. social events
☐ d. kindness to strangers

5. **ample**, page 141, col. 1, par. 3
"There was ample room to receive these guests without upsetting the routine ..."
☐ a. to be elaborate
☐ b. to have plenty of
☐ c. to be plain
☐ d. to be warm

6. **tenants**, page 141, col. 1, par. 4
"Since the tenants of the abbey were not always content, ..."
☐ a. occupants or inhabitants of a place
☐ b. guests for a period of time
☐ c. holders of property
☐ d. landlords of tenements

7. **reformers**, page 141, col. 2, par. 2
"As the discipline ... grew less strict, reformers started new orders of monks."
☐ a. former law breakers
☐ b. older monks
☐ c. do-gooders
☐ d. those who make changes

8. **regulated**, page 141, col. 2, par. 2
"The life ... was even more strictly regulated than ... in the early monasteries."
☐ a. to adjust to ensure good operation
☐ b. to exaggerate conduct
☐ c. to establish an appreciation
☐ d. to control or direct by rule

9. **ornamentation**, page 141, col. 2, par. 2
"... and the buildings he works in, though attractive, are without ornamentation."
☐ a. extremely overdone
☐ b. proper adornment
☐ c. very vulgar
☐ d. seasonal decorations

10. **largely**, page 142, col. 2, par. 3
"The English abbeys were largely destroyed for their wealth ..."
☐ a. in a big way
☐ b. by large instruments
☐ c. to a great extent
☐ d. in a thoughtless way

The word **manufacture** means to make by hand. We may use the same formula in discovering the meaning of **manuscripts**. The prefix **manu** comes from the Latin meaning **hand**. The root word *scriptus* means *written*. Originally, then, the word **manuscripts** mean those things which were written only by hand.

_____   _____   _____
Name   Date   Class

_____   _____
Total Number Right   Percent

144

Set 9

Set 9·A
Life Among
the Aztecs

Starting Time: Minutes _____ Seconds _____

Long before Europeans migrated to this continent, American Indians were making history. One of the most important groups of Indians in North America was the Aztecs, who lived in the high valley which is now Mexico City. The Aztecs had developed a standard of living equal to that of many Europeans of that time.

The Aztecs left records of various kinds. Some of their history is carved in stone, while some is written on long sheets of paper made from cactus plants or the bark of certain trees. The Aztecs built solidly constructed temples and houses. They were skilled in astronomy, law and government. And, in many ways, they were kind and gentle.

The Aztecs rose to power by way of their military abilities. Wars were often fought in order to capture enemies which could be sacrificed to the Aztec War God. Although such human sacrifice was shocking to the Europeans, it was a natural development of a civilization that combined religion and warfare. When the Spanish finally vanquished the Aztecs, the conquerors had to fight vigorously to stop the practice of human sacrifice.

According to tradition, in 1325—167 years before Columbus first landed on American shores—the Aztecs started to build their capital city, Tenochtitlan. This city later became the capital of the Spanish conquerors and, finally, of the Mexican republic.

Tenochtitlan was built on an island in a large lake. The city was connected to the mainland by causeways, which contained well guarded bridges. Since these bridges could be removed in case of danger, it was very difficult to attack Tenochtitlan from the edge of the lake.

When the Aztecs first settled in the Mexican valley, they did not have much land of their own. They gradually obtained land for farming by building islands in the lake. They also supported themselves by fishing and by trading with nearby tribes. The Aztecs learned a good deal from their more advanced neighbors. And, as their military power grew, they used the lands they conquered to start more farms.

By the end of the fifteenth century the Aztecs were the leaders of a united group of surrounding tribes. They received tributes from other tribes that they had conquered. Many of these tribes were frequently at the point of rebellion. Cortés, the Spanish conqueror, took advantage of this situation and allied his troops with those tribes who hated the Aztecs.

The Aztecs achieved great power by building upon the wealth of the tribes they conquered. Their capital was a great center of commerce, wealth and culture. Skilled architects and stone masons, aided by slave labor, built great temples and palaces, as well as comfortable houses. The Aztecs even had botanical gardens, which were unknown in Europe at that time.

To aid irrigation and travel throughout the city, the Aztecs built an elaborate canal system. They grew cotton and made fine clothes from it, which were often ornamented with gold, rare furs, and the bright feathers of tropical birds.

The Aztecs had no alphabet, but they kept records of their history by means of picture writing. They had a system of education which was run by their priests and priestesses. Their schools were open only to the upper classes.

The Aztecs had hospitals and doctors and surgeons who were probably quite as good as the 15th century European medical facilities and staffs. The Aztec's study of astronomy was so advanced that they were able to make a very accurate calendar and to predict eclipses. Their calendar is a famous relic of their civilization. It is a round, flat stone, three feet thick and twenty feet in diameter, with signs and pictures representing the days and months of the year.

An Aztec legend prophesied that one day a white god would come to them from the east and rule over them. Hernando Cortés, the Spanish captain, took advantage of this belief, which helped him greatly in his conquest of the Aztecs.

In 1519, the beautiful Aztec city of Tenochtitlan, with its gleaming white temples and palaces, dazzled the eyes of the invading Spaniards. It was built in a most attractive natural setting, and the Spaniards saw it first from the high peaks which surrounded the valley of Mexico.

What the Spanish soldiers found in the Aztec city surpassed their wildest dreams. There were shady parks and gardens, containing rare plants from all parts of Mexico. There were strange animals in the zoo. And there were many large, busy markets, where the Spaniards found articles of food, clothing, and handicrafts that they had never seen before.

When Cortés arrived at Tenochtitlan with his 450 Spanish soldiers and his Indian allies, the Aztec Emperor Montezuma received them and gave them quarters in the city. Cortés realized that he was in a dangerous position. He invited Montezuma to the Spanish camp, where Montezuma was held prisoner until he died.

After the death of their emperor, the Aztecs in Mexico revolted against the Spaniards. It was only after fierce fighting that the Aztecs were defeated and Spanish rule was established.

The Aztec country became an important part of the Spanish Empire. It was called New Spain, and Spanish priests came to establish Christianity in the new possession of the Spanish king. Mule trains, carrying the Aztecs' treasures, were sent down the hills to the coast. From there, the treasures were shipped to Spain.

Today, more than four centuries after the Spanish conquest, there are still many Indians living in Mexico who speak the language of the Aztecs. Modern Mexico and Mexicans are proud of their Aztec ancestry. Many of the Aztec customs have been preserved, and Mexican ways of living and eating show strong Aztec influence. Aztec designs are found in the pottery and painting of today. Many words of the Aztec language have been added to the Spanish spoken in the country. And some of the words (such as chocolate, tomato, ocelot, coyote, and avocado) have even become part of the English language.

Finishing Time: Minutes _____ Seconds _____

Life Among the Aztecs

COMPREHENSION: Answer the questions without looking back at the passage. When finished, correct your answers by checking with the answer key on page 183. Find your words per minute by looking in the chart on page 185. Enter both scores on graphs provided at the end of this book.

1. The Aztecs became powerful through their
   ☐ a. military ability.
   ☐ b. their knowledge of astronomy.
   ☐ c. ability in farming and cloth-making.
   ☐ d. government.

2. How long before the Spanish discovered America was the capital city of the Aztecs built?
   ☐ a. 300 years
   ☐ b. 193 years
   ☐ c. 167 years
   ☐ d. 120 years

3. The Aztec capital was first built
   ☐ a. on a mountain.
   ☐ b. in a swamp.
   ☐ c. on an island.
   ☐ d. on the shores of a lake.

4. Did the Aztecs use slave labor?
   ☐ a. Yes
   ☐ b. No
   ☐ c. Seldom
   ☐ d. Often

5. The Aztecs kept records by using
   ☐ a. their alphabet.
   ☐ b. picture writing.
   ☐ c. special round stones.
   ☐ d. religious sculptures.

6. Cortes' conduct with the Aztecs could best be called
   ☐ a. cruel.   ☐ c. unwise.
   ☐ b. treacherous. ☐ d. cunning.

7. The Aztec practice of human sacrifice was a natural outgrowth of a civilization that
   ☐ a. depended upon conquest to build wealth.
   ☐ b. developed outside the European traditions.
   ☐ c. often appeared shocking to Spanish conquerors.
   ☐ d. combined religion and warfare.

8. It was difficult to attack Tenochtitalan because
   ☐ a. ambushes could be set up on the mountains.
   ☐ b. the surrounding tribes were hostile.
   ☐ c. the bridges could be removed.
   ☐ d. Montezuma maintained a powerful army.

9. To aid irrigation, the Aztecs
   ☐ a. constructed canals.
   ☐ b. utilized rain water.
   ☐ c. built reservoirs.
   ☐ d. drained the mountain streams.

10. The Aztecs seemed interested primarily
    ☐ a. in useful, practical things.
    ☐ b. in beauty and ornaments.
    ☐ c. in luxury and furs.
    ☐ d. in beauty and utility.

Name _____   Date _____   Class _____

Reading Time: _____ _____ _____ _____ _____
              Minutes   Seconds   Words per minute   Total number right Percent

Life Among the Aztecs

CLOZE TEST: The following passage, taken from the selection you have just read, has words omitted from it. Fill in the blank without looking back at the passage. When finished, correct your answers by checking with the answer key on page 183.

A. Subject Matter Words Missing

When Cortés, with his 450 Spanish _____1_____ and his Indian allies, arrived at Tenochtitlan, the Aztec _____2_____, Montezuma, received them and _____3_____ them quarters in the city. Cortés _____4_____ that he was in a dangerous _____5_____. He invited Montezuma to the _____6_____ camp, where Montezuma was held _____7_____ until he died. After the death of their Emperor, the Aztecs in Mexico _____8_____ against the Spanish. It was only after _____9_____ fighting that the Aztecs were defeated, and Spanish _____10_____ was established.

B. Structure Words Missing

Today, more than four centuries _____1_____ the Spanish conquest, there are _____2_____ many Indians living in Mexico who speak _____3_____ language of the Aztecs. Modern Mexico _____4_____ Mexicans are proud of their Aztec ancestry. _____5_____ of the Aztec customs have been preserved, and Mexican ways _____6_____ living and eating show strong Aztec influence. Aztec designs are found _____7_____ the pottery and painting _____8_____ today. Many words of the Aztec language have been added _____9_____ the Spanish spoken in the country, and some of them (such _____10_____ chocolate, tomato, ocelot, coyote, and avocado) have even become a part of the English language.

Name		Date	Class

A. Number Right	Percent	B. Number Right	Percent

Life Among the Aztecs

VOCABULARY: The following words have been taken from the selection you have just read. Put an *X* in the box before the best meaning or synonym for the word as used in the selection.

1. **vanquished**, page 146, col. 1, par. 3
   "When the Spanish finally vanquished the Aztecs, ..."
   ☐ a. to defeat
   ☐ b. to frighten
   ☐ c. to send running
   ☐ d. to abuse

2. **vigorously**, page 146, col. 1, par. 3
   "... the conquerors had to fight vigorously ..."
   ☐ a. in a serious way
   ☐ b. just temporarily
   ☐ c. in an energetic way
   ☐ d. in a wretched manner

3. **advanced**, page 146, col. 2, par. 3
   "The Aztecs learned a good deal from their more advanced neighbors."
   ☐ a. being available
   ☐ b. being upgraded
   ☐ c. being promoted
   ☐ d. progressing beyond others

4. **tributes**, page 146, col. 2, par. 4
   "They received tributes from other tribes that they had conquered."
   ☐ a. words of gratitude
   ☐ b. violent arguments
   ☐ c. taxes and land
   ☐ d. gifts in appreciation

5. **rebellion**, page 146, col. 2, par. 4
   "Many of these tribes were frequently at the point of rebellion."
   ☐ a. an uprising against authority
   ☐ b. an organization of resisters
   ☐ c. a feeling of insubordination
   ☐ d. a carelessly formed group

6. **elaborate**, page 147, col. 1, par. 2
   "... the Aztecs built an elaborate canal system."
   ☐ a. too complicated
   ☐ b. worked out with care and detail
   ☐ c. up to date
   ☐ d. not a good type

7. **predict**, page 147, col. 1, par. 4
   "... to make a very accurate calendar and to predict eclipses."
   ☐ a. making a good guess
   ☐ b. to foretell
   ☐ c. to study about
   ☐ d. to keep a record of

8. **prophesied**, page 147, col. 1, par. 5
   "An Aztec legend prophesied that one day ..."
   ☐ a. to utter religious statements
   ☐ b. to speak the inspired word
   ☐ c. to act as a mediator
   ☐ d. to indicate beforehand

9. **surpassed**, page 147, col.. 1, par. 7
   "What the Spanish soldiers found ... surpassed their wildest dreams."
   ☐ a. to have contributed to
   ☐ b. to have satisfied
   ☐ c. to have gone beyond
   ☐ d. to have fulfilled mildly

10. **quarters**, page 147, col. 2, par. 1
    "... Montezuma received them and gave them quarters in the city."
    ☐ a. a place to stay
    ☐ b. a separate section of land
    ☐ c. a special district
    ☐ d. a rich estate

Surpass is from the French *surpasser* which means *to go beyond*. The prefix **sur** comes from another prefix **super** which is a prefix of **superiority**. **Surpasser** means to overpass or to go beyond.

Name _____   Date _____   Class _____

Total Number Right _____   Percent _____

Starting Time: Minutes _____ Seconds _____

About three hundred years ago, there were approximately half a billion people in the world. In the two centuries that followed the population doubled, and, by 1850, there were more than a billion people in the world. It took only 75 years for the figure to double once more, so that now the population figure stands at approximately three and one half billion. Each day the population of the world increases by about 150,000.

In former centuries the population grew slowly. Famines, wars, and epidemics, such as the plague and cholera, killed many people. Today, although the birth rate has not changed significantly, the death rate has been lowered considerably by various kinds of progress.

Machinery has made it possible to produce more and more food in vast areas, such as the plains of America and Russia. Crops have been increased almost everywhere and people are growing more and more food. New forms of food preservation have also been developed so that food need not be eaten as soon as it is grown. Meat, fish, fruit and vegetables can be dried, tinned or frozen, then stored for later use.

Improvement in communications and transportation has made it possible to send more food from the place where it is produced to other places where it is needed. This has helped reduce the number of famines.

Generally speaking, people live in conditions of greater security. Practices such as the slave trade, which caused many useless deaths, have been stopped.

Progress in medicine and hygiene has made it possible for people to live longer. People in Europe and North America live, on the average, twice as long as they did a hundred years ago. In other countries, too, people generally live much longer than they once did. Babies, especially, have a far better chance of growing up because of increased protection against infant disease. However, all countries do not benefit to the same degree from this progress in medicine and hygiene.

In Europe and North America, the growing population has had the advantage of greater quantities of natural resources and food. However, in some places, such as the monsoon countries of Asia, the birth rate has always been very high. Now, with better hygienic conditions and better medical care, fewer babies die; but the birth rate has not changed. This means that the population is growing very rapidly and that there is not enough food for everyone.

Half the world's people live in Asia, but most of them are concentrated in the coastal regions and on the islands. The same type of populace concentration is true of other continents, although they are often far less populated. There are still vast regions of the world where very few people live: the central regions of the larger continents, mountainous areas, deserts, the far north, and tropical jungles.

In prehistoric times, people from Africa and Asia migrated to other continents. Europe was occupied by people from the east, America by groups from Asia. In the nineteenth century, the population of Europe increased rapidly, and living conditions were sometimes difficult because of wars, famines, or political conditions. Many Europeans left their countries to find better conditions in America, Africa and Australia.

During the nineteenth and twentieth centuries, migrations have taken place within certain countries: the cities with their industries have attracted people away from the country. The possibility of earning a fixed salary in a factory or office was more attractive than the possibility of staying on the farm and having one's work destroyed by frost, storms, or droughts. Furthermore, the development of agricultural machinery made it possible for fewer people to do the same amount of work.

Thus, at the same time that the industrial revolution made it possible to produce goods more cheaply and more quickly in factories, an agricultural revolution also took place. Instead of leaving fields empty every third year, farmers began to plant clover or some other crop that would enrich the soil. Instead of using only animal fertilizer, farmers began to use chemical fertilizers to keep the soil rich. These methods have enabled French farmers, for example, to get five times as much wheat as was obtained from the same land two centuries ago.

In many countries farmers find it more profitable to raise only one crop or one kind of animal. They choose the kind that gives the best results. Then they sell all that they produce, instead of trying to grow a little of everything and consume what they grow. This is a more feasible type of operation because modern methods and machinery are adapted to specific animals and specific crops. There-fore, it would be too expensive to do all the work by hand, or to buy the equipment needed for several different kinds of farming.

At the same time, constant progress has been going on in industry. Fifty years ago it took a day to assemble the pieces of an automobile. Today one factory can produce one car in a minute. Today, too, it takes only one textile worker to supervise the production of as much cotton cloth as 4,000 workers could have produced in the eighteenth century. Modern industry needs large numbers of specialized workers. The less specialized workers are gradually being replaced by new machines. Large quantities of raw materials, sometimes brought from halfway around the world, are also needed. To work the machines, energy must be supplied from sources such as coal, water power, electricity and oil. And to build, maintain and improve modern factories, great financial resources are necessary. A factory is often the property of a society or a government, rather than the property of one person.

After producing its goods, industry must sell these goods to people. If a factory can produce more goods than it is able to sell in its own country, it tries to sell them to people of other countries. Thus, nowadays we see more and more trade agreements making it easier to exchange raw materials and manufactured goods between countries, and great advertising campaigns helping industries sell more goods.

Finishing Time: Minutes _____ Seconds _____

More People and More Products

COMPREHENSION: Answer the questions without looking back at the passage. When finished, correct your answers by checking with the answer key on page 183. Find your words per minute by looking in the chart on page 185. Enter both scores on graphs provided at the end of this book.

1. The population of the world is now approximately
   ☐ a. 2,000,000.
   ☐ b. 2,500,000.
   ☐ c. 3,000,000.
   ☐ d. 3,500,000.

2. Population has increased rapidly in the last 75 years because
   ☐ a. people have more children.
   ☐ b. various kinds of progress prolong lives.
   ☐ c. there are not as many wars.
   ☐ d. people do not need as much food.

3. Of all the people in the world, Asia contains
   ☐ a. one-fourth.
   ☐ b. one-third.
   ☐ c. one-half.
   ☐ d. two-thirds.

4. Which factor has *not* helped increase population?
   ☐ a. Progress in medicine
   ☐ b. Improvement in communications
   ☐ c. Machinery
   ☐ d. Centuries

5. According to the text, industry today needs
   ☐ a. unskilled workers.
   ☐ b. more government help.
   ☐ c. fewer raw materials.
   ☐ d. skilled workers.

6. Another title for this article could be
   ☐ a. "Progress and Population."
   ☐ b. "Cities Are Starving."
   ☐ c. "Agriculture and Industry."
   ☐ d. "Two Revolutions."

7. If present trends continue, industry
   ☐ a. will replace workers by machines.
   ☐ b. will sell more and more cars.
   ☐ c. will produce things that cost more.
   ☐ d. will try to find more customers.

8. It would seem to be desirable
   ☐ a. to stop the growth of population.
   ☐ b. to reduce the population of the monsoon countries.
   ☐ c. to send more people to the north.
   ☐ d. to try to make empty regions more habitable.

9. Specialization is more evident
   ☐ a. in industry but not in agriculture.
   ☐ b. in agriculture but not in industry.
   ☐ c. in agriculture and in industry.
   ☐ d. neither in agriculture nor industry.

10. Even if a farmer can grow many kinds of crops, he will often find it cheaper to specialize because
    ☐ a. he would not want to grow the same things as his neighbors.
    ☐ b. he would not be able to buy many pieces of farm machinery.
    ☐ c. he would not want to buy vegetables at the store.
    ☐ d. he would not be able to do all the work by hand.

Name _____ Date _____ Class _____

Reading Time: _____ _____ _____ _____ _____
              Minutes Seconds Words per minute Total number right Percent

More People and More Products

CLOZE TEST: The following passage, taken from the selection you have just read, has words omitted from it. Fill in the blank without looking back at the passage. When finished, correct your answers by checking with the answer key on page 183.

A. Subject Matter Words Missing

Thus, at the same _____1_____ that the industrial revolution made it _____2_____ to produce goods more cheaply and more _____3_____ in factories, an agricultural revolution also _____4_____ place. Instead of leaving fields empty every third _____5_____, farmers began to _____6_____ clover or some other crop that would _____7_____ the soil. Instead of using only animal fertilizer, the farmers began to use _____8_____ fertilizers to keep the soil rich. These methods have _____9_____ French farmers, for example, to get five times as much wheat as was obtainable from the same _____10_____ two centuries ago.

B. Subject Words Missing

During the nineteenth _____1_____ twentieth centuries, migrations have taken place within certain countries: _____2_____ cities with their industries have attracted people away _____3_____ the country. The possibility _____4_____ earning a fixed salary _____5_____ a factory _____6_____ office was more attractive _____7_____ the possibility of staying _____8_____ the farm and having one's work destroyed _____9_____ frost, storms, _____10_____ droughts.

Name _____   Date _____   Class _____

A. Number Right _____ Percent _____   B. Number Right _____ Percent _____

154

More People and More Products

VOCABULARY: The following words have been taken from the selection you have just read. Put an *X* in the box before the best meaning or synonym for the word as used in the selection.

1. **approximately**, page 151, col. 1, par. 1
"... there were approximately half a billion people ..."
□ a. close to
□ b. more than
□ c. most definitely
□ d. the same as

2. **considerably**, page 151, col. 1, par. 2
"... the death rate has been lowered considerably by various kinds of progress."
□ a. not too much
□ b. in some instances
□ c. by a fair amount
□ d. very greatly

3. **preservation**, page 151, col. 1, par. 3
"New forms of food preservation have also been developed ..."
□ a. to keep safe
□ b. to prepare to resist decay
□ c. to prepare by cooking
□ d. to set apart

4. **hygiene**, page 151, col. 2, par. 3
"Progress in medicine and hygiene has made it possible for people ..."
□ a. exercise schedules
□ b. food programs
□ c. vitamin and diet programs
□ d. rules of health and cleanliness

5. **advantage**, page 151, col. 2, par. 4
"... has had the advantage of greater quantities of natural resources ..."
□ a. some overabundance
□ b. great progress
□ c. best type
□ d. definite benefit

6. **populace**, page 152, col. 1, par. 1
"The same type of populace concentration is true of other continents ..."
□ a. common people
□ b. favorable groups
□ c. special types
□ d. prevailing groups

7. **enrich**, page 152, col. 1, par. 4
"... farmers began to plant ... some other crop that would enrich the soil."
□ a. to make abundant
□ b. to make finer in quality
□ c. to increase in quantity
□ d. to make more beautiful

8. **consume**, page 152, col. 1, par. 5
"... instead of trying to ... consume what they grow."
□ a. to eat up
□ b. to destroy
□ c. to waste
□ d. to preserve

9. **feasible**, page 152, col. 1, par. 5
"This is a more feasible type of operation because ..."
□ a. to be expensive
□ b. to be difficult
□ c. to be workable
□ d. to be simple

10. **financial**, page 152, col. 2, par. 2
"And to build ... factories, great financial resources are necessary."
□ a. important and rare
□ b. relating to money
□ c. relating to property
□ d. difficult to obtain

Preservation is a noun which comes from a combination of the prefix **pre** which can mean **beforehand**, the root word from the Latin *servare* which means *to keep* and the suffix **tion, expressing a state or action.** The definition as applied to the use in this selection obviously means to prepare beforehand so as to resist decomposition.

Name _____   Date _____   Class _____

Total Number Right _____   Percent _____

Set 9·C
Artificial
Waterways

Starting Time: Minutes _____ Seconds _____

It is impossible to answer the question, "Who built the first canal?" Perhaps some people long ago, living in a dry country, discovered that they could dig ditches to irrigate their fields with river water. And, naturally, in the days when boats were the most important means of transport, canals were the easiest means of reaching a place that was not on a river, but was at the same level as a river. Furthermore, a ditch joining two rivers proved both easy and time-saving for boat travel.

Today, most countries in the world have canals. Even in the twentieth century, goods can be moved more cheaply by boat than by any other means of transport. Some canals, such as the Suez or the Panama, save ships weeks of time by making their voyage a thousand miles shorter. Other canals permit boats to reach cities that are not located on the coast. Still other canals drain lands where there is too much water, help to irrigate fields where there is not enough water, and furnish water power for factories and mills.

The size of a canal depends on the kind of boats going through it. The canal must be wide enough to permit two of the largest boats using it to pass each other easily. It must be deep enough to leave about two feet of water beneath the keel of the largest boat using the canal.

Some canals have sloping sides, while others have sides that are nearly vertical. Canals that are cut through rock can have nearly vertical sides. However, canals with earth banks may crumble if the angle of their sides is too steep.

Some canals are lined with brick, stone, or concrete to keep the water from soaking into the mud. This also permits ships to go at greater speeds, since they cannot make the banks fall in by stirring up the water. In small canals with mud banks, ships and barges must limit their speed.

When the canal goes through different levels of water, the ships must be raised or lowered from one level to the other. This is generally done by means of locks. If a ship wants to go up to higher water, the lower end of the lock opens to let the boat in. Then this gate closes, and the water is let into the lock chamber from the upper level. This raises the level of the water in the lock until it is the same as the upper level of water. Now the upper gates can be opened to release the ship into the higher water. Of course there must always be enough water on the upper level to allow for the flooding of the lock. Sometimes a canal contains a series of locks when the difference in levels is very great.

In places where it does not rain very often, irrigation canals drain water from rivers or lakes and carry it to fields. Sometimes artificial lakes, such as the lake behind the Aswan Dam on the Nile River, provide the irrigation water.

In places where there is too much water, canals can drain the water off the land for use in farming. In Holland, acres and acres of land have been drained in this way. Since much of this drained land is below sea level, the water in the canals has to be pumped up to sea level. Dikes have been built in Holland to keep the sea from covering the land, as it did in the past.

Sometimes canals have to be built across deep valleys. Bridges or aqueducts are constructed for this purpose. The Romans often brought water to cities from great distances by building such bridges, at the top of which were canals. Some canals go through mountains by means of tunnels. One such tunnel, near Marseille, France, is over four miles long.

Canals existed in Egypt thousands of years ago. The great canal at Babylon, between the Tigris and Euphrates, was built about 2000 B.C. The Grand Canal of China, which is over 900 miles long, was begun about 2500 years ago, and took centuries to finish. During the seventeenth century, France built many canals that are still in use today. However, they are not so heavily traveled as they were a hundred years ago, before railways were built. One such canal is a short-cut between the Atlantic Ocean and the Mediterranean. In Russia, there are canals reaching from Leningrad to the Caspian Sea. Canals in Germany permit boats to go from the Black Sea to the North Sea. The Kiel Canal provides a passageway between the North Sea and the Baltic. In America, the Great Lakes are all connected by canals, enabling ships to go from the Atlantic Ocean and the St. Lawrence River to Lake Superior. Since the lakes are at different levels, they are connected by locks.

Many countries have built canals near the coast, and parallel to the coast. These waterways make it possible for boats to travel between ports along the coast without being exposed to the dangers of the open sea.

Canals are also used to carry water to mills and factories. The water from a river is kept at a higher level than the river until it reaches the wheel of the mill. Then the water is poured over the mill wheel, making it turn. The same principle is used in more modern factories and in hydroelectric generating plants. The force of the water, falling from a certain height, provides a cheap way of producing electricity.

When the planet Mars was first observed through a telescope, people saw that the round disk of the planet was criss-crossed by a number of strange blue-green lines. These were called "canals" because they looked the same as canals on earth that are viewed from an airplane. However, scientists are now certain that the Martian phenomena are really not canals. The photographs taken from space-ships have helped us to discover the truth about the Martian "canals."

Finishing Time: Minutes _____ Seconds _____

Artificial Waterways

COMPREHENSION: Answer the questions without looking back at the passage. When finished, correct your answers by checking with the answer key on page 183. Find your words per minute by looking in the chart on page 185. Enter both scores on graphs provided at the end of this book.

1. Where were canals first built?
    ☐ a. Suez
    ☐ b. Panama
    ☐ c. Holland
    ☐ d. No one knows.

2. A canal must be deep enough to leave how many feet of water beneath the keel of the largest boat using the canal?
    ☐ a. One foot of water
    ☐ b. Two feet of water
    ☐ c. Five feet of water
    ☐ d. Ten feet of water

3. The Aswan Dam was built primarily for what purpose?
    ☐ a. Navigation
    ☐ b. Irrigation
    ☐ c. Drainage
    ☐ d. Electricity

4. In Europe, canals were built primarily for
    ☐ a. navigation.
    ☐ b. irrigation.
    ☐ c. drainage.
    ☐ d. electricity.

5. Canals in soft, muddy land have sides which are
    ☐ a. straight.
    ☐ b. straight or sloping.
    ☐ c. sloping.
    ☐ d. lined with concrete.

6. A canal with earth sides may be lined with concrete, so that
    ☐ a. boats can go faster.
    ☐ b. the water will be cleaner.
    ☐ c. the water will flow faster.
    ☐ d. the canal will be less dangerous.

7. The water in the canals near the coast in Holland is
    ☐ a. above sea level.
    ☐ b. at sea level.
    ☐ c. below sea level.
    ☐ d. at a constantly changing level.

8. Compared to other means of water transport, canal boats are
    ☐ a. cheaper and sometimes faster.
    ☐ b. more expensive, but faster.
    ☐ c. cheaper, but more dangerous.
    ☐ d. more expensive and slower.

9. Are canals ever built parallel to the sea coast?
    ☐ a. No, because boats can use the sea.
    ☐ b. Yes, to protect boats from storms.
    ☐ c. No, because the sea can flood the canals.
    ☐ d. Yes, to protect boats from attacks.

10. Between which of the following is it impossible to go by canal?
    ☐ a. The North Sea and the Black Sea
    ☐ b. The Atlantic Ocean and the Mediterranean Sea
    ☐ c. The North Sea and the Baltic
    ☐ d. The Red Sea and the North Sea

Name _____   Date _____   Class _____

Reading Time: _____ _____   _____   _____ _____
              Minutes Seconds   Words per minute   Total number right Percent

Artificial Waterways

CLOZE TEST: The following passage, taken from the selection you have just read, has words omitted from it. Fill in the blank without looking back at the passage. When finished, correct your answers by checking with the answer key on page 183.

A. Subject Matter Words Missing

The size of a canal _____1_____ on the kind of boats going through it. The canal _____2_____ be wide enough to permit two of the _____3_____ boats using it to pass each other _____4_____. It must be deep enough to _____5_____ about two feet of water beneath the _____6_____ of the largest boat using the canal. Some canals have _____7_____ sides, while others have sides that are nearly vertical. Canals that are _____8_____ through rock can have nearly vertical sides. However, canals with earth _____9_____ may crumble if the angle of their sides is too _____10_____.

B. Structure Words Missing

Today most countries _____1_____ the world have canals. Even in _____2_____ twentieth century, goods can be moved more cheaply _____3_____ boat than by any other means of transport. _____4_____ canals, such as the Suez _____5_____ the Panama, save ships weeks _____6_____ time by making their voyage _____7_____ thousand miles shorter. Other canals permit boats _____8_____ reach cities that are _____9_____ located on the coast. Still other canals drain lands _____10_____ there is too much water.

Name		Date	Class

A. Number Right	Percent	B. Number Right	Percent

Artificial Waterways

VOCABULARY: The following words have been taken from the selection you have just read. Put an *X* in the box before the best meaning or synonym for the word as used in the selection.

1. **irrigate**, page 156, col. 1, par. 1
   "... they could dig ditches to irrigate their fields with river water."
   □ a. simple fertilizing
   □ b. supplying water
   □ c. complete flooding
   □ d. controlled planting

2. **transport**, page 156, col. 1, par. 2
   "...moved more cheaply by boat than by any other means of transport."
   □ a. carrying from one place to another
   □ b. manufacturing
   □ c. buying and selling
   □ d. storing and selling

3. **vertical**, page 156, col. 2, par. 2
   "Some canals have sloping sides, while others have sides that are nearly vertical."
   □ a. touching each other
   □ b. on the short side
   □ c. easily by-passed
   □ d. straight up and down

4. **release**, page 156, col. 2, par. 4
   "Now the upper gates can be opened to release the ship ..."
   □ a. to deliver
   □ b. to let go
   □ c. to raise
   □ d. to help tow

5. **artificial**, page 157, col. 1, par. 2
   "Sometimes artificial lakes, such as the lake behind the Aswan Dam ..."
   □ a. not formed by nature
   □ b. unusual
   □ c. shallow and useless
   □ d. used for show

6. **aqueducts**, page 157, col. 1, par. 4
   "Bridges or aqueducts are constructed for this purpose."
   □ a. a passage for traffic
   □ b. a structure to transport water
   □ c. a footbridge
   □ d. a structure designed for its beauty

7. **parallel**, page 157, col. 1, par. 6
   "Many countries have built canals near the coast, and parallel to the coast."
   □ a. an extension of
   □ b. similar to
   □ c. having the same direction
   □ d. across from

8. **hydroelectric**, page 157, col. 2, par. 2
   "The same principle is used ... in hydroelectric generating plants."
   □ a. high powered electricity
   □ b. water produced electricity
   □ c. undependable electricity
   □ d. automatic electricity

9. **generating**, page 157, col. 2, par. 2
   "The same principle is used ... in hydroelectric generating plants."
   □ a. electrical manufacturing
   □ b. electrical distributing
   □ c. electrical refining
   □ d. electrical producing

10. **phenomena**, page 157, col. 2, par. 3
    "... scientists are now certain that Martian phenomena are not really canals."
    □ a. surface lines
    □ b. scientist's observations
    □ c. observable circumstance
    □ d. a changing occurrence

The expression Trans-Atlantic Flight is a good one to illustrate the meaning of the prefix *trans* which is *across*. Our word **transport** is a combination of *trans*, a Latin prefix and *portare*, a Latin word which means *to carry*. The addition of the suffix **ation**, meaning act of, gives us **transportation**, the act of **transporting**.

Name _____ Date _____ Class _____

Total Number Right _____ Percent _____

Set 10

Set 10·A
An Empire
and Its Problems, I

Starting Time: Minutes _____ Seconds _____

A thousand years before Christ, Rome was merely a small Italian trading post on the banks of the Tiber River. For a time it was ruled by Etruscan kings who came down from the north. Soon, however, the merchants of Rome, who traded with the Greek cities in southern Italy, as well as the towns to the north, began to resent the domination of kings. The merchants preferred to set up a city-state, as the Greeks had done, governed by a Senate of influential persons. These persons were generally aristocrats who owned land, and they were appointed to the Senate by two Consuls who were elected by the citizens.

For a long time the common people, or plebeians, had little money or power. At one point the plebeians showed their discontent by leaving Rome and settling down in another city. This incident frightened the upper classes, or patricians, because they could not get along without the plebeians. As a result the patricians gave the plebeians some privileges, and the latter returned to Rome. Little by little it became possible for plebeians to attain high positions, even positions as high as Senator. Representatives of the plebeians, called tribunes, could veto the action of the Senate, and even of the Consuls, if necessary.

Romans had great respect for the government and its officials. Some plebeian families rose to positions of importance because of the service their members had rendered to Rome. After a time, the Senate, composed of highly respected men, became even more powerful than the Consuls, who could not make decisions without Senate approval.

There was, however, a large number of people who had no power and no rights. They were the slaves, who were brought from conquered territory, sometimes from very far away. They could be bought and sold, punished or liberated at the will of the masters. As Rome grew, the patricians became richer and often exploited the plebeians. Both groups exploited the slaves.

Rome began its expansion by taking possession of land around the city of Rome. Sometimes colonies of Roman citizens were settled in this land. Other times the people living there were given the privileges of citizenship in return for their support. Thus, more and more people served in the Roman army, which became stronger and more powerful.

In the third and fourth centuries before Christ, the Roman army fought in a series of wars. At the conclusion of these wars,

Rome had become the most important city in Italy. Its only important rival, at that point, was Carthage, across the Mediterranean in northern Africa.

The Carthaginians were the descendants of the Phoenicians, who had established a very rich, successful city. They were seamen and traders. When the Greeks, who had established cities in southern Italy, tried to stop Rome from expanding, the Carthaginians helped the Romans because they did not want the Greeks to become more powerful. After the Greeks were driven out, the Romans took possession of southern Italy and the Carthaginians took possession of Sicily.

Rome and Carthage did not remain friendly for long. They were too close together; and both cities were too powerful for peaceful coexistence. Carthage had already gained control of the coast of North Africa, from the Greek territory of Cyrene to the Straits of Gibraltar and southern Spain. The Carthaginians did not permit ships from any other city to sail through the straits or into the ports which they controlled. Unlike the Romans, the Carthaginian army was composed of paid soldiers from many places. Carthage was ruled by a group of rich merchants who made up the aristocracy. The Carthaginians also had large numbers of slaves.

In 264 B.C. the first of three long wars between Rome and Carthage began. These three wars were spread out over more than a hundred years, with intervals of peace in between. They were called the Punic Wars, and ended with the complete destruction of Carthage by the Romans. The best-known figure during these wars was the Carthaginian general, Hannibal, who harassed Rome for fifteen years during the second Punic War.

After the defeat of Carthage, Rome had no rival in the western Mediterranean world. Shortly afterward, Rome established provinces in the Eastern Mediterranean, too. Gold and slaves poured into Rome from the conquered lands. The lives of the rich Romans became more and more luxurious. The Roman governors who went out to rule the new provinces were interested chiefly in getting as rich as they could. They accomplished this by imposing high taxes and taking advantage of all they could get.

In Rome the demand for cloths, spices, and luxuries from other parts of the Roman Empire grew tremendously. To satisfy this demand Roman ships sailed regularly between Rome and the outposts. The ship owners became rich merchants and banks had to be established to handle all the money that was being amassed. The banks at Rome filled a line of booths on both sides of the market place, called the Forum. When a government official returned to Rome and built a beautiful new house, others wanted to do the same. Some made their old houses bigger by adding more rooms, a court with columns, and a library. They installed expensive furniture, statues, mosaics and paintings in their new or enlarged houses. The new houses sometimes had running water, baths, and sanitary conveniences. Sometimes there was central heating with a furnace that sent hot air through pipes into the rooms. Greek literature was translated, theaters were built, books were copied. Roman writers and artists not only copied Greek models, but created new works as well. Freed Greek slaves at Rome began to open schools for the education of Roman children, who had seldom learned to read and write in former years.

Some people felt that there was too much luxury. Laws were passed to restrain expensive habits, such as wearing showy jewelry and using carriages. However, these laws had little effect on the rich people who wished to display the luxuries that they could afford.

Finishing Time: Minutes _____ Seconds _____

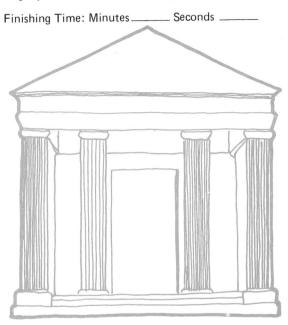

An Empire and Its Problems, I

COMPREHENSION: Answer the questions without looking back at the passage. When finished, correct your answers by checking with the answer key on page 183. Find your words per minute by looking in the chart on page 185. Enter both scores on graphs provided at the end of this book.

1. The Consuls in Rome were
   - ☐ a. appointed by the king.
   - ☐ b. elected by the landowning aristocrats.
   - ☐ c. elected by the citizens.
   - ☐ d. appointed by the Senate.

2. The plebeians obtained more power because
   - ☐ a. they showed their discontent.
   - ☐ b. they owned land.
   - ☐ c. they had friends in the Senate.
   - ☐ d. they had money.

3. The Carthaginians helped the Romans at one time because
   - ☐ a. they wanted to trade with Rome.
   - ☐ b. they wanted to conquer Rome.
   - ☐ c. they wanted to stop Greek power.
   - ☐ d. they wanted Roman soldiers to fight for them.

4. The only serious rival of Rome in the third century B.C. was in
   - ☐ a. Greece.
   - ☐ b. Italy.
   - ☐ c. Asia.
   - ☐ d. Africa.

5. Rome found Carthage difficult to defeat because of the work of
   - ☐ a. Caesar.
   - ☐ b. the Greeks.
   - ☐ c. Roman governors who loved luxury.
   - ☐ d. Hannibal.

6. The Romans set up a city-state governed by a Senate because
   - ☐ a. they were tired of the domination of kings.
   - ☐ b. they traded with Greek city-states.
   - ☐ c. Rome was not a big trading post.
   - ☐ d. the common people wanted power.

7. Rome became the most important city in Italy because of its
   - ☐ a. military victories. ☐ c. money.
   - ☐ b. trade   ☐ d. slaves.

8. Rome and Carthage fought each other because
   - ☐ a. the people loved luxury too much.
   - ☐ b. they both wanted Greek slaves to teach their children.
   - ☐ c. each wanted to become the most powerful city.
   - ☐ d. Rome was governed by merchants.

9. The rich Romans paid little attention to laws limiting luxury because
   - ☐ a. they had no respect for the law.
   - ☐ b. they wanted to live better.
   - ☐ c. they were not interested in spending too much money, anyhow.
   - ☐ d. they wanted to show how much they could buy.

10. Rome and Carthage were similar in that
    - ☐ a. they had the same government.
    - ☐ b. they both had citizen armies.
    - ☐ c. they depended on slaves.
    - ☐ d. they were interested in dividing the Mediterranean between them.

Name _____ Date _____ Class _____

Reading Time: _____ _____ _____ _____ _____
              Minutes   Seconds   Words per minute   Total number right   Percent

An Empire and Its Problems, I

CLOZE TEST: The following passage, taken from the selection you have just read, has words omitted from it. Fill in the blank without looking back at the passage. When finished, correct your answers by checking with the answer key on page 183.

A. Subject Matter Words Missing

For a long time the common _____ 1, or plebeians, had little money or _____ 2. At one point the plebeians showed their discontent by _____ 3 Rome and settling down in _____ 4 city. This incident frightened the upper _____ 5, or patricians, because they could not _____ 6 along without the plebeians. As a result the patricians _____ 7 the plebeians some privileges, and the latter _____ 8 to Rome. Little by little it became _____ 9 for plebeians to attain _____ 10 positions, even positions as high as Senator.

B. Structure Words Missing

A thousand years _____ 1 Christ, Rome was merely a small Italian trading post _____ 2 the banks of the Tiber River. _____ 3 _____ 4 a time it was ruled by Etruscan kings who came down _____ 5 the north. Soon, however, the merchants _____ Rome, who traded with _____ 6 Greek cities in southern Italy, _____ 7 well as the towns to the north, began to resent the domination _____ 8 kings. They preferred to set _____ 9 a city-state, as the Greeks had done, governed by _____ 10 Senate of influential persons.

Name _____   Date _____   Class _____

A. Number Right _____   Percent _____   B. Number Right _____   Percent _____

An Empire and Its Problems, I

VOCABULARY: The following words have been taken from the selection you have just read. Put an X in the box before the best meaning or synonym for the word as used in the selection.

1. **domination**, page 162, col. 1, par. 1
   "... the merchants ... began to resent the domination of kings."
   ☐ a. cruel method
   ☐ b. firm attitude
   ☐ c. complete control
   ☐ d. unfair wage system

2. **influential**, page 162, col. 1, par. 1
   "The merchants preferred to set up a city-state, ... governed by a Senate of influential people"
   ☐ a. those exercising power
   ☐ b. those most wealthy
   ☐ c. those most intelligent
   ☐ d. those properly elected

3. **liberated**, page 162, col. 2, par. 2
   "They could be bought and sold, punished or liberated ..."
   ☐ a. to be tortured
   ☐ b. to be released
   ☐ c. to be killed
   ☐ d. to be confined

4. **exploited**, page 162, col. 2, par. 2
   "... the patricians became richer and often exploited the plebians."
   ☐ a. treated kindly
   ☐ b. opporessed with fear
   ☐ c. treated with vengeance
   ☐ d. used for profit

5. **rival**, page 163, col. 1, par. 1
   "It's only important rival, at that point was Carthage, ..."
   ☐ a. having an association with
   ☐ b. being a friend to
   ☐ c. being an opponent of
   ☐ d. having a working relationship with

6. **coexistence**, page 163, col. 1, par. 3
   "They were too close together, and both cities were too powerful for peaceful coexistence."
   ☐ a. to live side by side
   ☐ b. to compete fairly
   ☐ c. to develop equally
   ☐ d. to ignore competition

7. **intervals**, page 163, col. 1, par. 4
   "These three wars were spread out ... with intervals of peace in between."
   ☐ a. a large area
   ☐ b. a kind of space
   ☐ c. a type of meeting
   ☐ d. a series of pauses

8. **imposing**, page 163, col. 1, par. 5
   "They accomplished this by imposing high taxes ..."
   ☐ a. to offer
   ☐ b. to lay upon
   ☐ c. to threaten with
   ☐ d. to indicate

9. **translated**, page 163, col. 2, par. 1
   "Greek literature was translated, theaters were built, books were copied."
   ☐ a. to express in another language
   ☐ b. to perform on stage
   ☐ c. to read in public
   ☐ d. to give the definitions of

10. **restrain**, page 163, col. 2, par. 2
    "Laws were passed to restrain expensive habits, such as wearing showy jewelry."
    ☐ a. to encourage
    ☐ b. to explain
    ☐ c. to prevent
    ☐ d. to obtain

The word **coexistence** is made up of the prefix **co** and the root word **exist** plus the suffix **ence. Co** is a prefix signifying **accompanying action. Exist** is from the Latin word *existere* and means *to have actual being.* The suffix **ence** is a suffix of nouns and denotes an action, state or quality.

Name _____   Date _____   Class _____

Total Number Right _____   Percent _____

Starting Time: Minutes _____ Seconds _____

Although the rich people in Rome lived well, there were still many poor people and slaves. The rich tried to keep the poor from revolting by providing "bread and circuses"—gifts of free bread and lavish games and contests. Among the most popular of the contests were the gladiator shows. The Roman politician who wanted to make himself popular with the people tried to show them what wonderful games he could provide for them. If his games proved popular, he could become the governor of a province and make himself very rich.

Since it was considered improper for a Roman senator or a prominent citizen to engage in work or business, a good number of them used their money to buy land. Thus, many small farms became part of large estates. Of course a great number of slaves was needed to work the land; and the slaves were often treated most cruelly. Finally, some of them rose in revolt under a gladiator named Spartacus. However, they were defeated and thousands of them were killed by the Roman soldiers.

Slave labor and the long wars began to ruin the small farms of Italy. The men were away so long fighting that there was nobody left to work the land. The women and children were often obliged to leave the farm, and the land became part of some rich man's estate. When the former farmers returned from the wars, there was no place for them to go but to Rome. In Rome, however, they could not always find work. So they lived on the free bread, went to the games and circuses, and added to the numbers of poor people already in Rome.

When the farmer-soldier came home and found that his farm was still there, he discovered he could not grow crops as cheaply as the great plantations with their huge numbers of slaves. When he sold what he grew, he found he did not get enough money for himself and his family to live. Thus, he was forced to sell the farm and go to the city, as so many others had done. The same situation was found in other parts of the Roman Empire. Greece, for example, was subjected to the taxes of the Roman governors and to the raids of the slave-pirates, who kidnapped many people to keep the slave market in Rome going.

Gradually, the power of the Senate became subject to the growing power of certain military men, such as Pompey and Caesar. Caesar and Pompey joined forces for a short time and, with the help of a rich Roman named

Crassus, formed a "triumvirate" which controlled the policies of the Roman government. Senators who feared Caesar's rise to power, however, soon asked Pompey to defend the powers of the Senate. When the Senate ordered Caesar to give up his military command, Caesar forced Pompey and his men to leave Italy and cross over to Greece. Pompey still had great power, for he had conquered many lands in the Eastern Mediterranean and he also had officers in Spain. Before the Spanish officers could assemble their forces completely, Caesar defeated Pompey's men in Spain. Then he returned to defeat Pompey's other followers in Greece. Pompey escaped to Egypt. Caesar followed him there, and Pompey was killed.

Caesar came back to Rome victorious. He started to reorganize the government, having himself named dictator. However, many people thought Caesar was too ambitious and that he wanted too much power for himself. They remembered the old Republic, where the Consuls were obliged to govern with the consent of the Senate. Although Caesar did not abolish the Senate, he filled it with many of his friends and supporters, so that he would not meet with much opposttion. This convinced his enemies that Caesar really wanted to make all the decisions himself, and not to be limited by the representatives of the Roman citizens. Consequently, Caesar was stabbed to death one day in the streets of Rome.

His adopted son, Octavian, and Caesar's friend, Marc Antony, avenged Caesar's death and defeated those who had opposed Caesar. Octavian gained control over most of the Roman Empire. Then he heard that Marc Antony and Cleopatra, the Egyptian queen, were planning to make themselves rulers of Rome. Octavian attacked Antony's ships and Antony was defeated. Antony committed suicide, and Cleopatra, not wishing to be captured and taken to Rome, also killed herself.

Rome had become supreme in the world of the Mediterranean, but Rome's republican government had completely disappeared. The Romans felt that a supreme ruler was necessary to govern the vast territories that had become part of the Empire. Although Octavian did not wish to destroy the republican form of government, the Senate gave him the title of "Augustus" and "First Citizen."

They also gave him control of the army. Thus, in the years that followed, the Roman state became in fact a military monarchy.

The masses of the people continued to live in poverty, while the upper classes lived luxuriously. A large army was maintained to defend the frontiers, but inside the Roman state there was a long period of peace. Literature and art flourished, and the poor people were again kept happy with bread and circuses. Laws were made that applied to all the Empire. In spirit, at least, these laws were very fair.

While the people inside the Roman Empire were enjoying a high degree of civilization, the "uncivilized" people who lived in the forests beyond the northern and eastern boundaries loved to fight and seize land whenever it seemed possible. To keep some of these tribes of people calm, the Roman government allowed them to stay inside the Roman Empire for brief periods in return for military service. The Romans themselves had become less and less desirous of serving in the legions.

Thus, more and more of the "barbarians" (as the people of the north were called) found their way into the Roman Empire. Tribes such as the Goths, the Vandals, and the Huns entered Roman territory, defeated the soldiers on guard, and marched into Rome itself. Finally, one of the barbarian generals declared himself king, and the Roman emperor was forced to run away. The Roman empire soon fell to pieces as a result of the many battles between its invaders.

Finishing Time: Minutes _____ Seconds _____

An Empire and Its Problems, II

COMPREHENSION: Answer the questions without looking back at the passage. When finished, correct your answers by checking with the answer key on page 183. Find your words per minute by looking in the chart on page 185. Enter both scores on graphs provided at the end of this book.

1. Roman politicians tried to make themselves popular by
   ☐ a. not taxing the poor people.
   ☐ b. making laws favorable to the poor.
   ☐ c. making many speeches.
   ☐ d. providing bread and circuses.

2. Small farms in Italy were ruined because
   ☐ a. the farmers had to go and fight.
   ☐ b. the rich men bought the land.
   ☐ c. the women and children did not work hard enough.
   ☐ d. the farmers had to go to Rome to work.

3. Caesar became stronger than Pompey because
   ☐ a. he had more men in his army.
   ☐ b. he controlled more land.
   ☐ c. he attacked Pompey's forces quickly.
   ☐ d. Pompey went to Egypt.

4. Antony died in the following manner:
   ☐ a. he was captured.
   ☐ b. he was executed.
   ☐ c. he caught fever.
   ☐ d. he killed himself.

5. The Roman republic ended because
   ☐ a. there were too many rich people.
   ☐ b. the Senate had most of the power.
   ☐ c. the Romans felt a strong ruler was better.
   ☐ d. the corrupt government needed reform.

6. While the Roman Empire grew, the Senate became
   ☐ a. more powerful.   ☐ c. richer.
   ☐ b. less powerful.   ☐ d. poorer.

7. Greece became a poor country under the Romans because
   ☐ a. the country was so much smaller than Italy.
   ☐ b. the farmers were no longer interested in farming.
   ☐ c. the taxes were so high.
   ☐ d. the prices kept going up.

8. The Senate ordered Caesar to give up his military command because
   ☐ a. they feared Caesar would have more power than the Senate.
   ☐ b. they preferred Pompey.
   ☐ c. they wanted to protect Greece and Spain.
   ☐ d. they feared a popular revolt.

9. Caesar was killed because
   ☐ a. his decisions were hard on the rich.
   ☐ b. he was too popular.
   ☐ c. he wanted to abolish the Senate.
   ☐ d. he seemed to want all the power for himself.

10. The greatest weakness of the Roman Empire was
   ☐ a. its concentration of power in the hands of one man.
   ☐ b. its generosity toward conquered peoples.
   ☐ c. the ruling class' love of luxury.
   ☐ d. the parasites and profiteers.

Name _____ Date _____ Class _____

Reading Time: _____ _____ _____ _____ _____
              Minutes Seconds Words per minute Total number right Percent

An Empire and Its Problems, II

CLOZE TEST: The following passage, taken from the selection you have just read, has words omitted from it. Fill in the blank without looking back at the passage. When finished, correct your answers by checking with the answer key on page 183.

A. Subject Matter Words Missing

Caesar _____ 1 _____ back to Rome victorious. He started to reorganize the _____ 2 _____, having himself named as dictator. Then he began to _____ 3 _____ the government of parasites and profiteers. However, many people _____ 4 _____ Caesar was too ambitious and wanted too much _____ 5 _____ for himself. They remembered the old Republic where the Consuls were obliged to _____ 6 _____ with the consent of the _____ 7 _____. Caesar did not _____ 8 _____ the Senate, but he filled it with many of his _____ 9 _____ and supporters, so that he would not meet with much _____ 10 _____.

B. Structure Words Missing

The masses _____ 1 _____ the people continued to live _____ 2 _____ poverty, while the upper classes lived luxuriously. _____ 3 _____ large army was maintained _____ 4 _____ defend the frontiers, _____ 5 _____ inside the Roman state there was a long period _____ 6 _____ peace. Literature and art flourished, _____ 7 _____ the poor people were again kept happy _____ 8 _____ bread and circuses. Laws were made that applied to _____ 9 _____ the Empire. In spirit, at least, these laws were _____ 10 _____ fair.

Name _____   Date _____ Class _____

A. Number Right _____ Percent _____   B. Number Right _____ Percent _____

An Empire and Its Problems, II

VOCABULARY: The following words have been taken from the selection you have just read. Put an *X* in the box before the best meaning or synonym for the word as used in the selection.

1. **lavish,** page 167, col. 1, par. 1
   "The rich tried to keep the poor from revolting by providing ... lavish games."
   □ a. having simplicity
   □ b. being ridiculous
   □ c. showing extravagance
   □ d. being freely given

2. **assemble,** page 168, col. 1, par. 1
   "Before the Spanish officers could assemble their forces completely, ..."
   □ a. bring together
   □ b. collect for a speech
   □ c. fit together
   □ d. gather for training

3. **dictator,** page 168, col. 1, par. 2
   "He started to reorganize the government, having himself named dictator."
   □ a. a popular leader
   □ b. a ruler in name only
   □ c. a wholesome ruler
   □ d. a ruler having absolute authority

4. **ambitious,** page 168, col. 1, par. 2
   "... Caesar was too ambitious ... he wanted too much power for himself."
   □ a. overly mean
   □ b. greedy for authority
   □ c. very untalented
   □ d. too unfair

5. **abolish,** page 168, col. 1, par. 2
   "Although Ceasar did not abolish the Senate, he filled it ..."
   □ a. approve of
   □ b. to support
   □ c. put an end to
   □ d. to defend

6. **avenged,** page 168, col. 1, par. 3
   "... Marc Antony, avenged Caesar's death and defeated those who had opposed Caesar."
   □ a. to mourn
   □ b. to argue against
   □ c. to deliberate about
   □ d. to retaliate for

7. **supreme,** page 168, col. 1, par. 4
   "Rome had become supreme in the world of the Mediterranean, ..."
   □ a. the best liked
   □ b. the easiest to reach
   □ c. the greatest in power
   □ d. the most demanding

8. **luxuriously,** page 168, col. 2, par. 2
   "... people continued to live in poverty while the upper classes lived luxuriously."
   □ a. in wealth
   □ b. in constancy
   □ c. in selfishness
   □ d. in productivity

9. **flourished,** page 168, col. 2, par. 2
   "Literature and art flourished ..."
   □ a. were unnecessary
   □ b. were successful
   □ c. were overdone
   □ d. were well liked

10. **invaders,** page 168, col. 2, par. 3
    "... as a result of the many battles between its invaders."
    □ a. those who are superior
    □ b. those who always destroy
    □ c. those who enter as the enemy
    □ d. those who gain land

Avenged is the past tense of the verb **to avenge.** It is formed by a variation of *ad* and *vengier,* a French word which means *revenge.* This meaning goes back to the Latin *vindicare, punish.* This prefix **a** is often used before words of French derivation. **To avenge** means to take vengeance or exact satisfaction for.

Name _____   Date _____   Class _____

Total Number Right _____   Percent _____

Set 10·C
Walking
in Space

Starting Time: Minutes _____ Seconds _____

The whole world seemed to be black, black nothingness. The sky was black with bright, shining stars that never twinkled. The sun, a white, burning disk, seemed to hang in the black velvet of the surrounding heavens. This was the scene that spread before the eyes of the first astronaut who left his spaceship to walk in outer space. The name of the Russian astronaut who performed this feat was Leonov; and the date of his walk in space was March 18, 1965. Several months later a similar feat was performed by the first American astronaut to walk in space. Both of these "space walkers" had spent months previous to their flight learning how to control their movements under the strange conditions which exist in space. Wearing their thick space suits, they learned to deal with an environment where there is neither weight nor gravity, neither "up" nor "down."

We do not realize how much we depend on the earth's gravity until we are deprived of it. Then our feet no longer stay on the ground; we float around in the air; and the slightest touch may send us drifting off in the opposite direction.

In the laboratories where astronauts are trained for their journeys, they are subjected to conditions that resemble those of flight.

It takes time for them to prepare for the great changes that occur in space. When the spaceship leaves the earth at tremendous speed, the astronauts feel as if they are being crushed against the spaceship floor. Later, when they leave the zone of the earth's gravitation, they are unable to stay in one place. Simple actions, such as eating and drinking, become very difficult to perform. You may get an inkling of what the astronauts have to deal with if you try to drink a glass of water while standing on your head or while just lying down.

The beginnings of man's conquest of space took place in 1958, seven years before Leonov's trip. The first successful launching of "Sputnik" demonstrated that it was indeed possible to send objects far enough out of range of earth's gravity so that they would not fall back to earth. Rather, such objects could be forced to revolve about the earth, just as the moon does. However, while the moon is so far from earth that it takes it a month to revolve around the earth, man-made satellites, which are closer to earth, can make a complete revolution in a few hours.

It was three years after the first satellite launching that a spaceship containing a man made a successful flight. The flight lasted less

172

than two hours, but it pointed the way to future developments.

Other planets are so far away that spaceships must attain tremendous speeds to reach them in a reasonable time. If spaceships were launched from space or from the moon, the absence of weight would permit the ships to be launched with great speed at reduced pressures. A relatively small explosion would be enough to send a ship off at a very fast rate. And, since there is no atmosphere in space as there is on earth, the spaceship would meet with no resistance. To illustrate this point, remember how strong the wind feels if we are traveling fast in a car; then imagine a car traveling through an area where there is no wind. The windless condition is comparable to the condition in outer space.

The first astronaut to walk in space, Leonov, and his companion, Beliaiev, began making preparations for the walk as soon as their spaceship was launched. The spaceship was equipped with a double door, which was fitted with a bellows between the ship and the outside. This made it possible for the astronaut, in his space suit with oxygen supply, to go first from the air-filled ship to the bellows. Then the air was let out of the bellows, and, while the man stepped outside, the air inside the ship remained at normal pressure. If the door had opened directly into space, the air in the ship would have rushed out and been lost when the door opened.

Leonov and Beliaiev practiced testing the doors several times after they had begun revolving around the earth. When the time came for Leonov to go out, his companion helped him attach the cable that was to keep him from floating away from the ship. Then Leonov entered the bellows, and the door closed behind him. As the air was let out of the bellows, he felt his suit swell up because of the air pressure inside. When there was no air left in the bellows, the outer door opened, and Leonov could see, simultaneously, the blackness of space and the blinding light of the sun.

If the sky appears blue to us on earth, it is because the earth's atmosphere absorbs a certain number of blue rays of sunlight. Out where there is no air, this phenomenon does not take place. On the earth, our atmosphere

diffuses light so that, when the sun is up, light seems to be everywhere. However, in the airless realms of outer space, strong lights, such as the sun, exist side by side with a dark similar to the dark of the blackest night. The absence of air also explains why the stars do not seem to twinkle in space, as they do from the earth.

Leonov reported that the earth appeared as a huge, round disk, filling a large part of the sky. He found that the relief of hills and mountains was more easily observed from that distance than from a plane flying at a few thousand feet.

While Leonov was outside the ship, he kept in touch by telephone with his companion and with the earth. He opened the shutter of the movie camera, which made a record of what he did and saw. When the signal was given for him to return to the ship, he was enjoying the cosmos so much that he was disappointed to have to stop his wanderings so soon.

Finishing Time: Minutes _____ Seconds _____

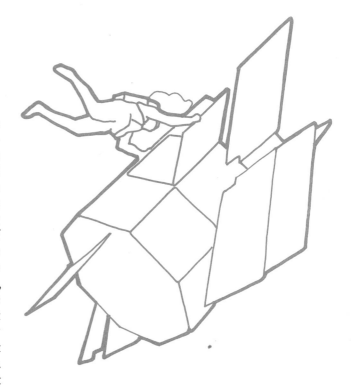

Walking in Space

COMPREHENSION: Answer the questions without looking back at the passage. When finished, correct your answers by checking with the answer key on page 183. Find your words per minute by looking in the chart on page 185. Enter both scores on graphs provided at the end of this book.

1. One of the greatest problems of space travel is
   ☐ a. the intense cold.
   ☐ b. the clouds.
   ☐ c. the absence of gravity.
   ☐ d. the blackness of the sky.

2. The first successful satellite was launched in
   ☐ a. 1947.
   ☐ b. 1956.
   ☐ c. 1958.
   ☐ d. 1962.

3. Artificial satellites go around the earth
   ☐ a. faster than the moon.
   ☐ b. at the same speed as the moon.
   ☐ c. more slowly than the moon.
   ☐ d. at the same speed as the earth itself.

4. The best place from which to launch a spaceship to other planets is probably
   ☐ a. the North Pole.
   ☐ b. the equator.
   ☐ c. Cape Kennedy.
   ☐ d. a satellite in space.

5. In space the sky does not appear blue because
   ☐ a. the sun does not shine there.
   ☐ b. there is no atmosphere.
   ☐ c. the earth's atmosphere takes all the blue rays.
   ☐ d. it is too cold.

6. Leonov's spaceship had a double door in order
   ☐ a. to prevent the loss of air.
   ☐ b. to accustom the astronaut to the darkness.
   ☐ c. to accustom the astronaut to the lack of air.
   ☐ d. to give him time to attach himself to the ship.

7. The stars do not seem to twinkle in space because
   ☐ a. they are so much nearer.
   ☐ b. the sun does not shine so brightly.
   ☐ c. the sky is so black.
   ☐ d. there is no atmosphere.

8. The first manned space flight lasted
   ☐ a. one day.
   ☐ b. almost six hours.
   ☐ c. less than one hour.
   ☐ d. less than two hours.

9. Leonov was attached to the spaceship by
   ☐ a. a kind of magnet.
   ☐ b. a light-weight, nylon cord.
   ☐ c. a bellows.
   ☐ d. a cable.

10. Leonov's space suit swelled up because
    ☐ a. of the intense cold.
    ☐ b. of the extra oxygen it was carrying.
    ☐ c. of the air pressure inside of it.
    ☐ d. of the air pressure outside of it.

___

Name _____ Date _____ Class _____

Reading Time: _____ _____ _____ _____ _____
              Minutes   Seconds   Words per minute   Total number right   Percent

174

Walking in Space

CLOZE TEST: The following passage, taken from the selection you have just read, has words omitted from it. Fill in the blank without looking back at the passage. When finished, correct your answers by checking with the answer key on page 179.

A. Subject Matter Words Missing

In the laboratories where astronauts are _____ 1 for their journeys, they are subjected to _____ 2 that resemble those of flight. It takes _____ 3 for them to prepare for the _____ 4 changes that occur in space. When the spaceship leaves the earth at _____ 5 speed, the astronauts feel as if they are being _____ 6 against the spaceship floor. Later, when they leave the _____ 7 of the earth's gravitation, they are _____ 8 to stay in one place. Simple actions, such as _____ 9 and drinking, become very difficult to_____ 10.

B. Structure Words Missing

If the sky appears blue _____ 1 us on earth, it is _____ 2 the earth's atmosphere absorbs a certain number _____ 3 blue rays of sunlight. Out where there is _____ 4 air, this phenomenon does not take place. _____ 5 the earth, our atmosphere diffuses light _____ 6 that, when the sun is up, light seems to be everywhere. _____ 7, in the airless realms of outer space, strong lights, _____ 8 as the sun, exist side by side _____ 9 a dark similar to the dark of _____ 10 blackest night.

Walking in Space

VOCABULARY: The following words have been taken from the selection you have just read. Put an X in the box before the best meaning or synonym for the word as used in the selection.

1. **disk**, page 172, col. 1, par. 1
"The sun, a white, burning disk, ..."
☐ a. a burning star
☐ b. a moving object
☐ c. a round, flat-like object
☐ d. a strange shaped object

2. **feat**, page 172, col. 1, par. 1
"Several months later a similar feat was performed ..."
☐ a. an ordinary task
☐ b. a noteworthy achievement
☐ c. a common deed
☐ d. something done

3. **subjected**, page 172, col. 1, par. 3
"... they are subjected to conditions that resemble those of flight."
☐ a. to be dominated by
☐ b. to be ruled by
☐ c. to be exposed to
☐ d. to be dependent of

4. **inkling**, page 172, col. 2, par. 1
"You may get an inkling of what the astronauts have to deal with ..."
☐ a. a complete picture
☐ b. some secret information
☐ c. a technical explanation
☐ d. some type of hint

5. **attain**, page 173, col. 1, par. 2
"... spaceships must attain tremendous speeds ..."
☐ a. to try
☐ b. to reach
☐ c. to affirm
☐ d. to enable

6. **comparable**, page 173, col. 1, par. 2
"The windless condition is comparable to the condition in outer space."
☐ a. opposed to comparison
☐ b. more severe
☐ c. just like another
☐ d. capable of being compared

7. **simultaneously**, page 173, col. 1, par. 4
"... Leonov could see simultaneously, the blackness of space and the blinding light of the sun."
☐ a. first one and then the other
☐ b. at the same time
☐ c. somewhat unclearly
☐ d. in an artificial way

8. **diffuses**, page 173, col. 1, par. 5
"... our atmosphere diffuses light so that ... light seems to be everywhere."
☐ a. able to disperse
☐ b. able to focus
☐ c. tends to concentrate
☐ d. able to inflict

9. **realms**, page 173, col. 2, par. 1
"However, in the airless realms of outer space, ..."
☐ a. a kingdom
☐ b. a frightening actuality
☐ c. a certain section
☐ d. the complete domain

10. **relief**, page 173, col. 2, par. 2
"He found that the relief of hills and mountains was more easily observed ..."
☐ a. position of
☐ b. elevation of land surfaces
☐ c. the sight of
☐ d. a dangerless place

Simultaneously comes from the Latin *simul* meaning *at the same time* and the Latin *taneus* meaning *momentary*. The definition we find in Webster's says **simultaneously** means existing or occurring at the same time. Finally, the suffix **ly** indicates that the word is an adverb.

Name _____   Date _____   Class _____

Total Number Right _____   Percent _____

Answer Key & Graphs

(The cloze exercises are scored by *exact* word replacement. Teachers may choose to allow synonyms.)

Set 1-A

Comprehension	1-b	2-c	3-a	4-d	5-b	6-b	7-b	8-a	9-d	10-d
Vocabulary	1-c	2-d	3-d	4-b	5-c	6-c	7-a	8-b	9-b	10-d

Cloze Test A
1. money   2. wagon   3. bigger   4. rent   5. indoors
6. room   7. could   8. stage   9. successful   10. times

Cloze Test B
1. or   2. on   3. a   4. the   5. to
6. of   7. as   8. not   9. to   10. a

Set 1-B

Comprehension	1-d	2-a	3-b	4-d	5-c	6-c	7-c	8-a	9-b	10-b
Vocabulary	1-c	2-b	3-b	4-a	5-d	6-c	7-b	8-a	9-d	10-c

Cloze Test A
1. art   2. colonized   3. important   4. control   5. expert
6. famous   7. island   8. prevent   9. secret   10. divulge

Cloze Test B
1. so   2. into   3. to   4. In   5. to
6. of   7. the   8. in   9. through   10. of

Set 1-C

Comprehension	1-a	2-c	3-b	4-d	5-a	6-c	7-b	8-b	9-a	10-a
Vocabulary	1-b	2-a	3-d	4-a	5-c	6-c	7-b	8-c	9-d	10-b

Cloze Test A
1. see   2. blurry   3. become   4. distant   5. opposite
6. reading   7. hold   8. glasses   9. clearly   10. shape

Cloze Test B
1. for   2. from   3. to   4. of   5. then
6. and   7. around   8. between   9. away   10. is

Set 2-A

Comprehension	1-c	2-b	3-b	4-a	5-c	6-b	7-a	8-d	9-d	10-d
Vocabulary	1-a	2-d	3-b	4-c	5-b	6-d	7-d	8-c	9-a	10-c

Cloze Test A
1. cooler   2. earth's   3. rays   4. cannot   5. easily
6. programs   7. travel   8. broadcast   9. longer   10. area

Cloze Test B
1. the   2. by   3. to   4. in   5. by
6. As   7. and   8. because   9. If   10. of

Set 2-B

Comprehension	1-a	2-c	3-c	4-c	5-d	6-c	7-c	8-b	9-d	10-c
Vocabulary	1-b	2-c	3-b	4-a	5-d	6-c	7-d	8-a	9-c	10-b

Cloze Test A
1. first   2. years   3. knew   4. guarded   5. carefully
6. trade   7. expensive   8. reign   9. monks   10. silkworms

Cloze Test B
1. still   2. because   3. of   4. as   5. so
6. to   7. ago   8. no   9. of   10. from

Set 2-C

Comprehension	1-c	2-c	3-a	4-c	5-d	6-d	7-b	8-c	9-d	10-a
Vocabulary	1-a	2-b	3-c	4-a	5-a	6-d	7-a	8-b	9-c	10-d

Cloze Test A
1. winter   2. weather   3. larger   4. entrance   5. several
6. water   7. stuck   8. prefer   9. single   10. diameter

Cloze Test B
1. on   2. but   3. in   4. no   5. by
6. the   7. until   8. above   9. with   10. or

Set 3-A

Comprehension	1-b	2-c	3-b	4-d	5-d	6-a	7-b	8-b	9-b	10-a
Vocabulary	1-b	2-d	3-a	4-b	5-a	6-c	7-c	8-c	9-b	10-c

Cloze Test A
1. taught 2. take 3. simple 4. come 5. strangers
6. keep 7. training 8. quickly 9. friends 10. invite

Cloze Test B
1. an 2. from 3. away 4. for 5. of
6. or 7. not 8. by 9. then 10. of

Set 3-B

Comprehension	1-a	2-b	3-c	4-a	5-b	6-a	7-b	8-c	9-b	10-d
Vocabulary	1-b	2-a	3-a	4-d	5-d	6-b	7-b	8-c	9-d	10-a

Cloze Test A
1. invention 2. send 3. place 4. human 5. find
6. wires 7. success 8. time 9. finally 10. first

Cloze Test B
1. in 2. because 3. for 4. If 5. to
6. the 7. of 8. that 9. because 10. where

Set 3-C

Comprehension	1-b	2-c	3-d	4-b	5-b	6-c	7-a	8-c	9-c	10-d
Vocabulary	1-b	2-c	3-a	4-a	5-c	6-b	7-b	8-d	9-b	10-c

Cloze Test A
1. grateful 2. happy 3. hoped 4. family 5. allowed
6. became 7. Indian 8. considerably 9. successful 10. bow

Cloze Test B
1. of 2. the 3. to 4. and 5. to
6. as 7. in 8. which 9. that 10. by

Set 4-A

Comprehension	1-c	2-c	3-a	4-d	5-b	6-d	7-d	8-a	9-d	10-c
Vocabulary	1-b	2-a	3-b	4-c	5-d	6-b	7-c	8-b	9-c	10-d

Cloze Test A
1. method 2. placed 3. kettles 4. food 5. replaced
6. add 7. cooked 8. knew 9. people 10. stewing

Cloze Test B
1. that 2. how 3. from 4. as 5. the
6. in 7. From 8. to 9. The 10. for

Set 4-B

Comprehension	1-a	2-a	3-c	4-a	5-b	6-b	7-b	8-b	9-d	10-a
Vocabulary	1-b	2-c	3-b	4-c	5-c	6-b	7-c	8-a	9-a	10-d

Cloze Test A
1. time 2. established 3. growing 4. planters 5. encouraged
6. trees 7. automobiles 8. industry 9. wild 10. economical

Cloze Test B
1. by 2. the 3. with 4. in 5. that
6. and 7. of 8. from 9. in 10. so

Set 4-C

Comprehension	1-c	2-b	3-a	4-a	5-a	6-b	7-d	8-b	9-c	10-d
Vocabulary	1-b	2-c	3-b	4-c	5-d	6-c	7-c	8-a	9-b	10-b

Cloze Test A
1. build 2. natural 3. protect 4. overhanging 5. caves
6. simple 7. easily 8. time 9. permanent 10. hunting

Cloze Test B
1. to 2. since 3. from 4. such 5. when
6. for 7. but 8. so 9. often 10. if

Set 5-A

Comprehension	1-c	2-b	3-a	4-d	5-c	6-c	7-d	8-c	9-a	10-c
Vocabulary	1-b	2-d	3-c	4-b	5-d	6-c	7-d	8-c	9-a	10-b

Cloze Test A

1. made	2. high	3. flew	4. took	5. balloon
6. fell	7. threw	8. clothes	9. safe	10. ascent

Cloze Test B

1. to	2. for	3. that	4. a	5. Under
6. enough	7. that	8. the	9. also	10. in

Set 5-B

Comprehension	1-c	2-b	3-b	4-c	5-a	6-b	7-d	8-b	9-b	10-a
Vocabulary	1-b	2-d	3-a	4-b	5-b	6-c	7-c	8-c	9-a	10-a

Cloze Test A

1. total	2. descendants	3. came	4. white	5. interest
6. control	7. mixed	8. usually	9. full-blooded	10. peoples

Cloze Test B

1. as	2. which	3. also	4. the	5. or
6. by	7. on	8. at	9. but	10. as

Set 5-C

Comprehension	1-c	2-d	3-c	4-b	5-a	6-d	7-b	8-b	9-d	10-c
Vocabulary	1-c	2-b	3-b	4-a	5-a	6-c	7-d	8-d	9-b	10-c

Cloze Test A

1. caterpillar	2. quiet	3. spin	4. protect	5. enemies
6. useful	7. becomes	8. hangs	9. attaches	10. surface

Cloze Test B

1. through	2. the	3. only	4. into	5. on
6. most	7. when	8. for	9. and	10. from

Set 6-A

Comprehension	1-a	2-c	3-a	4-c	5-d	6-c	7-b	8-c	9-a	10-b
Vocabulary	1-c	2-a	3-d	4-b	5-d	6-a	7-c	8-a	9-d	10-b

Cloze Test A

1. different	2. baked	3. found	4. people	5. language
6. written	7. baked	8. permanently	9. tablets	10. lands

Cloze Test B

1. more	2. than	3. a	4. in	5. of
6. over	7. to	8. then	9. up	10. of

Set 6-B

Comprehension	1-c	2-b	3-b	4-c	5-c	6-d	7-a	8-c	9-a	10-d
Vocabulary	1-a	2-a	3-a	4-b	5-d	6-c	7-c	8-c	9-b	10-b

Cloze Test A

1. able	2. atomic	3. oversee	4. hand	5. irrigate
6. fertile	7. internal	8. replace	9. artificial	10. master

Cloze Test B

1. thus	2. in	3. even	4. with	5. However
6. not	7. in	8. among	9. some	10. while

Set 6-C

Comprehension	1-a	2-b	3-c	4-d	5-a	6-a	7-b	8-c	9-a	10-c
Vocabulary	1-b	2-a	3-d	4-a	5-b	6-d	7-c	8-b	9-a	10-d

Cloze Test A

1. common	2. glass	3. connected	4. filled	5. slowly
6. completely	7. turned	8. sand	9. hour	10. bulb

Cloze Test B

1. of	2. still	3. the	4. for	5. in
6. In	7. during	8. to	9. which	10. of

Set 7-A

Comprehension	1-d	2-b	3-b	4-c	5-d	6-c	7-b	8-b	9-a	10-c
Vocabulary	1-a	2-d	3-b	4-b	5-c	6-b	7-d	8-a	9-b	10-c

Cloze Test A
1. domesticated 2. man's 3. tamed 4. animal 5. hybrid
6. beast 7. called 8. captivity 9. tamed 10. centuries

Cloze Test B
1. of 2. for 3. the 4. out 5. from
6. never 7. to 8. however 9. for 10. still

Set 7-B

Comprehension	1-a	2-a	3-c	4-d	5-c	6-c	7-b	8-c	9-d	10-b
Vocabulary	1-a	2-c	3-b	4-b	5-a	6-d	7-c	8-a	9-d	10-b

Cloze Test A
1. workers 2. know 3. same 4. meeting 5. bicycle
6. spending 7. young 8. show 9. country 10. minimum

Cloze Test B
1. not 2. of 3. also 4. Even 5. of
6. or 7. a 8. and 9. the 10. not

Set 7-C

Comprehension	1-c	2-c	3-c	4-d	5-a	6-d	7-d	8-c	9-b	10-a
Vocabulary	1-c	2-d	3-d	4-b	5-c	6-a	7-d	8-b	9-c	10-a

Cloze Test A
1. depends 2. example 3. baby 4. gave 5. bear
6. usually 7. instances 8. affection 9. killed 10. long

Cloze Test B
1. of 2. without 3. have 4. to 5. of
6. his 7. or 8. with 9. almost 10. on

Set 8-A

Comprehension	1-b	2-d	3-d	4-b	5-c	6-c	7-a	8-c	9-d	10-a
Vocabulary	1-b	2-d	3-a	4-a	5-c	6-c	7-d	8-b	9-b	10-c

Cloze Test A
1. many 2. taking 3. powder 4. uncleanliness 5. great
6. facilities 7. years 8. realize 9. people 10. regularly

Cloze Test B
1. when 2. with 3. no 4. and 5. when
6. with 7. from 8. on 9. of 10. over

Set 8-B

Comprehension	1-d	2-d	3-c	4-b	5-b	6-a	7-c	8-c	9-b	10-a
Vocabulary	1-b	2-d	3-b	4-a	5-c	6-b	7-c	8-d	9-c	10-c

Cloze Test A
1. limited 2. sending 3. placed 4. wider 5. see
6. clear 7. atmosphere 8. satellite 9. pictures 10. visible

Cloze Test B
1. of 2. by 3. and 4. by 5. all
6. what 7. with 8. As 9. ago 10. than

Set 8-C

Comprehension	1-d	2-b	3-c	4-c	5-c	6-b	7-d	8-b	9-a	10-d
Vocabulary	1-c	2-b	3-c	4-d	5-b	6-a	7-d	8-d	9-b	10-c

Cloze Test A
1. room 2. records 3. copied 4. lands 5. scholarly
6. great 7. preserved 8. today 9. years 10. bright

Cloze Test B
1. not 2. but 3. with 4. alike 5. at
6. by 7. for 8. a 9. the 10. to

Set 9-A
Comprehension	1-a	2-c	3-c	4-a	5-b	6-b	7-d	8-c	9-a	10-d
Vocabulary	1-a	2-c	3-d	4-c	5-a	6-b	7-b	8-d	9-c	10-a

Cloze Test A
1. soldiers 2. Emperor 3. gave 4. realized 5. position
6. Spanish 7. prisoner 8. revolted 9. fierce 10. rule

Cloze Test B
1. after 2. still 3. the 4. and 5. Many
6. of 7. in 8. of 9. to 10. as

Set 9-B
Comprehension	1-d	2-b	3-c	4-d	5-d	6-a	7-d	8-d	9-c	10-b
Vocabulary	1-a	2-c	3-b	4-d	5-d	6-a	7-b	8-a	9-c	10-b

Cloze Test A
1. time 2. possible 3. quickly 4. took 5. year
6. plant 7. enrich 8. chemical 9. enabled 10. land

Cloze Test B
1. and 2. the 3. from 4. of 5. in
6. or 7. than 8. on 9. by 10. or

Set 9-C
Comprehension	1-d	2-b	3-b	4-a	5-c	6-a	7-c	8-a	9-b	10-d
Vocabulary	1-b	2-a	3-d	4-b	5-a	6-b	7-c	8-b	9-d	10-c

Cloze Test A
1. depends 2. must 3. largest 4. easily 5. leave
6. keel 7. sloping 8. cut 9. banks 10. steep

Cloze Test B
1. in 2. the 3. by 4. Some 5. or
6. of 7. a 8. to 9. not 10. where

Set 10-A
Comprehension	1-c	2-a	3-c	4-d	5-d	6-a	7-a	8-c	9-d	10-c
Vocabulary	1-c	2-a	3-b	4-d	5-c	6-a	7-d	8-b	9-a	10-c

Cloze Test A
1. people 2. power 3. leaving 4. another 5. classes
6. get 7. gave 8. returned 9. possible 10. high

Cloze Test B
1. before 2. on 3. For 4. From 5. of
6. the 7. as 8. of 9. up 10. a

Set 10-B
Comprehension	1-d	2-a	3-c	4-d	5-c	6-b	7-c	8-a	9-d	10-c
Vocabulary	1-c	2-a	3-d	4-b	5-c	6-d	7-c	8-a	9-b	10-c

Cloze Test A
1. came 2. government 3. rid 4. thought 5. power
6. govern 7. Senate 8. abolish 9. friends 10. opposition

Cloze Test B
1. of 2. in 3. A 4. to 5. but
6. of 7. and 8. with 9. all 10. very

Set 10-C
Comprehension	1-c	2-c	3-a	4-d	5-b	6-a	7-d	8-d	9-d	10-c
Vocabulary	1-c	2-b	3-c	4-d	5-b	6-d	7-b	8-a	9-d	10-b

Cloze Test A
1. trained 2. conditions 3. time 4. great 5. tremendous
6. crushed 7. zone 8. unable 9. eating 10. perform

Cloze Test B
1. to 2. because 3. of 4. no 5. On
6. so 7. However 8. such 9. with 10. the

Words per Minute

Reading Time	Words per Minute	Reading Time	Words per Minute	Reading Time	Words per Minute
1:00	1000	2:30	400	4:00	250
1:05	923	2:35	387	4:05	245
1:10	857	2:40	375	4:10	240
1:15	800	2:45	364	4:15	235
1:20	750	2:50	353	4:20	231
1:25	706	2:55	343	4:25	226
1:30	667	3:00	333	4:30	222
1:35	632	3:05	324	4:35	218
1:40	600	3:10	315	4:40	214
1:45	571	3:15	308	4:45	210
1:50	545	3:20	300	4:50	207
1:55	522	3:25	293	4:55	203
2:00	500	3:30	286	5:00	200
2:05	480	3:35	279	5:05	197
2:10	462	3:40	273	5:10	194
2:15	444	3:45	267	5:15	190
2:20	429	3:50	261	5:20	187
2:25	414	3:55	255	5:25	185
				5:30	182

Rate

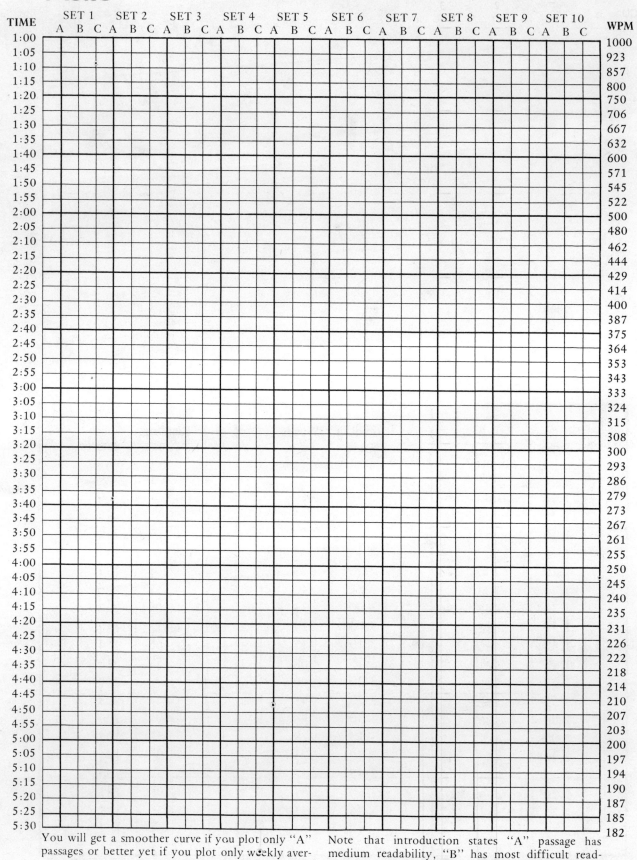

TIME	SET 1			SET 2			SET 3			SET 4			SET 5			SET 6			SET 7			SET 8			SET 9			SET 10			WPM
	A	B	C	A	B	C	A	B	C	A	B	C	A	B	C	A	B	C	A	B	C	A	B	C	A	B	C	A	B	C	
1:00																															1000
1:05																															923
1:10																															857
1:15																															800
1:20																															750
1:25																															706
1:30																															667
1:35																															632
1:40																															600
1:45																															571
1:50																															545
1:55																															522
2:00																															500
2:05																															480
2:10																															462
2:15																															444
2:20																															429
2:25																															414
2:30																															400
2:35																															387
2:40																															375
2:45																															364
2:50																															353
2:55																															343
3:00																															333
3:05																															324
3:10																															315
3:15																															308
3:20																															300
3:25																															293
3:30																															286
3:35																															279
3:40																															273
3:45																															267
3:50																															261
3:55																															255
4:00																															250
4:05																															245
4:10																															240
4:15																															235
4:20																															231
4:25																															226
4:30																															222
4:35																															218
4:40																															214
4:45																															210
4:50																															207
4:55																															203
5:00																															200
5:05																															197
5:10																															194
5:15																															190
5:20																															187
5:25																															185
5:30																															182

You will get a smoother curve if you plot only "A" passages or better yet if you plot only weekly averages. However, some users prefer to plot every drill.

Note that introduction states "A" passage has medium readability, "B" has most difficult readability and "C" passage has the easiest readability.

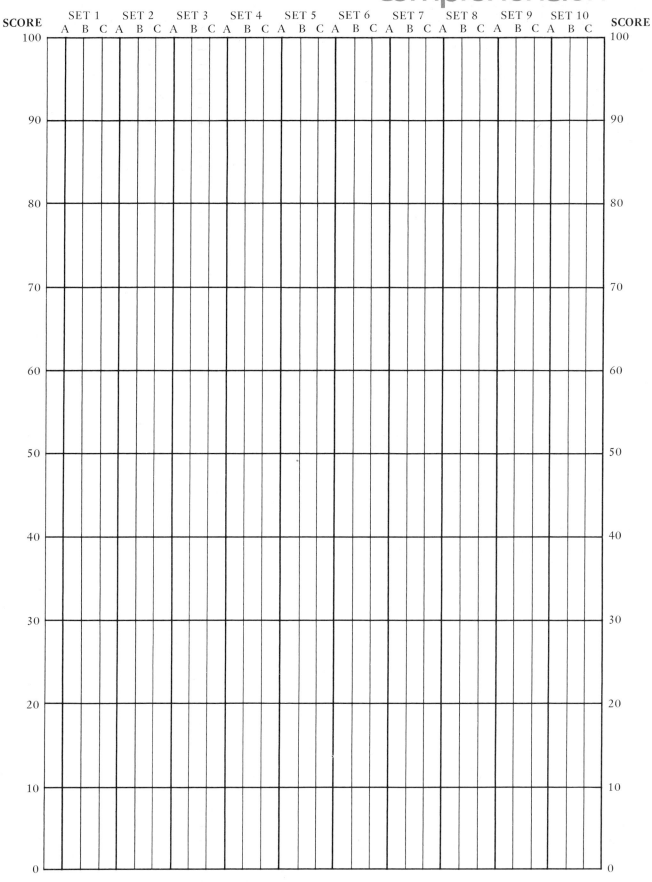

Cloze Test A

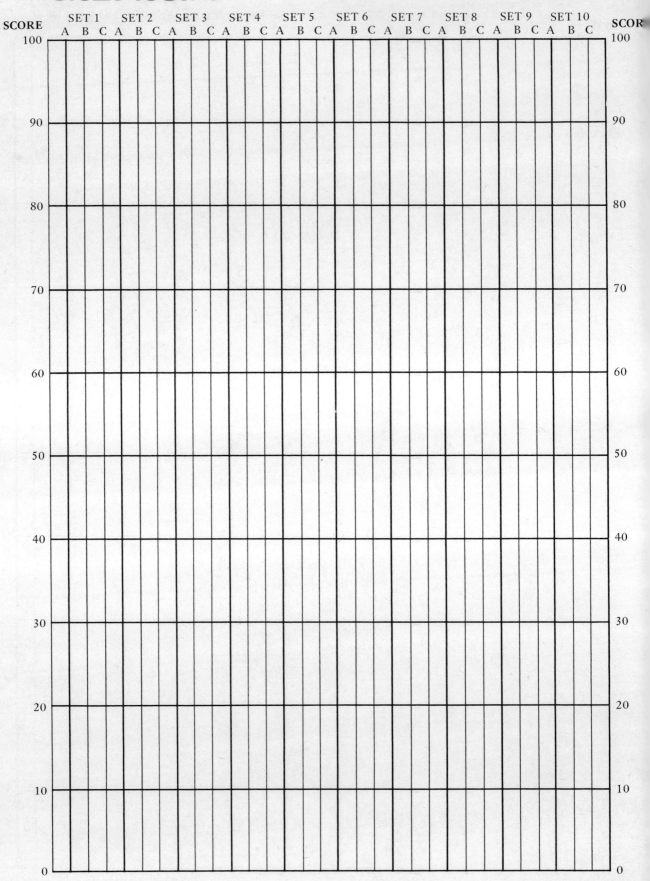

Cloze Test B

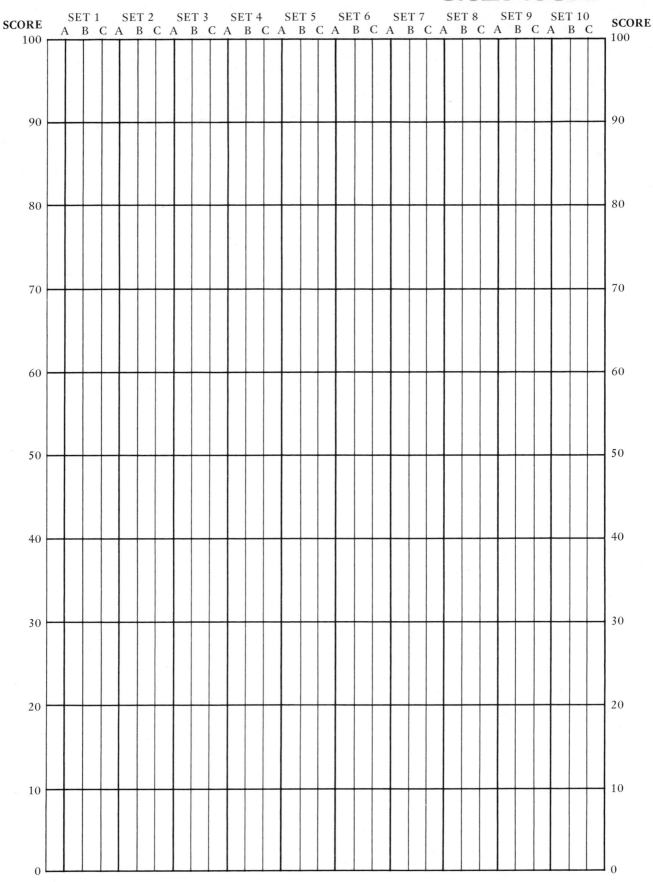

189

Vocabulary

SCORE	SET 1			SET 2			SET 3			SET 4			SET 5			SET 6			SET 7			SET 8			SET 9			SET 10			SCORE
	A	B	C	A	B	C	A	B	C	A	B	C	A	B	C	A	B	C	A	B	C	A	B	C	A	B	C	A	B	C	
100																															100
90																															90
80																															80
70																															70
60																															60
50																															50
40																															40
30																															30
20																															20
10																															10
0																															0